A Preview of

Active Server Pages +

Richard Anderson
Alex Homer
Rob Howard
Dave Sussman

Wrox Press Ltd. ®

A Preview of Active Server Pages +

Published by Wrox Press Ltd
Arden House, 1102 Warwick Road, Acock's Green, Birmingham B27 6BH, UK
Printed in USA
ISBN 1-861004-75-3

Trademark Acknowledgements

Wrox has endeavored to provide trademark information about all the companies and products mentioned in this book by the appropriate use of capitals. However, Wrox cannot guarantee the accuracy of this information.

Credits

Authors
Richard Anderson
Alex Homer
Rob Howard
Dave Sussman

Technical Architect
Chris Goode

Technical Editor
Sarah Drew

Category Managers
Joanna Mason
Dominic Lowe

Project Administrator
Jake Manning

Author Agents
Sarah Bowers
Sophie Edwards

Proof Reader
Christopher Smith

Technical Reviewers
Scott Guthrie
Mark Anders
Tom Kaiser
Bradley Millington
Erik Olsen
Lance Olsen
Zoltan Sekeres
Susan Warren
Eric Zinda

Production Manager
Laurent Lafon

Production Co-ordinator
Jonathan Jones

Illustrations
William Fallon

Index
Andrew Criddle

Cover Design
Shelley Frazier

About the Authors

Richard Anderson

Richard Anderson is an established researcher, software developer, and writer who spends his time working with Microsoft technologies, day in, day out. Having spent the better part of 10 years doing this, he is still remarkably sane. Richard currently works as an internet/product specialist for BMS (http://www.bms.uk.com) where he helps develop an enterprise level Internet payroll system, and works with some extremely cool technologies and people. Richard would like to say a special thanks to Matt Odhner (and NASA), Mark Anders, Scott Guthrie, Rob Howard, Sam, Alex, Tina, and Dave for making his last trip to Seattle so enjoyable and cool.

Alex Homer

Alex is a software developer and technical author living and working in the idyllic rural surroundings of the Derbyshire Dales in England. He came to computing late in life – in fact, while he was at school people still thought that the LED wristwatch was a really cool idea. Since then he has obtained a Bachelor of Arts degree in Mathematics, and so looked destined for a career painting computers. Instead, while not busy developing ASP components for Stonebroom Software (http://www.stonebroom.com), he prefers to install and play with the latest and flakiest beta code he can find and then write about it. You can contact him at alex@stonebroom.com or alex@stonebroom.co.uk.

Rob Howard

Rob is a developer and technology evangelist in Microsoft's early adopter group. He works with leading dot-coms to help them better understand, adopt, and employ best practices with new Microsoft technologies. When he's not writing code (or books) you can usually find him fly fishing in eastern Washington rivers. You can contact him at rhoward@microsoft.com.

Dave Sussman

Dave spent most of his professional life as a developer before realizing that writing was far more fun. He specializes in Internet and data access technologies, although just about any alpha or beta code gets him excited. Like Alex he lives in rural surroundings and therefore spends most of his time gazing out of the window at the birds and trees, instead of working. In his spare time he listens to his ludicrously expensive hi-fi and juggles. He dreams of a five ball Mills Mess.

Table of Contents

Table of Contents

Table of Contents

Table of Contents

Foreword

The Story of ASP+

Way back in late November, 1997, a small group of us from the Internet Information Server team at Microsoft started to discuss some new ways of creating web applications. Active Server Pages was really only about a year old at that point, and was becoming an incredibly popular technology. However, we had *just* sent IIS 4.0 and the NT Option Pack off to manufacturing, it was the start of the holiday season, and so things were pretty quiet at the office as people recuperated after the long grind. Therefore, taking advantage of this fact, Scott Guthrie and I started to debate endlessly what we liked and didn't like about ASP. While we loved the ease with which you could develop apps with ASP and the flexibility that it provided, there were a number of issues that we identified.

One of the first things that we decided was that ASP was too complicated, and that you had to write too much code. When we would tell people this, they often couldn't understand what we were talking about. "What do you mean? ASP isn't complicated, it's incredibly simple to use!" They were right – ASP is simple. However, while ASP code is easy to write, it tends to be very unstructured and gets really messy. We had seen some huge ASP pages that had tons of server script code intermixed with client script code and after a while it became mind-bogglingly difficult to figure out what was going on. So yes, the code was simple and straightforward, but there was always a ton of it!

Additionally, to do *anything* in ASP you always had to write code – there was no purely *declarative* method for doing anything. If you wrote an ad rotator component, for example, there was no way to just plop it down on the page and have it do anything. You always had to write some code. The reason was that ASP had no actual component model. Actually having a component model was made more difficult by the fact that an ASP page really defined a single function. You always started at the top of the page, and zipped right down to the bottom, executing your database queries, running your business logic, and generating HTML along the way. Therefore, *where* a component is placed in HTML determines *when* it gets to do its work.

So, if a component located towards the bottom of the page needs to do something *before* a component at the top of the page (say generate some data that is used by other components), you need to re-structure your code to do this. On the other hand, if you imagine how a VB Form works, it owns a set of controls, and the Form communicates with them by calling their methods and by raising events. All of the controls can be created, and then told to update their contents, databind, draw themselves, etc.

Tools support was another issue. The lack of a component-based, event-driven model definitely made developing tools for ASP difficult. And we were convinced that in order to really make developing web applications simple, we needed great tools support. We wanted to do for the Web what VB had done for Windows – make it so that anyone could write a rich application. Visual InterDev 6 presented such a model to developers, but to do so, it had to use lots of includes and generate tons of script code. Tools such as Visual Basic faced an additional obstacle to using ASP, namely that ASP could only support interpreted script languages. Surely a VB user would want to use real VB code!

From talking to customers, we had also become aware of a variety of other issues. For example, the fact that code was mixed with presentation was a real problem for a lot of people, especially when designers and developers were working together on a project. This also made scenarios such as supporting multiple client types and internationalizing an application very difficult.

The end of December is always a time of reflection, a time when you make your resolutions for the new year and vow to change some of your bad habits. Scott and I made a vow, too. We had been doing a lot of talking, but we had not been writing any code! So, we promised each other that we would create a prototype that we could use to demo the concepts that we had been developing. With that, Scott went home over the long New Year's weekend and returned in January 1998 with a working prototype.

This prototype, and the many that followed, were extremely valuable in that they allowed us to validate our ideas, and to communicate the vision with others. Of course, the first people that we had to show it to were my manager, David Treadwell, and his boss, J Allard. Now that everyone was back to work and ready to dig in, it was important for us to say "Hey, we've got some pretty cool stuff here, and we want to continue working on it!" Both were incredibly enthusiastic, and encouraged us to keep going. Eventually, they even gave us some resources to actually build it!

As we began building ASP+ for real, one of the first and most important decisions we had to make was how exactly to build it. We were one of the first groups at Microsoft to start building entirely on the NGWS Runtime. We chose it because we felt that it would provide the best development environment, not only for us, but for customers who build applications with ASP+. Developing on top of the runtime has turned out to be a great experience. We got huge productivity gains, and the richness of the underlying system is one of the main reasons that ASP+ is so rich. We really couldn't have written ASP+ without it. Additionally ASP+ is written entirely in C#, which proved to be a great language for building efficient, component based systems.

During the two and a half years since that first prototype, the team – now a fairly large organization – has worked hard to develop a rich, robust platform for Web applications. In addition to the issues that I listed previously, some the things that stand out in my mind about ASP+ and process of developing it are the following:

❑ Factored design. One of the best design decisions that we made was to completely factor ASP+ as a set of components. This allowed us to easily extend the model to do things such as low-level HTTP handlers, web services, plug-in authentication modules, and extensible state services.

❑ Scalability. We worked very hard to build a highly scalable model. Key things that we did were to create scalable state services, to address issues with using session state in a web farm, and web gardens, which is a strangely named technique for running a given application with multiple processes, each bound to a CPU in multi-proc boxes.

❑ Availability. We did lots of work to make ASP+ highly available. This included a new, high performance process model that could detect crashes, deadlocks and memory leaks and gracefully recover from them. The result is that an ASP+ app should never appear to be down!

❑ Working with tools. In order to truly "do for the Web what VB had done for Windows", it was critically important that we have great tools targeting ASP+. Luckily for us, the Visual Studio team had the exact same vision and devoted considerable resources to both creating tools for ASP+ and helping to create ASP+ itself. We viewed the design of ASP+ as a joint project with the VS team, and ASP+ is certainly a much richer product because of it. The end result is that Visual Studio 7 is a fantastic tool for building web applications and services that use ASP+.

Lastly, the greatest highlight of all is this – finally getting ASP+ into the hands of developers. And in order to really understand ASP+, it's critically important to have great books that explain it. How did this book come about? Well, it all started back in September of 1999. It was at the Wrox conference in Washington, D.C. that Scott Guthrie and I first publicly demonstrated ASP+. And it was there that we first talked to John Franklin from Wrox about the possibility of writing a book. We thought that Wrox would be the natural choice, because they have a history of writing great ASP and Windows DNA books. When I later presented ASP+ again at their London conference, in November of 1999, I had the chance to have lunch with all of the authors, and we talked about the book. They were all incredibly enthusiastic. Of course, at the time, they only knew a tiny bit about ASP+. They didn't know about the NGWS Runtime, Visual Studio, C#, or any of the other technologies that we were building. So, in reality, they didn't know *what* they were getting themselves into!

So there, in a nutshell, you have the story of ASP+. In closing, there are two groups of people that I would like to thank – one for what they've done, and one for what they are going to do. First, I would like to thank all of the people who built ASP+. They are an amazing group, and they've done fantastic work. I'm incredibly proud of them all. And finally, I would like to thank (in advance) all of the developers building the next generation of web applications and services with ASP+. We have spent a long time designing it, with the goal of allowing you to be successful and have a great time doing it.

Mark Anders
Product Unit Manager
NGWS Frameworks

Introduction

Microsoft's **Active Server Pages** technology is still a relatively new way to create dynamic Web sites and Web-based distributed applications. However, during its short life span, it has evolved to become the foremost tool in the Windows-oriented Web programmer's toolbox. This is probably due to the ease with which complex pages and applications can be created, combined with the ability to use home-grown custom components and existing Microsoft and 3rd party commercial components through the **Component Object Model** (COM/COM+) architecture.

However, there are new standards and technologies surfacing in the computing world. Of these, probably the most compelling is **Extensible Markup Language**, or XML. Along with its associated technologies like XML Style Language (XSL), XML Schemas, and the Simple Object Access Protocol (SOAP), it is rapidly changing the way we think about the design and construction of distributed applications of all types.

A New Kind of ASP

At the time of writing, Microsoft is working on the next generation of ASP, provisionally called **ASP+ Next Generation Web Services**. It makes it much easier to create dynamic and scalable Web applications, especially in the common areas of user-interaction, data handling, and asynchronous services. And, while it is completely changed under the hood, the techniques you use and your existing expertise are as valuable as in earlier versions. The aims of the new technology are:

- ❑ **Simplified development**. While ASP is great to get started with, and is fairly straightforward, as a page grows in complexity it can get messy. ASP+ makes even the richest pages easy to write.

- ❑ **Language independence**. While ASP enables different languages to be used, it's limited to script languages. ASP+ allows compiled languages to be used, providing better performance and cross-language compatibility.

❏ **Separation of code and content**. In many environments, developing a Web application utilizes the skills of a wide range of professionals – for example, you have programmers writing the code, and designers making the HMTL look good. Having both the code and the content intermixed in a single file that both of these groups need to operate on makes it difficult for them to work together. ASP+ allows code and content to be separated.

❏ **Simplified deployment**. There are difficulties encountered today with deploying components, where they have to be registered and they are locked by the operating system when in use. Configuration also has to be done through special applications. Both these factors make it hard to deploy, move or replicate your application as a single entity.

❏ **Support for multiple client types**. It's hard to create pages that work well with all the different types of clients that are using the Web. ASP+ provides rich server-side components that can automatically produce output specifically targeted at each type of client.

❏ **Support for 'Next Generation' Web Services**. ASP+ provides a new 'Web Services' feature that allows services to be created with native support for consuming and generating XML.

❏ **Improved availability**. ASP+ is more tolerant of application failures, memory leaks, etc. It can pro-actively restart processes that have failed to improve reliability and availability.

❏ **Improved scalability**. New session-state features make it easy to create applications that work well in Web farms (with multiple servers) and 'Web gardens' (single servers with multiple processors).

❏ **Improved tool support**. The rich, component based, event driven programming model that ASP+ implements makes it easier for tools from Microsoft (such as Visual Studio) and from other vendors to be integrated. This makes the development process much more like creating traditional applications, and the development environment can interact better to make the job even easier.

Many of these changes came about because the architecture of ASP+ is now much more modularized. Every page becomes a programmatically accessible fully compiled runtime object, and takes advantage of techniques like object-oriented design, just-in-time compilation, runtime support and dynamic caching. At the same time, the backward-compatible nature of ASP+ means that existing pages and applications can often be used as they stand, and the new features of ASP+ added to them over time. Alternatively, you can run ASP+ pages side by side with your existing ASP pages and migrate to ASP+ at your own pace.

A New Runtime Environment

In Chapter 1, we overview the features of ASP+ and describe the new structure and concepts that it involves. However, ASP+ is only a part of a larger Windows system service. It depends on a new runtime system called the **Next Generation Web Services Runtime** (NGWS Runtime). The runtime provides a completely new, highly efficient and scalable execution environment for ASP+ and for other applications and services.

This new runtime is the foundation on which ASP+ is built, and it provides all the capabilities needed to build the new generation of Web-based distributed applications and dynamic Web sites. The tight integration does mean, however, that you need to understand a bit more about what goes on under the hood to get the best from ASP+. Again, in Chapter 1, we'll look at the main issues that this involves.

What Does This Book Cover?

This book was written as Microsoft was about to release the first preview version of ASP+. This release is almost feature complete, and stable enough for developers to begin learning about and using the new technology. While we can't guarantee that the final release version will be identical, you can be sure that almost all of the concepts, examples and explanations we provide are accurate within the timeframe of the first full version of ASP+.

In this book, we attempt to explain just what ASP+ is all about, how you can use it, and what you can use it for. We start in **Chapter 1** with a look at the overall concepts of ASP+, why and how it has changed, and the things you should know to use it effectively. We also look briefly at the NGWS runtime framework, and see how this integrates with the ASP+ code we write.

Chapter 2 then goes on to look at how we can create dynamic pages with ASP+ in much the same way as we've done with ASP. However, the new architecture of ASP+ allows us to do a lot more than before with a lot less code – the programmer's dream. We show you how ASP+ allows objects that represent HTML controls and elements to be executed on the server, with all the supporting HTML and code required being generated automatically.

To extend the functionality of these server-based controls, we can also use templates and server-side data binding to modify the code that is created. In **Chapter 3**, we show how to add these features to your pages. ASP+ will ship with a new data access technology called ADO+, which is integrated into the data binding process to provide truly disconnected and versatile recordset capabilities.

In **Chapter 4**, we introduce and describe a range of advanced ASP+ programming techniques. This includes the new input validation features, reusable 'pagelet' components, output caching support, and techniques for handling errors and debugging your pages.

Chapter 5 introduces another brand new technique called ASP+ Web Services. It demonstrates how you can create XML Services that are accessible across the Internet. Together with a range of new server-side components that come with ASP+, these allow powerful business-to-business applications to be built without the need for the cumbersome techniques we've used in the past.

In **Chapter 6**, we move on to take a more in-depth technical look at the ASP+ Application Framework. To get the most from ASP+, you need to understand a little more about how requests and responses are managed, and how ASP+ application configuration differs from existing techniques. The good news is that it's much easier than ever before, through a far more flexible and extensible management system.

While the server-side controls provided with ASP+ are undoubtedly powerful and useful, you may need to create your own at some stage, or extend the controls that are provided. This might be in order to achieve new functionality, or to provide broader coverage for different kinds of client-side user agent. **Chapter 7** looks at how we can build our own server-side controls, and add them to the ASP+ environment.

Finally, in **Chapter 8**, we look at an application that was designed and built by Microsoft as an example of the way that ASP+ can be used. It takes advantage of many of the new features in ASP+ and the universal runtime, and will help you to get a feel for how complete applications can be created.

Who Is This Book For?

This book covers a product that is still under development, and as such it is aimed at experienced ASP developers who are working at the leading edge – rather than the casual ASP developer or beginner. For example, we do not cover the basics of COM, ASP, or the programming and scripting languages we use in this book.

However, the fact that (at the time of writing) the product is still a preview version does **not** mean that you can ignore it. ASP+ is going to arrive with the new NGWS runtime package, and it will probably also be part of the next release of Visual Studio (which should contain tools to help you work with ASP+).

So, our aim is to cover conceptual overviews of the product – including some of the background theory and explanation of why the product has developed along the lines it has. This is followed by deeper investigation of the features that developers will use first. We show how to take advantage of the new features quickly and with the minimum of fuss.

Providing that you have used ASP before, and are reasonably comfortable with the concepts, you should be able to use this book without requiring any other reference material (other than the SDK and Help files provided with the product). You should also be comfortable with the general principles of using COM to instantiate and use components, and the Visual Basic (or VBScript) languages. Some of the samples are written in other languages, such as C++, JScript and C# (read as "C Sharp") that are supported by the universal runtime framework, but you don't need to be fluent in these languages to be able to use this book.

Acknowledgements

While we depend on the software manufacturers to help us out with technical support and information for almost all the books we write, we must acknowledge the special situation within which this book was produced. Wrox has been at the forefront of ASP publishing since the first beginnings of this technology, and we are grateful for the regular support we receive from the developers and product managers at Microsoft.

This book, however, began life during a very early stage of the development of ASP+ and has provided us with a unique insight into the development of the product. It certainly could not have been written without the generous and timely assistance of many members of the ASP and COM+ teams at Microsoft, especially Mark Anders, Scott Guthrie, Brad Merrill, Brad Millington, Eric Andrae and the rest of the ASP+ team.

To all of you, thanks guys – we hope you like the result.

What You Need to Use this Book

To run all of the examples, you'll need to have the following software:

- ❑ Windows 2000
- ❑ Internet Explorer 5.5
- ❑ NGWS Runtime
- ❑ SQL Server 7

The complete source code for this book is available for download from our website, at http://www.wrox.com. Updates to the book will be available at http://www.wrox.com/beta

Conventions

To help you get the most from the text and keep track of what's happening, we've used a number of conventions throughout the book.

For instance:

> **These boxes hold important, not-to-be forgotten information that is directly relevant to the surrounding text.**

While the background style is used for asides to the current discussion.

As for styles in the text:

- ❑ When we introduce them, we **highlight** important words
- ❑ We show keyboard strokes like this: *Ctrl-A*
- ❑ We show filenames and code within the text like so: doGet()
- ❑ Text on user interfaces (and URLs) is shown as: Menu

We present code in two different ways:

```
In our code examples, the code foreground style shows new, important,
    pertinent code
while code background shows code that's less important in the present context,
    or which has been seen before.
```

Tell Us What You Think

We've worked hard to make this book as useful to you as possible, so we'd like to know what you think. We're always keen to know what it is you want and need to know.

We appreciate feedback on our efforts and take both criticism and praise on board in our future editorial efforts. If you've anything to say, let us know via e-mail:

feedback@wrox.com

or via the feedback links on our web site:

http://www.wrox.com

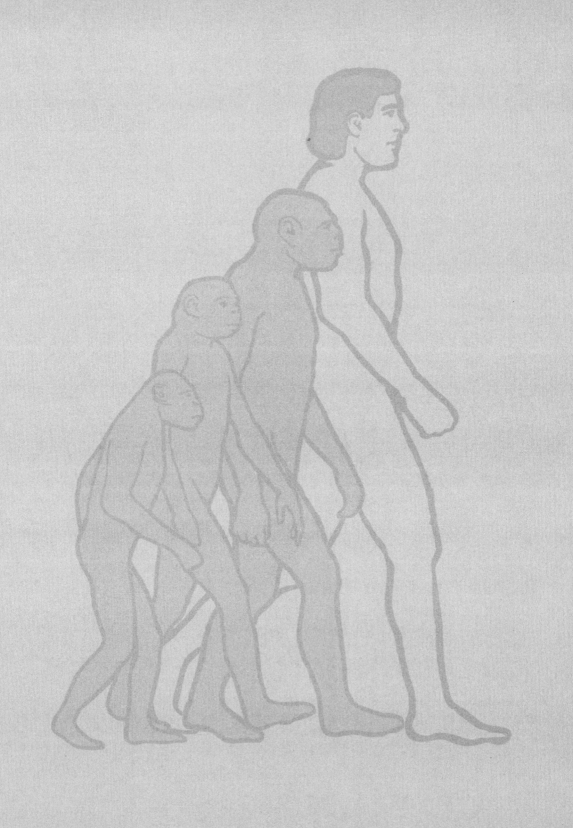

1

Introducing ASP+

Even though the ink is barely dry on the documentation for Active Server Pages 3.0, Microsoft is already hard at work on the next generation of their core server-side programming technology. In this chapter, we introduce this new product, and look at what it is all about. Currently called **ASP+ Next Generation Web Services** (though this name might yet change) we'll see why we need a new version of ASP, and explore the concepts behind its design and implementation. While this book is aimed predominantly at experienced developers who have used ASP before, we start out in this chapter by examining some of the core issues involved when you decide to migrate to ASP+.

ASP+ is designed to be backwards-compatible with earlier versions of ASP, with only minor changes required in some circumstances (we explore these further in the appendices). However, more to the point, you can install ASP+ on an existing Windows 2000 server alongside ASP 3.0. This allows you to experiment with the new version, without requiring a separate 'test bed' server. You can continue using existing ASP applications, and migrate them ASP+ when you are ready, so your investment in ASP is not lost.

But simply porting your applications to ASP+ will only give you a few of the benefits the new version offers. ASP+ has many new features that provide far greater ease of use, more power and better runtime efficiency, but to take advantage of them you will need to understand more about the way that ASP+ works.

As we are writing this book using a preview version of ASP+, we can't be exactly sure of all the features of the final release. But thanks to the information and assistance provided by the ASP+ team at Microsoft, we can be pretty sure that the content of the book will be reliable and useful with the final version. We'll also be maintaining a special Web site that is accessible from http://www.wrox.com/beta, where we'll document changes as the beta and final release versions appear, and provide some detailed information as well.

So, in this first chapter, we'll cover:

- ❑ How Active Server Pages has evolved since its inception

- ❑ What the new runtime framework is

- ❑ How ASP+ is different to ASP, and why

- ❑ A brief guide to getting started with ASP+

- ❑ Some of the changes expected in the final release version

We start with a look at the way that ASP and ASP+ have evolved, as this will help to set the background for understanding and working with the new product. For more information about working with COM+ and previous versions of ASP, check out Professional ASP 3.0, (ISBN 1-861002-61-0) from Wrox.

The Evolution of Active Server Pages

Although it seems to have been around forever, **Active Server Pages** is only some three-and-a-bit years old. Since its inception in late 1996, it has grown rapidly to become the major technique for server-side Web programming in the Windows environment (and on some other platforms using other implementations that accept the same or similar syntax, such as ChilliASP). But it didn't come from nowhere – the foundations lie much further back than that.

Dynamic Server-side Web Programming

Traditionally, dynamic Web pages have been created using server-side executable programs. A standardized Web server interface specification called the **Common Gateway Interface** (CGI) allows an executable program to access all the information within incoming requests from clients. The program can then generate all the output required to make up the return page (the HTML, script code, text, etc.), and send it back to the client via the Web server.

To make the programmer's life easier, and save having to create executable programs, languages such as Perl use an application that accepts text-based script files. The programmer simply writes the script, and the Web server executes it using a Perl interpreter.

Microsoft ISAPI Technologies

Microsoft introduced another Web server interface with their Web server, Internet Information Server. This is the **Internet Server Application Programming Interface** (ISAPI), and differs from the CGI in that it allows compiled code within a dynamic link library (DLL) to be executed directly by the Web server. As with the CGI, the code can access all the information in the client request, and it generates the entire output for the returned page.

Most developments in Microsoft's Web arena have been based on the ISAPI interface. One early and short-lived product was **dbWeb**, a data access technology that provided a range of searching, filtering and formatting capabilities for accessing data stored on the server, and for interacting with the client.

A second development was the **Internet Database Connector** (IDC). This proved a big hit with developers – not only because it was fast and efficient (unlike dbWeb), but also because it was a lot more generic and easier to program. IDC introduced the concept of **templates**, allowing programmers to easily adapt existing HTML pages to use its features and quickly build new applications around it.

IDC uses two text files for each 'page'. The first is a simple script that defines the way that the data should be collected from the server-based database. In essence, it is just a SQL statement plus some configuration information:

```
{this is the query file named getuserlist.idc}
Datasource: GlobalExampleData
Username: examples
Password: secret
Template: getuserlist.htx
SQLStatement:
+ SELECT DISTINCT UserName
+ FROM Person ORDER BY UserName;
```

The server executes this file to obtain the results recordset, then loads a template file:

```
{this is an extract from the template file named getuserlist.htx}
...
<TABLE>
  <TR>
    <TD>User name:</TD>
    <TD>
      <SELECT NAME=selUserName>
        <%BeginDetail%>
        <OPTION VALUE="<%UserName%>"><%UserName%>
        <%EndDetail%>
      </SELECT>
    </TD>
  </TR>
</TABLE>
...
```

The template is just an ordinary Web page, including HTML, text and other objects, but with one or more specially delimited placeholders inserted. And the syntax for these placeholders, and the other simple program code constructs that are supported, is eerily like ASP. Of course, it was from this that ASP actually evolved:

The Versions of ASP

So, it was in early 1996 that **Denali** (the codename for ASP) was released as a beta version 0.9 product, and it took the Web-development world by storm. The ability to execute code inline within a Web page was so simple and yet so powerful. With the provision of a series of components that could perform advanced features, most notably **ActiveX Data Objects** (ADO), it was almost child's play to create all kinds of dynamic pages.

The final release version of Active Server Pages 1.0, available as an add-on for IIS 3.0, was soon in use on Windows platforms all over the place. The combination of ASP with ADO enabled developers to easily create and open recordsets from a database. There's no doubt that this was one of the main factors for its rapid acceptance, because now you could create and open recordsets from a database within the script, and manipulate and output any values, in any order, almost any way you wanted.

In 1998, Microsoft introduced ASP 2.0 as part of the free **Windows NT4 Option Pack**. The major difference between this release of ASP and version 1.0 was in the way that external components could be instantiated. With ASP 2.0 and IIS 4.0, it is possible to create an ASP **application**, and within it run components in their own separate memory space (i.e. out of process). The provision of **Microsoft Transaction Server** (MTS) also made it easy to build components that can partake in transactions.

Windows 2000, COM+, and ASP 3.0

Early this year (2000), Windows 2000 arrived. This contains version 5.0 of IIS, and version 3.0 of ASP. Other than some minor additions to ASP, the core difference here is actually more to do with COM+. In Windows 2000, Microsoft combined MTS with the core COM runtime to create **COM+**. This provides a host of new features that make the use of components easier, as well as giving a much more stable, scalable and efficient execution platform.

Other than a few minor changes to the management interface, IIS has not changed a great deal on the surface. However, underneath, it now uses COM+ Component Services to provide a better environment for components to be executed within, including out of process execution as the default and the option to run each component in its own isolated process if required.

ASP+ and the Next Generation Web Services Framework

All this brings us to the present, with ASP+. The underlying structure of ASP+ is very different to that of previous versions, although from the 'outside' (as far as the developer is concerned) it does appear to offer a very similar interface. ASP+ is almost entirely component-based and modularized, and every page, object, and HTML element you use can be a runtime component object.

For this to perform efficiently, and provide a scalable solution, the management of these objects is a very necessary prerequisite. The new runtime environment carries out this management automatically, allowing ASP+ to become far more object-oriented in nature. This lets developers build more powerful applications by accessing these component objects in a far more granular and controlled manner.

On top of that, the object orientation of ASP+ provides extensibility for the environment as a whole. Developers can add to and extend the environment, both by creating new components or inheriting from the base classes that create them, and by over-riding selected behavior as required. Under the hood, the COM+ runtime manages the instantiation, pooling, and allocation of the objects automatically.

The Next Generation Web Services Framework

So, COM+ provides a framework of operating system services. But that's not the whole story. ASP+ is actually a part of a brand new **runtime framework** that provides support for all kinds of applications in Windows. The framework is a key part of of Microsoft's **Next Generation Web Services** or **NGWS**. When you install this, you get ASP+ as part of the package. The NGWS framework supports all other server-side programming techniques as well, such as a new managed component service, support for building executable applications and Windows Services, access to performance counter APIs and Event Log APIs, etc.

The NGWS framework extends the Component Object Model (COM) architecture that we use to create re-usable and interoperable software components by adding new and enhanced services for scalable distributed applications:

- ❏ A unified, rich set of programming libraries
- ❏ A secure, multi-language runtime engine
- ❏ Simplified application creation, deployment and maintenance
- ❏ Increased scalability for distributed applications
- ❏ Protection of existing software and training investments

We'll look at how it does all these things next.

What Is the NGWS Framework?

The integration of ASP into the operating system differs remarkably from earlier versions of ASP, which were basically just add-ons to the operating system. Up until now, ASP has been implemented through an ISAPI DLL named asp.dll, plus a few new system files and the ASP user components that came as part of the package (such as the Browser Capabilities component).

The NGWS framework reflects the information technology industry's changing view of the needs for creating, deploying, and maintaining Web services of all types – ranging from simple client applications to the most complex distributed architectures. The overall concept and strategy is part of the Windows **Distributed Internet Applications** (DNA) architecture.

However, the important part to recognize is that the framework is **not** just there for ASP+. It acts as a base for all kinds of applications to be built on Windows. The following diagram shows how the runtime framework supports **ASP+ Applications**:

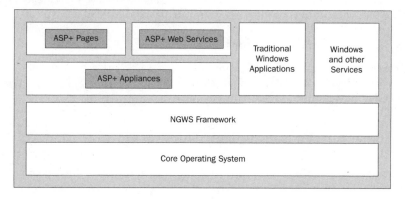

The NGWS framework provides an execution engine to run code, and a family of object oriented classes/components that can be used to build applications. It also acts as an interface between applications and the core operating system. You might ask why we need such a layer, when existing applications can talk to the core operating system and services quite easily. The reason is that it allows applications to use the operating system to best advantage, in a standard way that permits faster and simpler development – something that is increasingly necessary in today's competitive commercial environment.

To achieve these aims, the runtime framework implements many of the features that the programmer, or the specific programming language environment, had to provide themselves. This includes things like automatic garbage collection, rich libraries of reusable objects to meet the needs of the most common tasks, and improved security for applications. This last point, of course, is becoming more important with the spread of networked applications – especially those that run over the Internet.

A Common Intermediate Language

However, one of the biggest advantages that the runtime framework provides is a language-neutral execution environment. All code, irrespective of the source language, is compiled automatically into a standard **intermediate language** (**IL**) – either on command or when first executed (in the case of ASP+). The runtime framework then creates the final binary code that makes up the application and executes it. The compiled IL code is used for each request until the source code is changed, at which point the cached version is invalidated and discarded.

So, whether you use Visual Basic, C#, JScript, Perl or any of the other supported languages, the intermediate code that is created is (or should be) identical. And the caching of the final binary object code improves efficiency and scalability at runtime as well.

> *C# is the new language from Microsoft especially designed for use with the Next Generation Web Services framework and ASP+. It combines the power and efficiency of C++ with the simplicity of Visual Basic and JScript.*

One thing that this achieves is the ability to call from one language to another, and even inherit from objects created in one language and modify them within another language. For example, you can inherit an object that is written in C# in your VB program and then add methods or properties, or over-ride existing methods and properties. In fact, parts of the framework, and the entire ASP+ object model, are now implemented internally using C# rather than C++.

So, the new runtime framework introduces a true multi-language platform for programming any kind of application. As most of our current development is in the area of distributed applications, especially Internet- and Intranet-based applications, many the new features are directly aimed at this type of development.

The Web Application Infrastructure

The three sections shown highlighted in the previous diagram (and repeated in the next diagram) are those that implement ASP+ itself, and which we're interested in for this book:

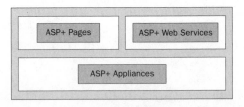

Together, these three sections implement the **Web Application Infrastructure** – the topic that we are concerned with in this book. Together with the new runtime framework, it provides a range of exciting new features:

User Interface Support

As part of the ASP+ libraries, there is a host of intelligent server-based rich controls for building Web-based user interfaces quickly and simply. They can output HTML 3.2 code for down-level browsers, while taking advantage of the runtime libraries for enhanced interactivity on richer clients such as Internet Explorer 4 and above.

These server-based controls can be also be reused to build controls composed of other controls, inheriting implementation and logic from these constituent controls.

Data Access Support

The NGWS framework provides a new version of ADO, called **ADO+**, which offers integrated services for accessing data – regardless of the format or location of that data. ADO+ presents an object-oriented view of relational data, giving developers quick and easy access to data derived from distributed sources.

ADO+ also improves support for, and to some extent relies on, XML. ADO+ can automatically persist and restore recordsets (or **datasets** as they are now called) to and from XML. As we'll see, this is particularly useful when passing data around the Web using ASP+ Web Services.

Scalability for Distributed Applications

Two of the major requirements for any Web-based application are a robust operating platform, and scalability to allow large numbers of multiple concurrent requests to be handled. The NGWS runtime provides these features by allowing automatic error and overload detection to restart and manage the applications and components that are in use at any one time. This prevents errant code or memory leaks from soaking up resources and bringing the server to a halt.

There are also new and updated system and infrastructure services, including automatic memory management and garbage collection, automatic persistence and marshaling, and evidenced based security. Together these features provide for more scalable and reliable resource allocation and application processing.

Existing Software and Training Investments

Despite all the changes to the core operating system and runtimes, great care has been taken to maintain backward compatibility with earlier versions of Windows, COM and ASP. In most cases, existing applications, COM and COM+ components, ASP pages, and other scripts and executables work under the NGWS runtime. Alternatively, you can update them in your own time as your business requirements demand.

> All ASP+ pages have the `.aspx` file extension, and this is mapped to the ASP+ runtime framework. This allows pages that have the `.asp` file extension to run unchanged under the existing ASP runtime.

How is ASP+ Different from ASP?

Having seen in outline how ASP+ is now an integral part of the operating system, we need to look at the other aspect. How, and why, is ASP+ different to earlier version of ASP? And just **how** different is it? Well, if you just want to run existing pages and applications, you probably won't notice the differences much at all. However, once you open up the ASP+ SDK or Help files, you'll see a whole new vista of stuff that doesn't look the least bit familiar.

Don't panic! We'll work through the main differences next. We'll start with a look at why Microsoft has decided that we need a new version of ASP, and how it will help you, as a developer, to meet the needs of the future when creating Web sites and applications. We'll follow this with a checklist of the major new features of ASP+, then examine each one in a little more detail. The remainder of the book then covers the new features one by one, explaining how you can use them.

Why Do We Need a New Version of ASP?

In the Introduction to this book, we listed the main motivations that Microsoft had when designing and developing ASP+. After all, considering that ASP has been so successful, why do we need a new version? There are really four main issues to consider:

- ❑ Currently, ASP can only be scripted using the basic non-typed languages such as VBScript and JScript (unless you install a separate language interpreter). While ASP does parse and cache the code for the page the first time it is executed, the limitations prevent more strongly-typed languages like Visual Basic and C++ from being used where this would be an advantage. ASP+ provides a true language-neutral execution framework for Web applications to use.

- ❑ It is also very easy to create huge ASP pages containing a spaghetti-like mixture of code, HTML, text, object declarations, etc. And it's hard to re-use code, unless you place it in separate 'include' files – not the best solution. In many environments, developing a Web application utilizes the skills of a wide range of professionals, for example, you have programmers writing the code, and designers making the HMTL look good. Having both the code and the content intermixed in a single file that both of these groups need to operate on makes it difficult for them to work together. ASP+ allows true separation of code and content.

- ❑ In previous versions of ASP, you have to write code to do almost anything. Want to maintain state in form fields? Write code. Want to validate data entered on the client? Write code. Want to emit some simple data values? Write code. Want to cache regions of pages to optimize performance? Write code. ASP+ introduces a real component model, with server-based controls and an event driven execution paradigm similar in concept to the way that a Visual Basic 'Form' works now. The new ASP+ server controls are declarative (i.e. you only have to declare them in order to get them to do something), and so you actually write less code – in fact, in many situations you don't have to write any code at all!

- ❑ The world out there is changing. The proportion of users on the Web that will access your site through an 'Internet device' such as a mobile cellular phone, personal digital assistant (PDA), TV set-top box, games console, or whatever else, will soon be greater that the number using a PC and a traditional Web browser. This means that we probably have to be prepared to do more work at the server to tailor our pages to suit a specific device. We'll also have to create the output in a whole new range of formats such as the Wireless Markup Language (WML). And, in addition to creating WML for rendering, new Internet devices and business applications are going to want to be able to send and receive XML data from Web applications. Doing this today from ASP requires you to manually use an XML parser, convert data to and from XML schemas, etc. ASP+ Web Services makes it much easier.

Besides all of this, the rapidly changing nature of distributed applications requires faster development, more componentization and re-usability, easier deployment, and wider platform support. New standards such as the Simple Object Access Protocol (SOAP), and new commercial requirements such as business-to-business (B2B) data interchange, require new techniques to be used to generate output and communicate with other systems. Web applications and Web sites also need to provide a more robust and scalable service, which ASP+ provides through proactive monitoring and automatic restarting of applications when failures, memory leaks, etc. are discovered.

So, to attempt to meet all these needs, ASP has been totally revamped from the ground up into a whole new programming environment. While there are few tools available to work with it just yet, Visual Studio 7.0 will be providing full support to make building ASP+ applications easy (both ASP+ Pages and ASP+ Services).

The rich, component based, event driven programming model is specifically designed to be 'tools friendly', and this support will be available for all Visual Studio languages – including VB, C++, and C#. And you can be sure that third party tool manufacturers will not be far behind.

The Big Advantages with ASP+

The biggest challenges facing the Web developer today must be the continued issues of browser compatibility, and the increasing complexity of the pages that they have to create. Trying to build more interactive pages that use the latest features of each browser, whilst still making sure that the pages will work on all the popular browsers, is a nightmare that refuses to go away.

And, of course, it will only get worse with the new types of Internet device that are on the way, or here already. In particular, trying to build pages to offer the same user-level capability to cellular phones as to traditional browser clients is just about impossible. The text-only 12-character by 3-line display of many cellular phones does tend to limit creativity and user interaction.

One obvious solution is to create output that is targeted at each specific client dynamically – or create multiple versions of the same site, one for each type of client. The second option is not attractive, and most developers would prefer the first one. However, this implies that every hit from every user will require some server-side processing to figure out what output to create.

If this is the case, why not automate much of the process? To this end, ASP+ introduces the concept of server controls that encapsulate common tasks and provide a clean programming model. They also help to manage the targeting of all the different types of client.

Server-side HTML Controls – Less Code to Write

ASP has always provided the opportunity to execute components on the server, and these components can generate sections of the page that is returned to the user. ASP+ extends this concept through **server controls**. All that's required to turn any HTML element into a server control is the addition of an extra attribute: `runat="server"`.

Any HTML element in a page can be marked this way, and ASP+ will then process the element on the server and can generate output that suits this specific client. And, as a by-product, we can do extra tricks – in particular with HTML `<form>` and the associated form control elements, where we can create the code to manage state during round trips to the server. This makes the programming experience less monotonous and dramatically more productive.

While the concept of having HTML elements that execute on the server may at first seem a little strange, as you'll see it adds a whole new layer of functionality to the pages, and makes them easier to write at the same time. What more could a programmer want?

The Problems with Maintaining State

One of the most cumbersome tasks when creating interactive Web sites and applications is managing the values passed to the server from HTML form controls, and maintaining the values in these controls between page requests. So one of the core aims of ASP+ is to simplify this programming task. This involves no extra effort on the part of the programmer, and works fine on all browsers that support basic HTML and above.

Take a look at the following section of code. This creates a simple form using HTML controls where the user can enter the name of a computer and select an operating system. OK, so this isn't a terribly exciting example in itself, but it illustrates a pretty common scenario used by almost every web application out there today. When the form page is submitted to the server, the values the user selected are extracted from the `Request.Form` collection and displayed with the `Response.Write` method. The important parts of the page are highlighted in the code listing:

```
<html>
  <body>
    <%
    If Len(Request.Form("selOpSys")) > 0 Then
      strOpSys = Request.Form("selOpSys")
      strName = Request.Form("txtName")
      Response.Write "You selected '" & strOpSys _
                    & "' for machine '" & strName & "'."
    End If
    %>
    <form action="pageone.asp" method="post">
      Machine Name:
      <input type="text" name="txtName">
      <p />
      Operating System:
      <select name="selOpSys" size="1">
        <option>Windows 95</option>
        <option>Windows 98</option>
        <option>Windows NT4</option>
        <option>Windows 2000</option>
      </select>
      <p />
      <input type="submit" value="Submit">
    </form>
  </body>
</html>
```

> **Although this is an ASP page (the file extension is `.asp` rather than `.aspx`), it will work just the same under ASP+ if we changed the extension to `.aspx`. Remember that the two systems can quite freely co-exist on the same machine, and the file extension just determines whether ASP or ASP+ processes it.**

This screenshot shows what it looks like in Internet Explorer 5. When the user clicks the Submit button to send the values to the server, the page is reloaded showing the selected values. Of course, in a real application, some the values would probably be stored in a database, or be used to perform some application-specific processing – for this example we're just displaying them in the page:

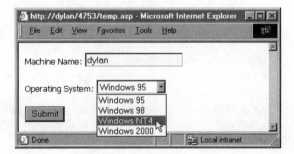

One problem is that the page does not maintain its **state**, in other words the controls return to their default values. The user has to re-enter them to use the form again. You can see this is the next screenshot:

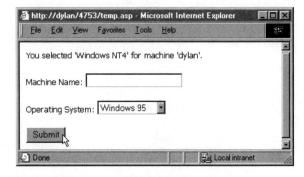

To get round this situation, we have to add extra ASP code to the page to insert the values into the controls when the page is reloaded. For the text box, this is just a matter of setting the value attribute with some inline ASP code, using the HTMLEncode method to ensure that any non-legal HTML characters are properly encoded. However, for the <select> list, we have to do some work to figure out which value was selected, and add the selected attribute to that particular <option> element. The changes required are highlighted below:

```
<html>
  <body>
    <%
    If Len(Request.Form("selOpSys")) > 0 Then
      strOpSys = Request.Form("selOpSys")
      strName = Request.Form("txtName")
      Response.Write "You selected '" & strOpSys _
                  & "' for machine '" & strName & "'."
    End If
    %>
    <form action="pageone.asp" method="post">
      Machine Name:
      <input type="text" name="txtName"
             value="<% = Server.HTMLEncode(Request("txtName")) %>">
      <p />
      Operating System:
      <select name="selOpSys" size="1">
        <option
        <% If strOpSys = "Windows 95" Then Response.Write " selected" %>
        >Windows 95</option>
        <option
        <% If strOpSys = "Windows 98" Then Response.Write " selected" %>
        >Windows 98</option>
        <option
        <% If strOpSys = "Windows NT4" Then Response.Write " selected" %>
        >Windows NT4</option>
        <option
        <% If strOpSys = "Windows 2000" Then Response.Write " selected" %>
        >Windows 2000</option>
      </select>
      <p />
      <input type="submit" value="Submit">
    </form>
  </body>
</html>
```

Now, when the page is reloaded, the controls maintain their state and show the values the user selected:

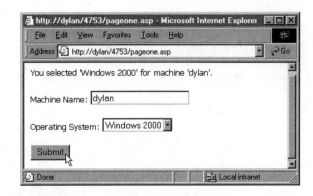

This page, named pageone.asp, *is in the* Chapter01 *directory of the samples available for the book. You can download all the sample files from our Web site at http://www.wrox.com.*

Controls that Automatically Maintain Their State

So, how does ASP+ help us in this commonly met situation? The next listing shows the changes required for taking advantage of ASP+ server controls that automatically preserve their state. We still use the Response.Write method to display the selected values. However, this time some of the elements on the page have the special runat="server" attribute added to them. When ASP+ sees these elements, it processes them on the server and creates the appropriate HTML output for the client:

```
<html>
  <body>
    <%
    If Len(Request.Form("selOpSys")) > 0 Then
      strOpSys = Request.Form("selOpSys")
      strName = Request.Form("txtName")
      Response.Write("You selected '" & strOpSys _
               & "' for machine '" & strName & "'.")
    End If
    %>
    <form runat="server">
      Machine Name:
      <input type="text" id="txtName" runat="server">
      <p />
      Operating System:
      <select id="selOpSys" size="1" runat="server">
        <option>Windows 95</option>
        <option>Windows 98</option>
        <option>Windows NT4</option>
        <option>Windows 2000</option>
      </select>
      <p />
      <input type="submit" value="Submit">
    </form>
  </body>
</html>
```

You can clearly see how much simpler this ASP+ page is than the last example. When loaded into Internet Explorer 5 and the values submitted to the server, the result appears to be just the same:

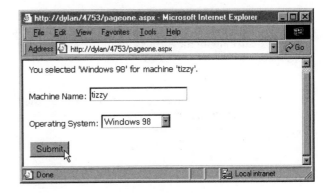

This page, named `pageone.aspx`, *is in the* `Chapter01` *directory of the samples available for the book. You can download all the sample files from our Web site at* http://www.wrox.com.

How Do the Server-Side Controls Work?

How is this achieved? The key is the `runat="server"` attribute. To get an idea of what's going on, take a look at the source of the page from within the browser. It looks like this:

```
<html>
  <body>
    You selected 'Windows 98' for machine 'tizzy'.
    <FORM name="ctrl0" method="post" action="pageone.aspx" id="ctrl0">
    <INPUT type="hidden" name="__VIEWSTATE" value="a0z1741688109__x">
      Machine Name:
      <INPUT type="text" id="txtName" name="txtName" value="tizzy">
      <p />
      Operating System:
      <SELECT id="selOpSys" size="1" name="selOpSys">
        <OPTION value="Windows 95">Windows 95</OPTION>
        <OPTION selected value="Windows 98">Windows 98</OPTION>
        <OPTION value="Windows NT4">Windows NT4</OPTION>
        <OPTION value="Windows 2000">Windows 2000</OPTION>
      </SELECT>
      <p />
      <input type="submit" value="Submit">
    </FORM>
  </body>
</html>
```

We wrote this ASP+ code to create the `<form>` in the page:

```
<form runat="server">
   ...
</form>
```

When the page is executed by ASP+, the output to the browser is:

```
<FORM name="ctrl0" method="post" action="pageone.aspx" id="ctrl0">
   ...
</FORM>
```

You can see that the action and method attributes are automatically created by ASP+ so that the values of the controls in the form will be POSTed back to the same page. ASP+ also adds a unique id and name attribute to the form as we didn't provide one. However, if you do specify these, the values you specify will be used instead.

> If you include the method="GET" attribute, the form contents are sent to the server as part of the query string instead, as in previous versions of ASP, and the automatic state management will no longer work.

Inside the form, we wrote this ASP+ code to create the text box:

```
<input type="text" id="txtName" runat="server">
```

The result in the browser is this:

```
<INPUT type="text" id="txtName" name="txtName" value="tizzy">
```

You can see that ASP+ has automatically added the value attribute with the text value that was in the control when the form was submitted. It has also preserved the name attribute we provided, and added an id attribute with the same value.

For the <select> list, we wrote this code:

```
<select id="selOpSys" size="1" runat="server">
  <option>Windows 95</option>
  <option>Windows 98</option>
  <option>Windows NT4</option>
  <option>Windows 2000</option>
</select>
```

ASP+ obliged by outputting this HTML, which has a selected attribute in the appropriate <option> element:

```
<SELECT name="selOpSys" id="selOpSys" size="1">
  <OPTION value="Windows 95">Windows 95</OPTION>
  <OPTION selected value="Windows 98">Windows 98</OPTION>
  <OPTION value="Windows NT4">Windows NT4</OPTION>
  <OPTION value="Windows 2000">Windows 2000</OPTION>
</SELECT>
```

Again, a unique id attribute has been created, and the <option> elements have matching value attributes added automatically. (If we had provided our own value attributes in the page, however, these would have been preserved.)

The Page VIEWSTATE

The other change is that ASP+ has automatically added a HIDDEN-type control to the form:

```
<INPUT type="hidden" name="__VIEWSTATE" value="a0z1741688109__x">
```

This is how ASP+ can store ambient state changes of a page across multiple requests – i.e. things that don't automatically get sent back and forth between the browser and server between Web requests. For example, if the background color of a server control had been modified it would use the VIEWSTATE hidden field to remember this between requests. The VIEWSTATE field is used whenever you post back to the originating page. In Chapter 2, we discuss this topic in more detail.

> So, as you can see, there really aren't any 'magic tricks' being played. It's all standard HTML, with *no* client-side script libraries, and *no* ActiveX controls or Java applets. An equally important point is that *absolutely no state* is being stored on the server. Instead, values are simply posted to the server using standard methods. Values are preserved and maintained across requests simply by the server controls modifying the HTML before the pages are sent to the client.

Server-side Code in ASP+

To display the values in the page, we used code that is very similar to that we used in the ASP example earlier on:

```
...
If Len(Request.Form("selOpSys")) > 0 Then
  strOpSys = Request.Form("selOpSys")
  strName = Request.Form("txtName")
  Response.Write("You selected '" & strOpSys _
             & "' for machine '" & strName & "'.")
End If
...
```

However, one of the other great features of ASP+ and server controls is that they are available to the code running on the server that is creating the page output. The ASP+ interpreter insists that each one has a unique id attribute, and therefore *all* the server controls (i.e. the elements that have the runat="server" attribute) will be available to code against. This means that we no longer have to access the Request collection to get the values that were posted back to the server from our form controls – we can instead refer to them directly using their unique id:

```
...
If Len(selOpSys.value) > 0 Then
  Response.Write("You selected '" & selOpSys.value _
             & "' for machine '" & txtName.value & "'.")
End If
...
```

Visual Basic Code in ASP+

In the ASP page we've just seen, the script was assumed to be VBScript (we didn't specify this, and VBScript is the default unless you change the server settings). In ASP+, there is no support for VBScript. Instead, the default language is Visual Basic ("VB"), which is a superset of VB. So, our code is being compiled into IL and executed by the runtime.

The compiler and runtime for Visual Basic that is included with ASP+ is the new version 7.0 (good news – you don't need to buy a separate copy!). There are a few implications in this, which we summarize in Appendix **B** of this book.

The most important thing to note straight away is that all method calls in VB7 must have the parameter list enclosed in parentheses (much like JScript and JavaScript). In VBScript and earlier versions of VB, this was not required – and in some cases produced an error. You can see that we've enclosed the parameter to the `Response.Write` method in parentheses in our example.

Secondly, VB7 has no concept of 'default' methods or 'default' properties, so we now must provide the method or property name. You'll probably come across this first when working with ADO recordsets where the syntax must be:

```
fieldvalue = objRecordset.Fields("fieldname").value
```

Server-side Event Processing – A Better Code Structure

Of course, if we are going to have HTML elements that execute on the server, why not extend the concept even more? ASP+ changes each page into a server-side object, and exposes more properties, methods and events that can be used within your code to create the content dynamically. Each page becomes a tree of COM+ objects that can be accessed and programmed individually as required.

Using Server-side Control Events

To see how we can take advantage of this to structure our pages more elegantly, take a look at the following code. It shows the ASP+ page we used in our previous example, but with a couple of changes. This version of the page is named `pagetwo.aspx`:

```
<html>
  <body>
    <script language="VB" runat="server">
      Sub ShowValues(Sender As Object, Args As EventArgs)
        divResult.innerText = "You selected '" _
          & selOpSys.value & "' for machine '" _
          & txtName.value & "'."
      End Sub
    </script>
    <div id="divResult" runat="server"></div>
    <form runat="server">
      Machine Name:
      <input type="text" id="txtName" runat="server">
      <p />
      Operating System:
      <select id="selOpSys" size="1" runat="server">
        <option>Windows 95</option>
        <option>Windows 98</option>
        <option>Windows NT4</option>
        <option>Windows 2000</option>
      </select>
      <p />
      <input type="submit" value="Submit"
             runat="server" onserverclick="ShowValues">
    </form>
  </body>
</html>
```

Firstly, notice that we've replaced the inline ASP+ code with a `<script>` section that specifies VB as the language, and includes the `runat="server"` attribute. Inside it, we've written a Visual Basic function named `ShowValues`. In ASP+, functions and subroutines must be placed inside a server-side `<script>` element, and not in the usual `<%...%>` script delimiters – we'll look at this in more detail in the next chapter.

We've also added an HTML `<div>` element to the page, including the `runat="server"` attribute. So this element will be created on the server, and is therefore available to code running there. When the VB subroutine is executed, it sets the `innerText` property of this `<div>` element.

Notice also how it gets at the values required (e.g. those submitted by the user). Because the text box and `<select>` list also run on the server, our code can extract the values directly by accessing the `value` properties of these controls. When the page is executed and rendered on the client, the `<div>` element that is created looks like this:

```
<div id="divResult">You selected 'Windows NT4' for machine 'lewis'.</div>
```

Connecting Server-side Control Events To Your Code

By now you should be asking how the VB subroutine actually gets executed. Easy – in the `<input>` element that creates the Submit button, we added two new attributes:

```
<input type="submit" value="Submit"
       runat="server" onserverclick="ShowValues">
```

The `runat="server"` attribute converts the HTML element into a server-side control that is 'visible' and therefore programmable within ASP+ on the server. The `onserverclick="ShowValues"` attribute then tells the runtime that it should execute the `ShowValues` subroutine when the button is clicked. Notice that the server-side event names for HTML controls include the word `"server"` to differentiate them from the client-side equivalents (i.e. `onclick`, which causes a client-side event hander to be invoked).

The result is a page that works just the same as the previous example, but the ASP+ source now has a much more structured and 'clean' format. It makes the code more readable, and still provides the same result – without any client-side script or other special support from the browser. If you view the source code in the browser, you'll see that it's just the same:

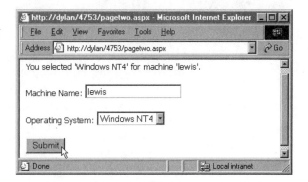

This page, named `pagetwo.asp`, *is in the* `Chapter01` *directory of the samples available for the book. You can download all the sample files from our Web site at http://www.wrox.com.*

You'll see how we can improve the structure even more, by separating out the code altogether, in Chapter 2. And, even better (as with earlier versions of ASP) we can add our own custom components to a page or take advantage of a range of server-side components that are provided with the NGWS framework.

Many of these can be tailored to create output specific to the client type, and controlled by the contents of a template within the page.

The ASP+ Application Framework

As a by-product of the modularization of ASP+, developers can also access the underlying runtime framework if they need to work at a lower level than the ASP+ page itself. As well as the information made available through the traditional ASP objects such as `Form`, `QueryString`, `Cookies` and `ServerVariables`, developers can also access the underlying objects that perform the runtime processing.

These objects include the entire page context, the **HTTP Modules** that process the requests, and the **Request HTTP Handler** objects. It is also possible to access the raw data streams, which are useful for managing file uploads and other similar specific tasks. We look at this whole topic in detail in Chapter 6.

Compilation and Rich Language Support – Enhanced Performance

When a page or Web service is first activated by the client, ASP+ dynamically compiles the code, caches it, and then reuses this cached code for all subsequent requests until the original page is changed – at which point the compiled code version is invalidated and removed from the cache. You can see this as a delay the first time that an ASP+ page is executed, while the response to subsequent requests is almost instant.

Because the compilation is to the **intermediate language** (rather than the processor-level binary code), any language can be used as long as the compiler outputs code in this intermediate language. In fact, a number of independent vendors are already working on different languages (including Cobol).

And, because the intermediate language code is common across languages, each language can inherit from all others and call routines that were originally written in all the other languages. The efficient component management services provided by the runtime also ensure that the compiled code in the page executes much more efficiently than would be possible using the earlier versions of ASP.

A Checklist of the New Features

The major features that ASP+ provides over earlier versions of ASP are:

❑ **Pages** that use the new server-side controls to automate state management in the page, and reduce the code you have to write. Because ASP+ pages have a programming model similar to VB Forms, we also refer to ASP+ pages as Web Forms.

❑ **HTML Server-side Controls** can be used to generate the HTML elements in the page output, and allow code to be used to set the properties (i.e. attributes) of these controls at runtime. They also allow events raised by the elements to be detected and appropriate code executed on the server in response to these events.

❑ **Rich Controls** that run on the server can be used to create more complex HTML elements and objects in the page output. ASP+ includes a calendar control and a range of grid, table, and list controls. These controls can also take advantage of server-side data binding to populate them with values.

❑ **Web Services** allow developers to create classes that are generally not rendered as visible output, but instead provide services to the client. For example, they can include functions that return specific values in response to a request.

❑ **Configuration and Deployment** is now easier, with the use of human-readable XML-format configuration files. Components no longer need to be registered on the server (no more regsvr32!), and applications can be deployed using file copy commands, the FrontPage server extensions or FTP.

❑ **Application and Session State Management** is extended to provide a persistent and more scalable environment for storing values relevant to specific clients and applications. In particular, a user's session state can now easily be maintained in a Web farm.

❑ **Error Handling, Debugging, and Tracing** features have been greatly extended and improved. Each page can have its own 'error page', and can also display values that are used in the page code as it executes – providing a 'trace' facility. Debugging can also be carried out across languages – allowing you to single step seamlessly from one language to another, for example from code in a VB page into a C++ component.

❑ **Security Management Features** now allow many different kinds of login and user authentication to be used. Instead of the default browser login prompt (with Windows 2000 and NTLM authentication), custom login pages can be created and managed by ASP+. It is also easier to manage users depending on the role or group they belong to.

❑ **Custom Server-side Caching** allows developers to store all kinds of values and objects locally on the server for use in ASP+ pages. The runtime can also cache the *output* from ASP+ pages. This can provide a huge performance boost in situations where a dynamically created page is the same for many visitors, such as a product catalog.

❑ **A Range of Useful Components** are shipped with ASP+. These class libraries can help to make writing Web applications easier. Examples include: the 'SendMail' component, encryption/decryption components, components for defining custom performance counters, components for reading and writing to the NT event log, components for working with MSMQ, network access components (replacements for WinInet), data access components, etc.

Features such as the intrinsic Request and Response objects (and the Form, QueryString, Cookies, and ServerVariables collections that they implement) are compatible with earlier versions of ASP. However, they have gained a lot of new properties and methods that make it easier to build applications. There is also access to the ObjectContext object for use by any existing ASP components. However, there are some new methods and properties available for the intrinsic ASP objects, as well as other issues that affect how existing pages, components and applications perform under ASP+. See Appendix A for more details.

ASP+ Pages

ASP+ Pages are described in detail in Chapters **2**, **3** and **4**. The four big advantages that ASP+ Pages provide are:

❑ **Controls can encapsulate reusable functionality**. This allows them to automate and simplify a lot of the common programming tasks, such as state management, validation, data manipulation, etc. that require specific coding in previous versions of ASP.

❑ **Code is 'cleaner' and easier to read**. The encapsulation of code in server controls, combined with the ability to use proper event handling techniques in your pages, allows a more structured design. Reusability of previously tested and optimized controls also means that development is faster.

❑ There is **better support for code and user interface development tools**. These can provide true WYSIWYG editing of pages, management of controls properties, and easy access to methods and events of the controls.

❑ It **removes the dependency of ASP on non-typed script languages** such as VBScript and JScript. Code can be written in any of the ASP+ supported languages, such as Visual Basic, C++, C#, Perl, etc. It can also be written as separate modules and used within the page, rather than as traditional inline code.

The ASP+ Control Families

ASP+ provides a series of new server controls that can be instantiated within an ASP+ page. From the developer's point of view, the advantage of using these controls is that server-side processing can be carried out on events raised by client-side controls.

The server controls provided with ASP+ fall into four broad categories or 'families':

❑ **Intrinsic controls** that create HTML-style elements on the client. They can create intelligent controls that automatically maintain state and provide extra features, or just plain HTML elements.

❑ **List controls** that can automatically produce lists of all kinds on the client. In conjunction with server-side data binding, they can also populate the lists with data from databases, XML files, etc. – using only a few lines of code.

❑ **Rich controls** output client-side HTML, and in some cases client-side script as well, in order to create more complex types of controls or interface elements on the client. An example is the 'Calendar' control, which detects the browser type and creates corresponding code to complement the features of that browser.

❑ **Validation controls** are non-visible controls that make it easy to do client-side or server-side validation when creating forms for the user to fill in and post back to the server. There is a range of these controls, allowing complex validation to be carried out easily.

All of these controls are designed to produce output that can run on **any** Web browser (you'll see this demonstrated in several places within the book). There are no client-side ActiveX controls or Java applets required. We'll look at each of these control types in more detail next.

The ASP+ Intrinsic Controls

In the example we looked at earlier in this chapter, we saw how ASP+ provides a series of **Intrinsic Controls** that are intelligent. In other words, they can be executed on the server to create output that includes event handling and the maintenance of **state** (the values the controls display). In Chapters 2, 3, and 4, we look at how we can use these controls in more detail, and explore their various capabilities.

However, to overview the aims of the new ASP+ Intrinsic Controls, we can say that they serve three main purposes:

❑ They allow the developer to interact with the control on the server when the page is being created, in particular by setting the values of properties or reacting to events that are raised on the client.

❑ They automatically create the appropriate HTML to preserve their current state, so that they display the correct values as selected by the user when the page is reloaded – without requiring the developer to write code to do this.

❑   They make development simpler and faster, and promote reusability and better page design and structure by encapsulating the repetitive code required for these tasks within the control.

The basic intrinsic controls are used by simply inserting the equivalent HTML into the page, just as you would in earlier versions of ASP, but adding the `runat="server"` attribute. The elements that are implemented as specific objects in the preview version of ASP+ are:

`<table>`	`<tr>`	`<th>`	`<td>`
`<form>`	`<input>`	`<select>`	`<textarea>`
`<button>`	`<a>`	`<img>`	

As in HTML, the `<input>` server control depends on the value of the `type` attribute. The output that the control creates is, of course, different for each value.

All other HTML elements in an ASP+ page that are marked with the `runat="server"` attribute are handled by a single generic HTML server control. It creates output based simply on the element itself and any attributes you provide or set server-side when the page is being created.

There is also a set of new ASP+ controls that can be defined within the page, and which are prefixed with the namespace 'asp'. These controls expose properties that correspond to the standard attributes that are available for the equivalent HTML element. As with all server controls, you can set these properties during the server-side `Load` events of the page, or add them as attributes in the usual way, but using the special property names. When rendered to the client, the properties are converted into the equivalent HTML syntax.

For example, to create an instance of a `ListBox` control, we can use:

```
<asp:ListBox visibleItems="3" runat="server">
  <asp:ListItem>Windows 98</asp:ListItem>
  <asp:ListItem>Windows NT4</asp:ListItem>
  <asp:ListItem>Windows 2000</asp:ListItem>
</asp:ListBox>
```

At runtime (in the preview version) the ASP+ code above creates the following HTML, and sends it to the client:

```
<SELECT name="ListBox0" size="3">
    <OPTION value="Windows 98">Windows 98</OPTION>
    <OPTION value="Windows NT4">Windows NT4</OPTION>
    <OPTION value="Windows 2000">Windows 2000</OPTION>
</SELECT>
```

A summary of the 'asp'-prefixed intrinsic controls looks like this:

ASP+ Intrinsic Control	HTML Output Element
`<asp:Button>`	`<input type="submit">`
`<asp:LinkButton>`	`<a href="jscript:__doPostBack(...)">...<a>`
`<asp:ImageButton>`	`<input type="image">`

Table continued on following page

ASP+ Intrinsic Control	HTML Output Element
`<asp:HyperLink>`	`<a href="...">...</a>`
`<asp:TextBox>`	`<input type="text" value="...">`
`<asp:CheckBox>`	`<input type="checkbox">`
`<asp:RadioButton>`	`<input type="radio">`
`<asp:DropDownList>`	`<select>...</select>`
`<asp:ListBox>`	`<select size="...">...</select>`
`<asp:Image>`	`<img src="...">`
`<asp:Label>`	`<span>...</span>`
`<asp:Panel>`	`<div>...</div>`
`<asp:Table>`	`<table>...</table>`
`<asp:TableRow>`	`<tr>...</tr>`
`<asp:TableCell>`	`<td>...</td>`

These controls provide more standardized property sets than the HTML controls, and make it easier to implement tools that can be used for designing and building ASP+ pages and applications.

The ASP+ List Controls

Many day-to-day tasks involve the listing of data in a Web page. In general, this data will be drawn from a data store of some type, perhaps a relational database. The aim of the ASP+ **List Controls** is to make building these kinds of pages easier. This involves encapsulating the functionality required within a single control or set of controls, saving development time and making the task easier.

The server-side ASP+ controls that generate the user interface can also manage tasks such as paging the list, sorting the contents, filtering the list, and selecting individual items. Finally, they can use the new server-side data binding features in ASP+ to automatically populate the lists with data. The three standard controls that are used to create lists are the **Repeater**, **DataList**, and **DataGrid** controls.

The **Repeater** control is the simplest, and is used simply to render the output a repeated number of times. The developer defines templates that are used to apply styling information to the `header`, `item`, `footer` and `separator` parts of the output that is created by the control. To create a table, for example, the `header` and `footer` information is used (as you would expect) for the header and footer of the table (the `<thead>` and `<tfoot>` parts in HTML terms). The `item` template content is applied to every row of the table that is generated from the repeated values – probably the records from a data store of some type. There is also the facility to use an `alternatingItem` template to apply different styles to alternate rows. The `separator` information defines the HTML output that will be generated after each row and before the next one.

The **DataList** control differs from the **Repeater** control in that it provides some intrinsic formatting of the repeated data as well as accepting the same kinds of template values as the **Repeater** control. The **DataList** control renders additional HTML (outside of that defined in its templates) to better control the layout and format of the rendered list, providing features such as vertical/horizontal flow and style support. However, unlike the **Repeater** control, it can also be used to edit the values in the elements on demand, and detect changes made by the user.

The richest of the list controls is the **DataGrid** control. The output is an HTML table, and the developer can define templates that are used to apply styling information to the various parts of the table. As well as being able to edit the values in the table, the user can also sort and filter the contents, and the appearance is similar to that of using a spreadsheet. However, as the output from the control is simply HTML, it will work in all the popular browsers.

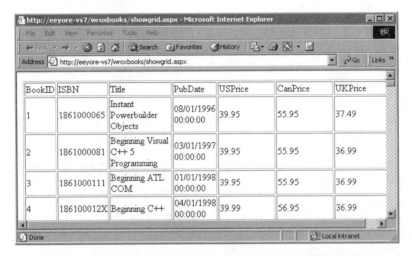

There are two other more specialized types of list control included with ASP+. These are the **RadioButtonList** and **CheckboxList** controls. In effect, they simply render on the client a list of HTML radio button or checkbox elements, with captions applied using span elements. However, you can easily specify the layout, i.e. if the items should appear listed horizontally across the page or vertically down it, or within an HTML table. You can also control the alignment of the text labels, and arrange for the list to automatically post back the selected values.

The ASP+ Rich Controls

The preview version of ASP+ ships with three **Rich Controls** that provide specific functions not usually available in plain HTML. Examples of these are the **Calendar** and **AdRotator** controls. Also due in later releases are **TreeView**, **ImageGenerator**, and other controls.

To give you some idea of what these custom controls can do, take a look at the screenshot below:

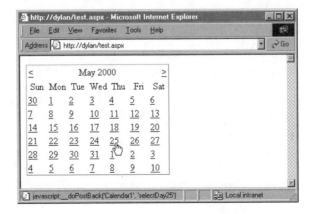

This was generated using this simple code:

```
<form runat="server">
  <asp:Calendar runat="server" />
</form>
```

The ASP+ Validation Controls

One common task when working with HTML forms in a Web application is the validation of values that the user enters. They may have to fall within a prescribed range, be non-empty, or even have the values from several controls cross-referenced to check that the inputs are valid.

Traditionally, this has been done using either client-side or server-side scripts, often specially written for each form page. In ASP+, a range of **Validation Controls** is included. These make it easy to perform validation checks – both client-side and server-side.

Three types of validation control are provided. The **RequiredFieldValidator** control, **CompareValidator** control, **RangeValidator** control, and **RegularExpressionValidator** control perform various types of checks to ensure that that a control contains a specific value, or matches the value in another control. The **CustomValidator** control passes the value that a user enters into a control to a specified client-side or server-side function for custom validation. The **ValidationSummary** control collects all the validation errors and places them in a list within the page.

Each one of these controls (except the **ValidationSummary** control) is linked to one or more HTML controls through the attributes you set for the validation control. They can automatically output the text or character string you specify when the validation fails. You can also use the `IsValid` method of the `Page` object to see if any of the validation controls detected an error, and provide custom error messages.

Some of the controls also detect the browser type, and can output code that performs validation client-side without requiring a round-trip to the server. If this is not possible, code to do the validation during the submission of the values to the server is output instead. We look in detail at how we can use these controls in Chapter 4.

You'll see most of the controls we've discussed described in more detail in Chapter 2. The more complex topics associated with them, such as templates, server-side data binding and ADO+ are covered in Chapter 3. Chapter 4 looks at the validation controls, and other advanced techniques in ASP+ pages. We also look at how you can build your own custom server-side controls in Chapter 7.

ASP+ Web Services

As the march of XML through traditional computing territory continues unabated, more and more of the ways that we are used to doing things are changing. One area is the provision of programmatic services that can be consumed by remote clients, especially where the server and client are running on different operating system platforms. The **Simple Object Access Protocol** (SOAP) is an XML grammar that allows clients to take advantage of the services provided by a remote server or application, by providing the requests in a standard format.

ASP+ includes support for the creation of suitable server or application objects that accept SOAP requests, and return the results in SOAP format. The technology is called **Web Services**, and allows developers to create these objects quickly and easily within the COM+ 2.0 framework.

These objects are also automatically discoverable and described to clients using the XML-based **Service Description Language** (SDL).

You simply create the object using normal server-side code as a `public class`, in any of the supported languages, and include one or more methods that the client can access marked with the special [`Web Method`] indicator. These are known as custom attributes. Other methods that are not marked as such are private, and cannot be accessed by clients. No knowledge of COM+ or HTTP itself is required, and the source for these service objects is just text files.

Web Services allows custom business service objects to be created quickly and easily by ASP+ developers. The client can access them synchronously or asynchronously, using the `HTTP-GET`, `HTTP-POST` or `HTTP-SOAP` methods that provide extra flexibility. As with other objects in ASP+, the source is compiled, cached and executed under the runtime. We explore the whole concept of Web Services in Chapter 5.

ASP+ Configuration and Deployment

In earlier versions of ASP, a file named `global.asa` could exist in the root directory of a virtual application. This file defined global variables and event handlers for the application. However, all other configuration details for the entire Web site were made in the Internet Services Manager snap-in to the MMC. The settings made in Internet Services Manager are stored in the IIS metabase, which is a server-based machine-readable file that specifies the whole structure of the Web services for that machine.

This has at least one major disadvantage. It requires the administrator or developer to access the metabase using either Internet Services Manager (it can be used remotely to access another machine on the LAN), the equivalent HTML pages, or custom pages that access the metabase through the Active Directory Services Interface (ADSI).

The Global Configuration File – config.web

In ASP+, all the configuration details for all Web applications are kept in human-readable files named `config.web`. The default `config.web` file is in the `Program Files\COM2OSDK\` directory and this specifies the settings that apply to any applications or directories that do not over-ride the defaults. The standard format for the configuration files is XML, and each application inherits the settings in the default `config.web` file.

The `config.web` file specifies a whole range of settings for the application, including the HTTP Modules and Request Handlers that are to be used to handle each request. This provides a completely extensible and flexible architecture, allowing non-standard HTTP protocol handling to be carried out if required. We examine configuration files and their use in Chapter 6.

The Application Definition File – global.asax

As in ASP 2.0 and 3.0, it is also possible to use a definition file that specifies the actions to take when an application starts and ends, and when individual user sessions start and end. This file is named `global.asax` (note the `.asax` file extension), and is stored in the root directory for each application.

The existing ASP event handlers `Application_OnStart`, `Application_OnEnd`, `Session_OnStart`, and `Session_OnEnd` are supported in `global.asax`, as well as several new events such as `Application_BeginRequest`, `Security_OnAuthenticate`, and others. And, as before, the `global.asax` file can be used to set the values of global or session-level variables and instantiate objects. We look at the use of `global.asax` files in Chapter 6.

ASP+ Application and Session State

One of the useful features in previous versions of ASP that developers were quick to take advantage of was the provision of global and user-level scope for storing values and object instances. This uses the Application and Session objects in ASP, and these objects are still present in ASP+. Although backwards compatible, however, the new Application and Session objects offer a host of extra features.

Using Application State

As in previous versions, each ASP application running on a machine has a single instance of the Application object, which can be accessed by any pages within that application. Any values or object references remain valid as long as the application is 'alive'. However, when the global.asax file is edited, or when the last client Session object is destroyed, the Application object is also destroyed.

Using the Application object for storing simple values is useful, and there are the usual Lock and Unlock methods available to prevent users from corrupting values within it through concurrent updates to these values. This can, however, cause blocking to occur while one page waits to access the Application object while it is locked by another page.

Note that when a page finishes executing or times out, or when an un-handled error occurs, the Application object is automatically unlocked for that page.

Bear in mind the impact of storing large volumes of data in an Application object, as this can absorb resources that are required elsewhere. You also need to ensure that any objects you instantiate at Application-level scope are thread safe and can handle multiple concurrent accesses. Another limitation in the use of the Application object is that it is not maintained across a Web farm where multiple servers handle user requests for the same application, or in a 'Web garden' where the same application runs in multiple processes within a single, multi-processor machine.

Using Session State

While the Application object is little changed from earlier versions of ASP, the Session object in ASP+ has undergone some quite dramatic updating. It is still compatible with code from earlier versions of ASP, but has several new features that make it even more useful.

The biggest change is that the contents of the Session object can now (optionally) be stored externally from the ASP+ process, in a new object called a **Session State Store**. It is managed by a new Windows service called the **State Server Process**, and this persists the content of all users Session objects – even if the ASP+ process they are running under fails. It also removes the content of sessions that have terminated through a time-out or after an error.

Alternatively, the Session content can be serialized out into a temporary SQL Server database table, where ASP+ talks directly to SQL Server. This means that it can be reloaded after an application or machine failure, providing a far more robust implementation of Session object storage than previous versions. It's therefore ideal for applications that require a session-level state management feature, for example a shopping cart.

This new state storage system also has another direct advantage. When using a Web farm to support a large-scale application or Web site it has always been a problem managing sessions, as they are not available across the machines in the Web farm.

The new ASP+ Session State Store can be partitioned across multiple servers, so that each client's state can be maintained irrespective of which server in the Web farm they hit first.

At last, ASP+ also allows session state to be maintained for clients that don't support cookies. This was proposed in earlier versions of ASP, but never materialized. Now, by using a special configuration setting, you can force ASP+ to 'munge' the session ID into the URL. This avoids all of the previously encountered problems of losing state information, for example when the URLs in hyperlinks do not use the same character case as the page names.

Finally, the State Server Process will also be able to expose information about the contents of the Session State Store, which will be useful for performance monitoring and administrative tasks such as setting maximum limits for each client's state. We examine the way that sessions can be managed in Chapter 6.

ASP+ Error Handling, Debugging, and Tracing

Error handling and debugging has long been an area where ASP trailed behind other development environments like Visual Basic and C++. In ASP+, there are several new features that help to alleviate this situation. It's now possible to specify individual error pages for each ASP+ page, using the new ErrorPage directive at the start of an ASP+ page:

```
<%@Page ErrorPage="/errorpages/thispage.aspx"%>
```

If a 'Not Found', 'Access Forbidden' response is generated, or an 'Internal Server Error' (caused by an ASP code or object error) occurs while loading, parsing, compiling or processing the page, the custom error page you specify is loaded instead. In this page, you can access the error code, the page URL, and the error message. The custom error page, or other error handler, can alternatively be specified in the config.web file for an application.

If no error page is specified then ASP+ will load its own error page, which contains far more detail than before about the error and how to rectify it. Settings in the config.web file also allow you to specify that this information should only be presented to a browser running on the Web server, and in this case remote users will just receive a simple error indication. Alternatively, you can create a procedure in the ASP+ page that captures the HandleError event, and doing so also prevents the default error page from being displayed.

Another welcome new feature is that Visual Basic now supports the try...catch...finally error handling technique that has long been the mainstay in languages like C++, and more recently in JScript. More details of this can be found in Appendix B. ASP+ also improves debugging techniques by including a new **Debugger** tool. This is the same debugger that is supplied with Visual Studio, allowing local and remote debugging.

Finally, ASP+ now includes comprehensive tracing facilities, so you no longer need to fill your pages with Response.Write statements to figure out what's going on inside the code. Instead, by turning on tracing at the top of the page with the new Trace directive, you can write information to the Trace object and have it rendered automatically as an HTML table at the end of the page. Tracing can also be enabled for ASP+ applications by adding instructions to the config.web file. The trace information automatically includes statistics that show the response time and other useful internal parameters:

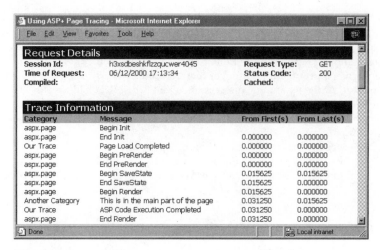

On top of this, a Web-based viewer is provided that allows you to examine the contents of the `TraceContext` object's log file. We look at the whole topic of error handling, debugging and tracing in Chapter 4.

Other ASP+ Features

To finish of this brief tour of the new features in ASP+, we'll look at some other topics that fall under the 'general' heading. These include security management, sending e-mail from ASP+ pages, and server-side caching.

New Security Management Features

In Chapters 4 and 6, you'll see how ASP+ implements several new ways to manage security in your pages and applications. As in ASP 3.0, the Basic, Digest and NTLM (Windows NT) authentication methods can be used. These are implemented in ASP+, using the services provided by IIS in earlier versions of ASP. There is also a new authentication technique called **Passport Authentication**, which uses the new Managed Passport Profile API. It's also possible to assign users to roles, and then check that each user has the relevant permission to access resources using the `IsCallerinRole` method.

An alternative method is to use custom form-based authentication. This technique uses tokens stored in cookies to track users, and allows custom login pages to be used instead of the client seeing the standard Windows Login dialog. This provides a similar user experience to that on amazon.com and yahoo.com. Without this feature, you need to write an ISAPI Filter to do this – with ASP+ it becomes trivially simple.

Server-Side Caching

ASP+ uses server-side caching to improve performance in a range of ways. As well as caching the intermediate code for ASP pages and various other objects, ASP has an **output cache** that allows the entire content of a page to be cached and then reused for other clients (if it is suitable).

There is also access to a custom server-side cache, which can be used to hold objects, values, or other content that is required within the application. Your pages and applications can use this cache to improve performance by storing items that are regularly used or which will be required again. The cache is implemented in memory only (it is not durable in the case of a machine failure), and scavenging and management is performed automatically by the operating system.

Getting Started with ASP+

Having seen what ASP+ is all about, and some details of the technologies that support it behind the scenes, it's time to get your hands dirty and build some applications. You can download the sample files for this book to run on your own server, and modify and extend them yourself. But first, if you haven't already done so, you must install ASP+.

The latest version of ASP+ can be downloaded from the Microsoft Web site. At the time of writing, the exact location of the download was unknown, but you can reach it via our support website at http://www.wrox.com/beta. It is also available as a CD for a minimal cost, and is part of Visual Studio 7.

As for tools, at the time of writing we are using the usual ASP developer's friend, Windows NotePad. Of course, you can continue to use Visual InterDev or any other development tool you wish that supports ASP – it just won't be much help with the new object syntax and server-side controls in ASP+. But as long as it doesn't mangle any code that it does not recognize, it will be fine until better tools become available.

And, if like us you're a confirmed 'simple text editor' ASP developer, you might like to try one of the alternatives to Windows NotePad that offers extra features. Our current favorite is TextPad (http://www.textpad.com/).

Installing ASP+

Installing ASP+ is just a matter of running the executable setup file. However, you should ensure that you have installed Internet Explorer version 5.5 first. If not, download it or install it directly from http://msdn.microsoft.com/downloads/webtechnology/ie/iepreview.asp.

Make sure that you close **all** other applications before installing IE 5.5, as it updates many of the Windows 2000 operating system files. Once installation is complete, you are ready to run ASP+. No other configuration is required at the moment, as the default configuration will do nicely for our first experimental efforts.

Creating an ASP+ Application

In ASP 2.0 and 3.0, it's necessary to take some definite actions to create an ASP application, especially if you want to run any components that the application uses in a separate process. The good news is that, with ASP+, none of this is actually required. And you don't have to register any ASP+ components either.

As we saw earlier, a file named config.web controls the configuration of an ASP+ application. It is stored in the root folder of that application. However, there is a default config.web file (automatically installed in your Program Files\COM20SDK\ folder when you install the runtime) that is used for all ASP+ applications. So, all you have to do to get started is create a subdirectory under your InetPub\WWWRoot folder and place your ASP+ pages there.

Of course, you can still create a folder outside the WWWRoot directory, and set up a virtual directory to point to it in the **Internet Services Manager** if required (as in previous versions of ASP). There is no need to set any of the configuration options in the **Application Settings** section of the **Properties** dialog for this application, or in the **Configuration** dialog – the default settings will work fine:

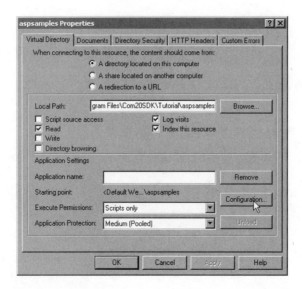

Later, you can add a `config.web` file and a `global.asax` file to the application's root folder if required to specify the configuration settings and application-level event handlers.

Testing Your Installation

Once you've installed the ASP+ runtime framework (and Internet Explorer 5.5 for the preview version of ASP+), you can try it out. An easy way to confirm that it's working is to run one of the sample files we provide. The simple example page named `pageone.aspx` that we looked at earlier is included in the `Chapter01` folder of the samples for this book (available from http://www.wrox.com/).

Simply copy it to the `InetPub\WWWRoot` directory on your server and open it from a browser using the URL http://localhost/pageone.aspx or http://your_server_name/pageone.aspx. You should get this:

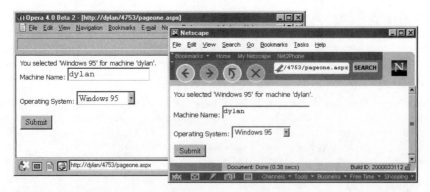

We've used Netscape Navigator 6 and Opera 4 here to prove that the page doesn't depend on the unique capabilities of Internet Explorer.

If the page doesn't work, check out the 'read me' text file that comes with ASP+ for late-breaking information. Alternatively, have a look at the SDK documentation provided with ASP+, or available at the Microsoft Web site, to see a full description and the remedy for any error message that you get.

Once you are up and running, the next step is to take a look at the Quick Start tutorials. There are examples of all kinds of ASP+ pages, Web services, and applications that you can try out and view the source code. Open the samples from http://localhost/quickstart/ or http://machinename/quickstart/:

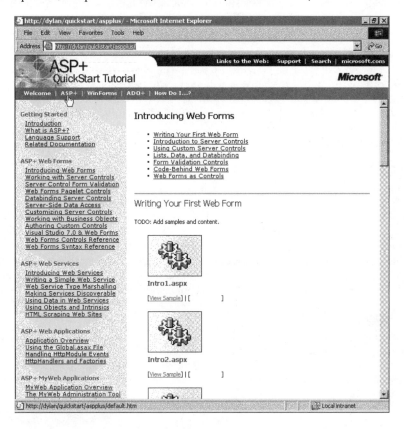

About the ASP+ Final Release

Obviously, the preview version of ASP+ and the runtime framework that we are using is not absolutely complete. However, it is classed as being 'feature complete', which means that only minor changes and additions are expected between now and the final release. In this last section, we'll examine some of the things that you can expect to see in the final release that are not available, or that aren't yet working properly.

Multiple Windows Platform Support

The final version of the NGWS framework and ASP+ is aimed at all of the current and recent Windows platforms, including Windows 2000, Windows NT4, Windows 95 and Windows 98. The preview release, however, is only designed for use on Windows 2000 Server and Windows 2000 Professional. The versions for Windows 95 and Windows 98 will be limited-functionality 'personal' versions, but will allow these operating systems to provide a local source for the execution of ASP+ pages. This will be useful for building applications designed for running locally.

XHTML Compliance

At the moment, the output generated by the server-side ASP+ controls is basic HTML 3.2, and is not XHTML compliant. Good coding practice suggests that all Web pages should be compliant with the new XHTML recommendations from the World Wide Web Consortium (W3C), so as to allow them to be manipulated if required by an XML parser or other application that expects content to be well-formed in XML terms.

A complete specification of XHTML version 1.0 can be obtained from the W3C Web site at http://www.w3.org/TR/xhtml1, and Microsoft will attempt to generate XHTML-compliant HTML code from server-side components in the final release of ASP+. However, as some popular browsers can behave oddly when confronted with XHTML, the final level of support is difficult to judge at the moment.

Client-Specific Output Formats

Most of the intelligent server-side controls supplied in the preview version of ASP+ only output standard HTML 3.2. However, some (such as the validation controls we look at in Chapter 4) do detect Internet Explorer 4 and above, and generate output that takes advantage of the DHTML capabilities of this browser. This provides better performance and a better user experience, as it dramatically reduces the need for round-trips to the server each time the user changes the selected data in the control.

In the later beta and release versions of ASP+, there will be more controls of this type. There will also be controls aimed at creating output in different formats entirely, for example Wireless Markup Language (WML). This might be a separate set of controls in some cases; however, due to the extreme incompatibilities between the user interfaces and client capabilities for these types of Internet device.

New Administration Tools

Finally, the release version of ASP+ will include administration tools allowing you to configure and maintain applications more easily. You can expect to see tools to manage the `config.web` configuration files and `global.asax` application files. There should also be graphical interfaces for viewing application performance, and examining detailed trace information while debugging complete applications.

Summary

In this chapter, we've attempted to provide a complete overview of what is new and what has changed in ASP+, compared to earlier versions of ASP. ASP+ is the new generation of Microsoft's successful Active Server Pages technology, and represents a real advance in ease of use and power.

ASP+ is designed to remove many of the existing limitations of ASP, such as the dependence on script languages, poor support for object-oriented design and programming techniques, and the need to continuously re-invent techniques for each page or application you build. Instead, ASP+ combines the ability to build more complex and powerful applications, with a reduced requirement for the developer to write repetitive code. For example, the process of maintaining values in HTML form controls and posting these values back to the server ('round tripping') requires quite a lot of code to maintain the state within the page. ASP+ does all this work for you automatically.

At the same time, the world out there is changing. The proportion of users that will access your site through an 'Internet device' such as a mobile cellular phone, personal digital assistant (PDA), TV set-top box, games console, or other device will soon be greater that the number using a PC and a traditional Web browser. ASP+ provides solutions that help to reduce the work required for coping with these disparate types of client.

The rapidly changing nature of distributed applications requires faster development, more componentization and re-usability, and wider general platform support. New standards such as the Simple Object Access Protocol (SOAP) and new commercial requirements such as business-to-business (B2B) data interchange require new techniques to be used to generate output and communicate with other systems. To meet all these requirements, ASP has been totally revamped from the ground up into a whole new programming environment that includes:

❑ **Pages** that use the new server-side controls to automate state management in the page, and reduce the code you have to write.

❑ **HTML Server-side Controls** that can be used to generate the HTML elements in the page output, and allow code to be used to set the properties (i.e. attributes) of these controls at runtime. They also allow events raised by the elements to be detected and appropriate code executed on the server in response to these events.

❑ **Rich Controls** that run on the server can be used to create more complex HTML elements and objects in the page output. ASP+ includes a calendar control and a range of grid, table and list controls. These controls can also take advantage of server-side data binding to populate them with values.

❑ **Web Services** that allow developers to create pages that are generally not rendered as visible output, but instead provide services to the client. For example, they can include functions that return specific values in response to a request.

❑ Better **Configuration and Deployment**, with the use of human-readable XML-format configuration files. Components no longer need to be registered on the server (using regsvr32), and applications can be deployed using file copy commands, the FrontPage server extensions, or FTP.

❑ Extended **Application and Session State Management** that provides a persistent and more scalable environment for storing values relevant to specific clients and applications.

❑ Improved **Error Handling, Debugging, and Tracing** features. Each page can have its own 'error page', and can also display values that are used in the page code as it executes, providing a 'trace' facility.

❑ New **Security Management Features**, which allow many different kinds of login and user authentication to be used. Instead of the default browser login prompt, custom login pages can be used with Windows 2000 and NTLM authentication. It is also easier to manage users depending on the role or group they belong to.

❑ **Custom Server-side Caching** allows developers to store all kinds of values and objects locally on the server for use in ASP+ pages. The runtime can also cache the *output* from ASP+ pages. This can provide a huge performance boost in situations where a dynamically created page is the same for many visitors, such as a product catalog.

❑ **A Range of Useful Components** are shipped with ASP+. These class libraries can help to make writing Web applications easier. Examples include: the 'SendMail' component, encryption/decryption components, components for defining custom performance counters, components for reading and writing to the NT event log, components for working with MSMQ, network access components (replacements for 'WinInet'), data access components, etc.

In the remainder of this book, we'll examine all thee topics in more detail, and show you how you can use ASP+ to build powerful and interactive Web-based distributed applications more quickly and efficiently than ever before.

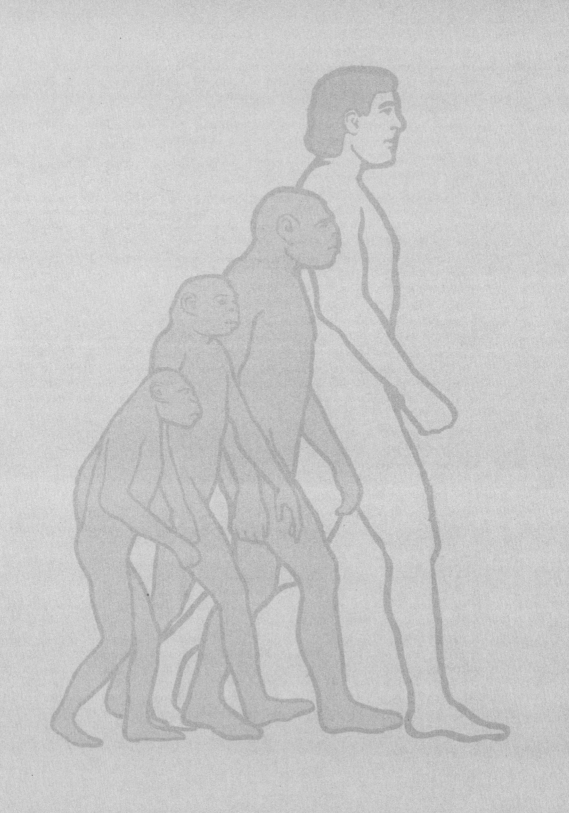

2

ASP+ Pages

In the previous chapter we examined the problems with the existing ASP architecture, and how ASP+ has been designed to overcome some of these. Obviously not every problem with designing Web applications is cured by ASP+, but the new environment is such a leap forward in many ways, that many of the problems have been solved.

We also showed you how a simple ASP page could be converted to ASP+ to make use of some of the new built in features, such as control state, but now it's time to look at ASP+ pages in more detail. So, in this chapter we are going to look at:

- ❑ The way ASP+ pages can make your code cleaner
- ❑ How to program against the ASP+ Object Model
- ❑ What Web Controls are, and how they can be used
- ❑ How the different families of Web Controls target different uses
- ❑ How the Web Controls have an Object Model

By the end of the chapter you'll see how great ASP+ is as a development environment, and the rich set of facilities it has to offer.

Coding Issues

In the previous chapter we looked at two of the main disadvantages of existing ASP applications – those of state management, and the coding model. ASP+ introduces a new way of coding, and for those of you who have programmed in event driven languages such as Visual Basic or DHTML scripters, then this model will seem familiar, although it might seem a little alien to programmers who have only coded in script languages in ASP. However, it's extremely simple, providing many advantages, and leads to much more structured code. No longer is the code intermixed with the HTML, and the event driven nature means the code is easily separated into related blocks.

We previously saw how this worked for an OnClick event on a server control, and how the code to be run was broken out into a separate event procedure. That example showed a list of operating systems in a SELECT element. Using lists like this is extremely common, and often the list of items is generated from a data store. So, let's look at the difference between an ASP page and a new ASP+ page to do the same thing.

Coding the Old Way

To produce a list of items from a data store in ASP you have to loop through the list of items, manually creating the HTML. When the item is selected, the form is then posted back to the server. Your code can look something like this:

```
<html>

<form action="OldAsp.asp" method="post">

   Please select your delivery method:
   <select id="ShipMethod" Name="ShipMethod" size="1">
<%
   Dim rsShip
   Dim SQL
   Dim ConnStr
   Dim ItemField

   Set rsShip = Server.CreateObject("ADODB.Recordset")

   SQl = "select * from Shipping_Methods"
   ConnStr = "Driver={SQL Server}; Server=localhost; " & _
             "Database=AdvWorks; UID=sa"

   rsShip.Open SQL, ConnStr

   While Not rsShip.EOF
     Response.Write "<option value='" & _
                    rsShip("ShippingMethodID") & "'>" & _
                    rsShip("ShippingMethod") & "</option>"
     rsShip.MoveNext
   Wend

   rsShip.Close
   Set rsShip = Nothing
%>
   </select>
```

```
      <br>
      <input type="submit" value="Place Order">
   </form>

<%
   If Request.Form("ShipMethod") <> "" Then
      Response.write "<br>Your order will be delivered via " & _
                     Request.Form("ShipMethod")
   End If
%>
</html>
```

There's nothing very complex about this code – it loops through a Recordset building a select list, and allows the user to select a value and submit that back to the server. In many situations you'd probably build some sort of database query or update based upon the selected value, but in our example we are printing out the selected value:

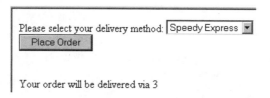

Notice that only the ID is available in the submitted page. That's fine if we're going to use it in some form of data query, but not if we need to display it again.

Coding in ASP+ Pages

Before we look at how the above ASP page would be coded in ASP+, let's start by examining the event order. In ASP+ we have a structured set of events, so our code can be placed in these, rather than interspersed with the HTML. The event order is:

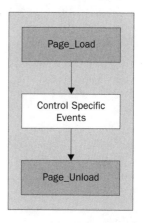

The Page_Load event is always the first event, and is fired **every** time the page is loaded. After that any control specific events that are implemented are fired, and finally the Page_Unload is **always** fired last.

Since our Web controls can be accessed server-side, this means we can put the loading of data into them in the Page_Load event.

For example, rewriting the original ASP page in ASP+ we get:

```
<%@ Import Namespace="System.Data" %>
<%@ Import Namespace="System.Data.ADO" %>

<html>
<head>

<script language="VB" runat="server">

  Sub Page_Load(Source As Object, E As EventArgs)

      Dim myCommand As ADOCommand
      Dim myReader  As ADODataReader
      Dim SQL       As String
      Dim ConnStr   As String

      SQl = "select * from Shipping_Methods"
      ConnStr = "Provider=SQLOLEDB; Data Source=(local);_
                 Initial Catalog=AdvWorks; User ID=sa"

      myCommand = New ADOCommand(SQL, ConnStr)
      myCommand.ActiveConnection.Open()

      myCommand.Execute(myReader)

      While myReader.Read()
        ShipMethod.Items.Add(New ListItem(myReader.Item("ShippingMethod"), _
                         myReader.Item("ShippingMethodID")))
      End While

  End Sub

  Sub PlaceOrder_click(Source As Object, E As EventArgs)

    YouSelected.Text = "Your order will be delivered via " & _
                    ShipMethod.SelectedItem.Text

  End Sub

</script>

<form runat="server">

  Please select your delivery method:

  <asp:DropDownList id="ShipMethod"
      runat="server"/>

  <br/>

  <asp:button id="PlaceOrder" Text="Place Order"
      onclick="PlaceOrder_Click"
      runat="server"/>
```

```
    <br/>

    <asp:Label id="YouSelected" runat="server"/>
</form>
</html>
```

Let's look at this code in detail to see what the changes are and why they've been done, starting with the HTML form:

```
<form runat="server">

    Please select your delivery method:

    <asp:DropDownList id="ShipMethod"
        runat="server"/>

    <br/>

    <asp:button id="PlaceOrder" Text="Place Order"
        onclick="PlaceOrder_Click"
        runat="server"/>

    <br/>

    <asp:Label id="YouSelected" runat="server"/>
</form>
```

This has three ASP+ Web controls – a drop down list, and button, and a label. We'll explain more about these throughout the chapter, but for now we want to concentrate on the event side of things. So, just remember that these are server-side controls, and can therefore be accessed from within our server-side code. Now let's look at the coding bits in more detail.

One important point to note is that for server controls to take part in postback, they must be within a server-side form control. For example:

```
<form runat="server">

    ' controls go here

</form>
```

At the start of the page we place the Import statements, to tell ASP+ which code libraries we wish to use. The two below are for data access, and we'll explain more about these in the next chapter:

```
<%@ Import Namespace="System.Data" %>
<%@ Import Namespace="System.Data.ADO" %>

<html>
<head>
```

The Page_Load Event

Next we start the script block, and define the `Page_Load` event. Remember this will be run every time the page is loaded.

```
<script language="VB" runat="server">

   Sub Page_Load(Source As Object, E As EventArgs)
```

So, within this event we want to query the database and build our list. We're not going to explain the following data access code, since it's covered in the next chapter, but it's roughly equivalent to the code in the previous example, simply creating a set of records.

```
       Dim myCommand As ADOCommand
       Dim myReader  As ADODataReader
       Dim SQL       As String
       Dim ConnStr   As String

       SQl = "select * from Shipping_Methods"
       ConnStr = "Provider=SQLOLEDB; Data Source=(local);_
                   Initial Catalog=AdvWorks; User ID=sa"

       myCommand = New SQLCommand(SQL, ConnStr)
       myCommand.ActiveConnection.Open()

       myCommand.Execute(myReader)
```

Once the records are created, we add them to the list (`ShipMethod`). In the ASP example we actually had to create the HTML OPTION elements in the loop, but in the ASP+ page we can just use the `Add` method of the list to add items. We showed earlier that the list is declared to run server-side, so we can just call its methods and properties server-side. This is more like the Visual Basic programming environment, where we're dealing with controls.

```
       While myReader.Read()
          ShipMethod.Items.Add(New ListItem(myReader.Item("ShippingMethod"), _
                             myReader.Item("ShippingMethodID")))
       End While
```

At this stage the code in the `Page_Load` event has finished. On the first load there are no control events to run, so processing will continue with the `Page_Unload` event, if implemented.

Web Control Events

When we select an item in the list and click the button, we invoke the postback mechanism. Our button was defined as:

```
    <asp:button id="PlaceOrder" Text="Place Order"
          onclick="PlaceOrder_Click"
          runat="server"/>
```

The `onclick` property identifies the name of the procedure to be run when the button is clicked. Remember that this is server-side event processing, so there is no special client-side code.

When this button is clicked the form is submitted back to itself, and the defined event handler is run:

```
Sub PlaceOrder_Click(Source As Object, E As EventArgs)

    YouSelected.Text = "Your order will be delivered via " & _
                        ShipMethod.SelectedItem.Text

End Sub
```

This just sets the text of a label to the value selected:

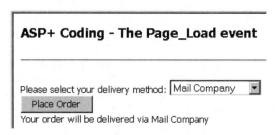

This shows one interesting point. Because the list control is a server control we have access not only to the value, but also to the text of the selected item. This wasn't possible (at least not easily) with the ASP page.

So, let's just reiterate these points:

❑   Server based controls can be accessed from server code.

❑   The `Page_Load` event is run every time the page is loaded.

❑   The control event is only run when fired by a server control.

There is, however, one big flaw with our code above. Because the `Page_Load` runs every time the page loads, the code in it will be run even under a postback scenario. That means we are performing the data query and filling the list every time, so whatever the user selected would be overwritten (as well as being unnecessary).

The Page.IsPostBack Property

The `Page.IsPostBack` property is designed to counter this problem, as it is a Boolean value that is set to `True` whenever the page has been posted to (for example, when running the event procedure for a control). We can use this property in the `Page_Load` event so that our data access code is only run the first time the page is loaded:

```
Sub Page_Load(Source As Object, E As EventArgs)

    If Not Page.IsPostBack Then

        Dim myCommand As ADOCommand
        Dim myReader  As ADODataReader
        Dim SQL       As String
        Dim ConnStr   As String

        SQl = "select * from Shipping_Methods"
        ConnStr = "server=localhost;uid=sa;pwd=;database=AdvWorks"
```

```
myCommand = New SQLCommand(SQL, ConnStr)
myCommand.ActiveConnection.Open()

myCommand.Execute(myReader)

While myReader.Read()
  ShipMethod.Items.Add(New ListItem(myReader.Item("ShippingMethod"),_
                       myReader.Item("ShippingMethodID")))
End While
End If

End Sub
```

The Page ViewState

We've now ensured that this code runs only when the page is first loaded. We don't have to worry about the contents of the list disappearing because the contents are held within the ViewState. We won't show it here as the contents aren't reader friendly, but this contains everything about the current state of the control.

The ViewState means that you don't have to do anything at all to preserve the contents of controls during postback.

Web Controls

In the previous chapter when we looked at the improvements in the code structure, we showed code responding to an event using the HTML SELECT element. These standard HTML controls are all very well, and have been designed to map one to one with their HTML equivalents. And this is one of their problems, since you do not automatically get the benefits of the uplevel ASP+ controls. For example, consider the background color. For a SPAN you set the CSS `style` property, and on a table you set the `BGColor` property. The ASP+ controls provide a consistent model, whereby you can just set the `BackColor` property on all controls, and the correct HTML is automatically rendered.

There are four sets of Web Controls:

- ❑ Intrinsic Controls, which map to simple HTML elements
- ❑ List Controls, to provide data flow across a page
- ❑ Rich Controls, to provide rich UI and functionality
- ❑ Validation Controls, to provide a variety of data validation

As we go through this chapter you'll see examples from all of these families, and some will be covered in more detail in the next chapter when we look at data and data binding.

HTML Controls or ASP+ Controls

At this stage you might be questioning the actual need for HTML controls that work server-side, as well as ASP+ controls. That's a question that the ASP+ team have asked themselves several times, but they opted for the flexible approach, allowing the user to decide.

For example, consider the following from Chapter 1:

```
<input type="text" id="txtName" runat="server">
```

This uses the HTML control, but includes the `runat="server"` attribute to make it available for server-side programming. How does this differ from the following?

```
<asp:TextBox id="txtName" runat="server"/>
```

Well, once it's rendered it doesn't differ at all. The first produces the following HTML:

```
<INPUT name="txtName" id="txtName" type="text">
```

And the second produces this HTML:

```
<input name="txtName" type="text" id="txtName">
```

So, if there's no difference, which should you use? Well, as one member of the ASP+ team puts it "it's a lifestyle choice". Use whichever set of controls you feel happier with. The HTML controls keep you closer to the actual content, but they don't offer the uplevel functionality (such as consistent naming and so on). On the other hand, the ASP+ controls provide a more consistent programming model, but divorce you a little from the actual content output. Through the rest of this book we'll be using the ASP+ controls.

Using Web Controls

You use Web Controls in the same way as you use HTML controls. The only difference is that they must have the `runat="server"` attribute set. You don't have to do anything special to access this code library, as it's available by default, but you do have do ensure you use the correct tag prefix (or code namespace as it is sometimes called) when using the control. For example, a normal HTML list control is added to the page like this:

```
<select id="ShipMethod">
```

An ASP+ list control has the following form:

```
<asp:ListBox id="ShipMethod">
```

The code namespace is the `asp:` at the beginning of the control name. The reason we have the tag prefix, is to ensure that controls with the same names can be uniquely identified. This might not seem a big problem, but when you realize you can author your own controls, you can see what a problem this might be. We suspect there will also be a large third party market for controls, so it's extremely important that they are named correctly.

The Object Model

An important point to remember is that Web Controls (and all controls for that matter) are objects, and are fully supported by all of the usual things that objects have: methods, properties and events.

Properties and Methods

Once a Web Control has been added to an ASP+ page, you can set properties and call methods at will. You've already seen one example of this – the `DropDownList`:

```vb
<script language="vb" runat="server">

  Sub Page_Load(Source As Object, E As EventArgs)

    . . .

        ShipMethod.Items.Add(
                    New ListItem(myReader.Item("ShippingMethod"), _
                                 myReader.Item("ShippingMethodID")))

  End Sub

  Sub PlaceOrder_Click(Source As Object, E As EventArgs)

    YouSelected.Text = "Your order will be delivered via " & _
                    ShipMethod.SelectedItem.Text

  End Sub

</script>

  <asp:DropDownList id="ShipMethod"
```

In the `Page_Load` event we are calling the `Add` method of the `ShipMethod` control (a listbox), to programmatically add items to the list. In the `PlaceOrder_Click` procedure we are setting the `Text` property of a label. For anyone who has worked in DHTML or Visual Basic this isn't anything new, but it is a big leap forward for ASP server-side code.

Responding to Events

In the previous chapter you saw that the new object model allows us to respond to client-side events within server-side code. If you've done any client-side programming you might well be used to that, but this new model allows for cross-browser compatibility, by rendering pure HTML to the client, and responding to events on the server.

The use of server-side events is the same as for client event processing – you just specify the event name, and then the event procedure to be run when the event is fired:

```
<asp:Button id="FooBtn" onclick="FooBtn_onclick">
```

You then implement the event procedure as follows (in VB):

```vb
Sub FooBtn_onclick(Sender As object, E As EventArgs)
```

In C# the procedure declaration would be:

```csharp
void FooBtn_onclick(Object Sender, EventArgs E)
```

The most common event you'll be responding to will be the OnClick event, although the controls do support other events. For a list of these you need to consult the documentation for the particular control.

Control Families

Now that we've described the reasons for using Web Controls, let's look at the control families in detail. Remember that there are four of them:

❑ Intrinsic Controls, which map to simple HTML elements

❑ List Controls, to provide data flow across a page

❑ Rich Controls, to provide rich UI and functionality

❑ Validation Controls, to provide a variety of data validation

In this chapter we'll be covering the Intrinsic Controls and the Rich Controls. The List controls are covered in Chapter 3, when we look at data and data binding, and the Validation Controls are covered in Chapter 4, when we look at advanced ASP+ Page features.

Intrinsic Controls

The Intrinsic Controls are designed to provide replacements for the standard set of HTML controls. So, why do we need replacements, especially since the existing HTML controls can be run server-side? Simply put, it's consistency. One of the problems with HTML has been its lack of consistent naming for similar controls. Consider the case of an inputting data, as there are many forms this can take:

```
<input type="radio">
<input type="checkbox">
<input type="button">
```

Although these are all input controls, they all behave in a different manner, and should really be different controls, such as:

```
<asp:RadioButton>
<asp:CheckBox>
<asp:Button>
```

Text input in HTML is the opposite of this, with two controls performing the same task:

```
<input type="text">
<textarea>
```

Both of these provide areas for text input – the first only allows a single line, while the second allows multiple lines. A more sensible solution is a single control, where you can specify the number of lines:

```
<asp:TextBox rows="1">
<asp:TextBox rows="5">
```

As well as having a set of properties relating specifically to the control, the Web Controls also accept standard HTML properties. That's because these controls actually render HTML on the client, so they map HTML properties through to the rendered HTML.

We'll look at these controls in more detail, taking them in related groups.

Control Transfer

There are four types of controls that allow passing of control back to the server:

❑ Button, which acts as a standard submit button. Use this when you want to perform normal postback to the server.

❑ LinkButton, which allows custom processing before postback is actually received on the server. This allows you to have a button and perform server-side scripting instead of the normal postback routine. It is the only intrinsic control that relies on client-side scripting.

❑ ImageButton, which is a standard image button. Use this when you want to display an image that performs postback to the server.

❑ Hyperlink, which performs the actions of an a tag.

This gives us a flexible set of ways of performing postback, and the use of each control is similar:

```
<html>
<form runat="server">

  <table border="0">
    <tr>
      <td>A WebButton control</td>
      <td><asp:Button id="AdvWorksWebBtn"
              Text="Click here for Adventure Works"
              onclick="AdvWorksWebBtn_Click"
              runat="server"/></td>
    </tr>
    <tr>
      <td>A LinkButton control</td>
      <td><asp:LinkButton id="AdvWorksLinkBtn"
              Text="Click here for Adventure Works"
              onclick="AdvWorksLinkBtn_Click"
              runat="server"/></td>
    </tr>
    <tr>
      <td>An ImageButton control</td>
      <td><asp:ImageButton id="AdvWorksImg"
              ImageURL="/advworks/images/Frontartcomp.jpg"
              OnClick="AdvWorksImg_Click"
              runat="server"/></td>
    </tr>
    <tr>
      <td>A HyperLink control</td>
      <td><asp:HyperLink id="AdvWorks"
              NavigateURL="/advworks"
              Text="Click here for Adventure Works"
              runat="server" /></td>
    </tr>
```

```
      </table>

  </form>

  <script language="vb" runat="server">

    Sub AdvWorksImg_Click(Sender As Object, _
                          E As ImageClickEventArgs)

      Page.Navigate ("//localhost/advworks")

    End Sub

    Sub AdvWorksWebBtn_Click(Sender As Object, E As EventArgs)

      Page.Navigate ("//localhost/advworks")

    End Sub

    Sub AdvWorksLinkBtn_Click(Sender As Object, E As EventArgs)

      Page.Navigate ("//localhost/advworks")

    End Sub

  </script>
  </html>
```

In all cases I've decided to navigate to another page, but since this page runs on the server, you can perform any processing you like. The output of this code would look like this:

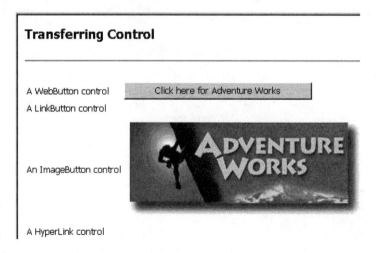

They all achieve the same purpose in this example, but you see the difference when you look at the generated HTML:

The `Button` control generates a normal submit button:

```
<input type="submit" name="AdvWorksWebBtn"
       value="Click here for Adventure Works"
       id="AdvWorksWebBtn">
```

The `LinkButton` generates an a tag, but actually posts back to the server:

```
<a id="AdvWorksLinkBtn"
   href="javascript:__doPostBack('AdvWorksLinkBtn', '')">
   Click here for Adventure Works
   </a>
```

The `ImageButton` generates a normal image input control:

```
<input type="image" name="AdvWorksImg" id="AdvWorksImg"
       src="/advworks/images/Frontartcomp.jpg" border="0">
```

The `HyperLink` generates a standard a tag that performs normal redirection:

```
<a id="AdvWorks" href="/advworks">
   Click here for Adventure Works</a></td>
```

Which you use depends on how you want your page to look and the processing you need to achieve. The general advice is:

- ❑ `Hyperlinks` don't postback to the server. They directly navigate from one page to another, and are the most efficient way to navigate. However, they assume that no values typed on the origin page need to be accessed or saved before the navigation takes place.

- ❑ `Buttons` and `ImageButtons` enable you to postback, with the server code having free reign on all client values. You **could** then do a navigation from within one of these event handlers – you could also just as easily update the page and then have it automatically redisplay back to the client.

- ❑ `LinkButton` looks like a hyperlink on the client, but actually causes a postback to the server when clicked. This is the one control we'll look at that requires client-side javascript support in order for it to work. If you don't want to require client-side script support you might want to consider using an ImageButton or Button instead.

Text Entry

The `TextBox` is the only text entry control, since it not only handles both single and multi line entry, but also password entry too. For example, imagine this form:

This is created with the following:

```
<html>
<head>

<script language="vb" runat="server">

   Sub SubmitBtn_Click(Sender As Object, E As EventArgs)

      YouEntered.Text = "Hi " & Name.Text & _
                        ". You live at " & Address.Text & _
                        " and your password is " & Password.Text

   End Sub

</script>

<form runat="server">

  <table border="0">
    <tr>
      <td>Name</td>
      <td><asp:TextBox id="Name" runat="server" /></td>
    </tr>
    <tr>
      <td>Address</td>
      <td><asp:TextBox id="Address" TextMode="MultiLine"
              Rows="5" Columns="30" runat="server" /></td>
    </tr>
    <tr>
      <td>Password</td>
      <td><asp:TextBox id="Password" TextMode="Password"
              runat="server" /></td>
    </tr>
    <tr>
      <td></td>
      <td><asp:Button id="SubmitDetailsBtn" text="Submit"
              onclick="SubmitBtn_Click" runat="server" /></td>
    </tr>
  </table>

  <p><asp:Label id="YouEntered" runat="server" /></p>

</form>
```

It's pretty obvious stuff. Although the three text entry controls are all TextBox controls, they use different modes. The first uses the default of single line, whereas the second use MultiLine mode and specifies the size of the text box. The third specifies the mode to be Password, so whatever is typed in is not echoed back to the screen. This sort of form is typical for collecting user information from people visiting your site. In our event procedure for the button we just display the details back to the user, but this could just as easily update a database.

Selections

Selections are catered for by the following controls:

- ❑ CheckBox, which allows multiple options to be selected.
- ❑ RadioButton, which allows only a single button to be selected.
- ❑ ListBox, which provides a list of items, allowing single or multiple selection.
- ❑ DropDownList, which provides a drop down list allowing only a single selection.

Since these give different options, we'll examine them separately.

CheckBoxes

CheckBoxes are analogous to the HTML input type checkbox, and have only four properties:

- ❑ Checked, to indicate whether or not the check box is selected.
- ❑ Text, which is the text to display.
- ❑ TextAlign, to indicate whether the text appears to the left or right of the check box. This can be the value Left or Right, and defaults to Left.
- ❑ AutoPostBack, to indicate whether or not changing the state of the check box automatically posts back to the server.

For example, consider the following code:

```
<html>
<head>

<script language="vb" runat="server">

  Sub UpdateDetails_Click(Sender As Object, E As EventArgs)

    Dim Details As String

    If BrochureChk.Checked Then
      Details = "We will send a brochure to: " & Address.Text & "<br/>"
    End If

    If MailChk.Checked Then
      Details &= "You will be added to out mailing list, " & _
                 "using this email address:" & _
                 EmailAddress.Text & "<br/>"
    End If

    If FriendChk.Checked Then
      Details &= "We will send your details to your friend at: " & _
                 FriendEmailAddress.Text
    End If

    SelectionDetails.Text = Details

  End Sub
```

```
    </script>

<form runat="server">

    <table border="0">
        <tr>
            <td><asp:CheckBox id="BrochureChk" Text="Send me a brochure"
                    runat="server" /></td>
            <td><asp:TextBox id="Address" TextMode="MultiLine"
                    Rows="5" Columns="30" runat="server"/></td>
        </tr>
            <td><asp:CheckBox id="MailChk" Text="Add me to the mailing list"
                    checked="true" runat="server" /></td>
            <td><asp:TextBox id="EmailAddress" columns="50" runat="server"/></td>
        </tr>
            <td><asp:CheckBox id="FriendChk" Text="Recommend a friend"
                    runat="server"/></td>
            <td><asp:TextBox id="FriendEmailAddress" columns="50"
                    runat="server"/></td>
    </table>

    <br/>

    <asp:Button id="UpdateDetails" Text="Update Details"
        onclick="UpdateDetails_Click"
        runat="server"/>

    <p>
        <asp:Label id="SelectionDetails" runat="server"/>
    </p>

</form>
</html>
```

This contains three check boxes, along with three text boxes, a command button and a label. When the button is clicked, its event procedure sees whether each check box is selected, and if so, sets the string to be output in the label:

Check Boxes

☑ Send me a brochure   `1 Anyplace`
                        `Anywhere`

☐ Add me to the mailing list `me@here.com`
☑ Recommend a friend   `him@there.com`

Update Details

We will send a brochure to: 1 Anyplace Anywhere
We will send your details to your friend at: him@there.com

AutoPostBack

If you want a more immediate return to the server, you can set the `AutoPostBack` property of the check box and set an associated event procedure:

```
<asp:CheckBox id="BrochureChk" Text="Send me a brochure"
    OnCheckedChanged="BrochureChk_Changed"
    AutoPostBack="true" runat="server" />
```

This means that every time the check box is selected or cleared, a postback will occur. Although this gives a more immediate response, it's not useful for all situations, and should be used carefully, since it could make your application appear slower, since postbacks happen more frequently.

RadioButtons

Radio buttons are similar to check boxes, with the addition of allowing only one item in a group to be selected. For this you set the `GroupName` property of the radio buttons to be the same. For example, imagine a list of suitable delivery methods for an order page:

```
<asp:RadioButton ID="Standard" GroupName="Delivery"
    Text="Standard - 7 to 10 days" Checked="true"
    runat="server" />
<br />
<asp:RadioButton ID="Medium" GroupName="Delivery"
    Text="Medium - 3 to 7 days" runat="server" />
<br />
<asp:RadioButton ID="Fast" GroupName="Delivery"
    Text="Fast - Next working day" runat="server" />
```

You could then add the order button and its associated event procedure:

```
<asp:Button id="ProcessOrder" onclick="ProcessOrderBtn_Click"
    Text="Process Order" runat="server" />
```

```
Sub ProcessOrderBtn_Click(Sender As Object, E As EventArgs)

    Dim Message As String

    Message = "Thank you for you order. It will arrive in "

    If Standard.Checked Then
      Message += "7 to 10 days."
    Elseif Medium.Checked Then
      Message += "3 to 7 day."
    Else
      Message += " tomorrow."
    End If

    ThankYou.Text = Message

End Sub
```

Within the event procedure you only need to test the `Checked` property of each radio button.

ListBoxes and DropDownLists

There are two differences between list boxes and drop down lists. The first is that a drop down list only shows one item at a time. Leading from this is that the drop down list can only have one item selected, whereas the list box can have more than one item selected. This is controlled by the `SelectionMode` property, which can be `Single` for only a single item, or `Multiple` for multiple item selection.

There are three ways of getting the items into these lists. You've seen the first way, by use of the `Add` method, where you programmatically add items to the list. The second is by way of the `ListItem` control:

```
<asp:ListBox id="ListBox" runat="server">
  <asp:ListItem selected="true">Item One</asp:ListItem>
  <asp:ListItem>Item Two</asp:ListItem>
  <asp:ListItem>Item Three</asp:ListItem>
</asp:ListBox>
```

This is much the same as the way you add OPTION elements to a SELECT list in HTML.

The third is to use the `DataSource` property, where the items are taken from a collection (such as an array). For example:

```
Dim catList As new ArrayList

catList.add ("Item One")
catList.add ("Item Two")
catList.add ("Item Three")

DropDown.DataSource = catList
DropDown.DataBind()
```

Data binding is covered in more detail in the next chapter.

To examine the different selection modes, have a look at the code below:

```
<html>
<head>

<script language="vb" runat="server">

  Sub Page_Load(Sender As Object, E As EventArgs)

    If Not Page.IsPostBack Then

      ListsAdd ("North Face Sunspot")
      ListsAdd ("Polar Star")
      ListsAdd ("Big Sur")
      ListsAdd ("Cascade")
      ListsAdd ("Everglades")
      ListsAdd ("Parka")
      ListsAdd ("Sierra")

    End If

  End Sub
```

```
    Sub ListsAdd(item As String)

        DropDown.Items.Add(item)
        ListBoxSingle.Items.Add(item)
        ListBoxMultiple.Items.Add(item)

    End Sub

    Sub ShowSelectionsBtn_Click(Sender As Object, E As EventArgs)

        ' the drop down list only has one selection possible
        DropDownSelection.Text = DropDown.SelectedItem.Text

        ' as does the single selection mode list box
        ListBoxSingleSelection.Text = ListBoxSingle.SelectedItem.Text

        ' but the multi-selection could have more than one item
        Dim item As ListItem
        Dim sel  As String = ""

        For Each item In ListBoxMultiple.Items
          If item.Selected Then
            sel += item.Text + "<br/>"
          End If
        Next

        ListBoxMultipleSelection.Text = sel

    End Sub

</script>

<form runat="server">

  <table border="0">
    <tr>
      <td>You can only select one here<br/>
          <asp:DropDownList id="DropDown" runat="server" />
      </td>
      <td><asp:Label id="DropDownSelection" runat="server"/></td>
    </tr>
    <tr>
      <td>And you can only select one here<br/>
          <asp:ListBox id="ListBoxSingle" runat="server" />
      </td>
      <td><asp:Label id="ListBoxSingleSelection" runat="server"/></td>
    </tr>
    <tr>
      <td>But you can select more than one here by
          using the control key<br/>
          <asp:ListBox id="ListBoxMultiple" SelectionMode="Multiple"
              runat="server" />
      </td>
      <td><asp:Label id="ListBoxMultipleSelection" runat="server"/></td>
    </tr>
  </table>
```

```
    <br />

    <asp:Button id="ShowSelections" Text="Show Selections"
        onclick="ShowSelectionsBtn_Click" runat="server" />

</form>
</html>
```

The code here is quite simple. There are three selection boxes – one drop down list, one single selection list box and one multiple list box. The Page_Load event procedure simply loads all three with some values. In the event procedure for the button, we simply show the selected values. For the multiple selection mode we have to loop through each item in the list checking to see if it has been selected:

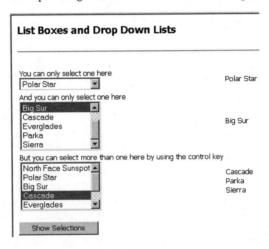

Images

The Image control is a replacement for the standard HTML image control, and really doesn't require much in the way of explanation. Its use is simple:

```
<asp:Image ImageURL="//localhost/advworks/images/dboots5.gif"
        AlternateText="A picture of some boots"
        runat="server" />
```

Containers

Container controls are controls designed to be parent controls, with other controls within them. You've already seen use of one of them – the Label control, which actually renders to a SPAN element.

The Panel renders to a DIV element, and is great for encompassing other controls, and is particularly useful when you need a group of controls to change their visibility. For example:

```
<asp:Panel id="ControlsPanel" runat="server">

    Some arbitrary controls:<br/><br/>
    <asp:Label Text="A Label" runat="server"/><br/>
    <asp:TextBox Text="A TextBox" runat="server"/><br/>

</asp:Panel>
```

Since the label and text box are contained within the panel, you could set the style of the panel such that it is hidden, and all child controls will also be hidden.

The `Table`, `TableRow` and `TableCell` map directly onto the TABLE, TR and TD elements in HTML, and are useful for building up tables that require server-side processing. For example:

```
<asp:Table id="ItemsTable" runat="server">
  <asp:TableRow>
    <asp:TableCell>R1 C1</asp:TableCell>
    <asp:TableCell>R1 C2</asp:TableCell>
    <asp:TableCell>R1 C3</asp:TableCell>
  </asp:TableRow>
  <asp:TableRow>
    <asp:TableCell>R2 C1</asp:TableCell>
    <asp:TableCell>R2 C2</asp:TableCell>
    <asp:TableCell>R3 C3</asp:TableCell>
  </asp:TableRow>
</asp:Table>
```

A far easier way to create tables is to use the DataGrid control, which creates rows and cells based on collections of data. This is covered in the next chapter.

Rich Controls

The controls described so far map fairly well onto their HTML equivalents, but just like the standard controls in Visual Basic, there's room for more. In VB we've seen a large market for advanced controls, with rich functionality, and although this has happened in the ASP market, it's not been to such an extent.

Since one of the tenets of ASP+ is its ease of use, you'll not be surprised to learn that an advanced set of controls comes with it. There are only two in the beta release, but we expect to see more from Microsoft in the final release, as well as a host from third parties.

AdRotator

The displaying of advertisements on Web pages is one of the few ways of making money on the Web. ASP originally shipped with an Ad Rotator, and this functionality has been encapsulated into a server-side control. It is extremely simple to use. First you must create the file of ads – this is an XML file, and takes the form:

```
<Advertisements>

  <Ad>
    <ImageUrl>/AdvWorks/images/AD_1.PNG</ImageUrl>
    <TargetUrl>http://www.astro-bikes.com</TargetUrl>
    <AlternateText>The Astro Mountain Bike Co</AlternateText>
    <Keyword>Biking</Keyword>
    <Impressions>80</Impressions>
  </Ad>

</Advertisements>
```

For each advertisement you require, just add an `Ad` element. Within this, you have the following:

- ❑ `ImageURL` is the URL of the image to display.
- ❑ `TargetUR1` is the URL of the target Web site.
- ❑ `AlternateText` is the text to display when the mouse is over the image.
- ❑ `Keyword` is optional, and specifies a category for the advertisement. This can then be used in the `KeywordFilter` property of the component.
- ❑ `Impressions` indicates the relative weighting for the ad.

To include the rotator in your page, you just add the control:

```
<asp:adrotator AdvertisementFile="/advworks/xml/ads.xml"
    BorderColor="black" BorderWidth="1" runat="server"/>
```

This gives you an ad which rotates through the `AdvertisementFile`:

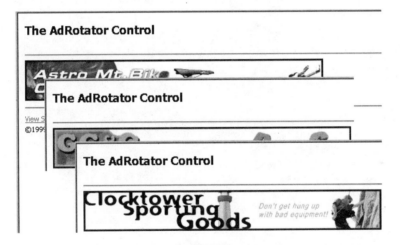

The XML file is also extensible, allowing you to add extra elements. For example:

```
<Advertisements>

  <Ad>
    <ImageUrl>/AdvWorks/images/AD_1.PNG</ImageUrl>
    <TargetUrl>http://www.astro-bikes.com</TargetUrl>
    <AlternateText>The Astro Mountain Bike Co</AlternateText>
    <Keyword>Biking</Keyword>
    <Impressions>80</Impressions>
    <Caption>Bikes that are out of this world</Caption>
  </Ad>

</Advertisements>
```

This extra element can then be made available in the event procedure for the component:

```
<asp:adrotator AdvertisementFile="/advworks/xml/ads.xml"
    BorderColor="black" BorderWidth="1"
    OnAdCreated="Ad_Created"
    runat="server"/>
<br/>
<asp:Label id="Caption runat="server"/>

<script language="vb" runat="server">

  Sub Ad_Created(Source As Object, E As AdCreatedEventArgs)

    If e.AdProperties("Caption") <> "" Then
      AdCaption.Text = e.AdProperties("Caption")
    End If

  End Sub

</script>
```

Now, when an ad is created, the event procedure is run. This procedure checks to see if the property `Caption` has some text, and if so, it outputs it into the caption label. In this way you can easily customize your ads.

Calendar

The other control initially supplied is the `Calendar` control, which provides a rich calendar. Like the AdRotator it's extremely simple to use, although it does offer a great deal of customisation. Let's start with a simple example first:

```
<asp:Calendar runat="server"/>
```

This gives the following simple output:

Pretty simple, but also pretty dull, so let's make it look better:

```
<asp:Calendar runat="server"
    BackColor="Beige" ForeColor="Brown"
    BorderWidth="3"
    BorderStyle="Solid" BorderColor="Black"
    CellSpacing="2" CellPadding="2"
    ShowGridLines="true"
/>
```

Now we have a different look:

Now, how about a bit more advanced formatting:

```
<ASP:Calendar CssClass="calstyle" runat="server"
    BackColor="Beige" ForeColor="Brown"
    BorderWidth="3"
    BorderStyle="Solid" BorderColor="Black"
    CellSpacing="2" CellPadding="2"
    ShowGridLines=true

    TitleStyle-BorderColor="darkolivegreen"
    TitleStyle-BorderWidth="3"
    TitleStyle-BackColor="olivedrab"
    TitleStyle-Height="50px"

    DayHeaderStyle-BorderColor="darkolivegreen"
    DayHeaderStyle-BorderWidth="3"
    DayHeaderStyle-BackColor="olivedrab"
    DayHeaderStyle-ForeColor="black"
    DayHeaderStyle-Height="20px"

    DayStyle-Width="50px"
    DayStyle-Height="50px"

    TodayDayStyle-BorderWidth="3"

    WeekEndDayStyle-BackColor="palegoldenrod"
    WeekEndDayStyle-Width="50px"
    WeekEndDayStyle-Height="50px"

    SelectedDayStyle-BorderColor="firebrick"
    SelectedDayStyle-BorderWidth="3"

    OtherMonthDayStyle-Width="50px"
    OtherMonthDayStyle-Height="50px"
/>
```

You can see that this has a rich set of styles available for customization, and gives the output overleaf:

I won't go into detail explaining what the various styles are since it's fairly obvious.

Calendar Functionality

There are two events that are useful to respond to – when the date changes, and when the month changes. These can be hooked into the control in the following manner:

```
<asp:Calendar id="cal"
    OnSelectionChanged="cal_OnSelectionChanged"
    OnVisibleMonthChanged="cal_OnVisibleMonthChanged"
    runat="server"/>
```

Let's take the OnSelectionChanged event procedure first:

```
Sub cal_OnSelectionChanged(Source As Object, E As EventArgs)

  CurrentDate.Text = cal.SelectedDate.ToString()

End Sub
```

Here we simply set the Text property of a Label control to the currently SelectedDate. We have to convert it to a string first, because the selected date is a property of type DateTime. Using this event procedure you can synchronize other events, such as database queries dependent on the date.

For the month changing, the event procedure is as follows:

```
Sub cal_OnVisibleMonthChanged(Source As Object,
                        E As MonthChangedEventArgs)

  CurrentMonth.Text = E.NewDate.ToString()
  PreviousMonth.Text = E.PreviousDate.ToString()

End Sub
```

Notice that the second parameter to the event procedure is not just EventArgs, but contains more specific information. In fact, all it contains are two properties – NewDate, which is the new month, and PreviousDate, which is the previous month. Both of these dates are full dates, and are the first day of the month. This is easily seen when we run the sample:

Currently Date = 07/20/2000 00:00:00
Currently Selected Month = 07/01/2000 00:00:00
Previously Selected Month = 08/01/2000 00:00:00

Here the current date shows the selected date, while the current and previous months show the first day of the appropriate month. If you only required the month names, then you could apply formatting to these dates.

By default the calendar only allows selection of single dates. However, the SelectionMode property allows us to choose between the following:

❑   None, where no selection of dates is allowed.

❑   Day, where only the day can be selected.

❑   DayWeek, where a day or a whole week can be selected.

❑   DayWeekMonth, where a day, and whole week, or a whole month can be selected.

When in DayWeek mode, you get an extra column added to the beginning of each week, and selecting this selects the whole week:

When in DayWeekMonth mode you also get an extra selection at the beginning of the month:

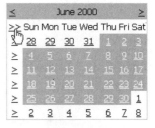

When you have multiple date selections like this, you can't use the SelectedItem property to determine which date has been selected, because more that one has. Instead you need to use the SelectedItems collection, which contains a DateTime for each date selected. So you could then change the selection event procedure to the following:

```
Sub cal_OnSelectionChanged(Source As Object, E As EventArgs)

  Dim sel As Integer

  sel = cal.SelectedDates.Count
  If sel = 1 Then
    CurrentDate.Text = cal.SelectedDate.ToString()
  Else
    CurrentDate.Text = cal.SelectedDates.Item(0) & " to " & _
                       cal.SelectedDates.Item(sel - 1)
  End If

End Sub
```

Here we check to see how many items have been selected. If it's only one, then we just display that one date. If more than one, then we show the first and the last in the range. You could also use a `For Each` construct to loop through all of the selected dates.

Date Ranges

You can also set ranges from code by using the `SelectRange` method of the calendar, which accepts two dates – that start and end of the range. So, you could easily add two more calendar controls to allow selection of the start and end dates, and then add a button to set the range on our existing calendar:

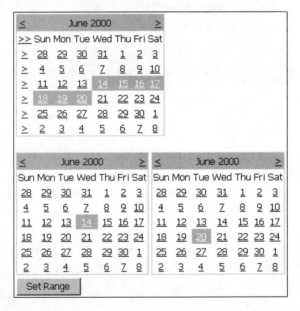

The code for the button looks like this:

```
Sub SetRangeBtn_Click(Source As Object, E As EVentArgs)

  cal.SelectedDates.SelectRange(calFrom.SelectedDate, calTo.SelectedDate)

End Sub
```

All in all, the calendar offers a great deal of functionality, with very little coding involved. That's the beauty of rich controls.

Other Rich Controls

The other set of rich controls that will be supplied with this beta are the Validation Controls, to aid in all types of form validation. These are covered in detail in Chapter 4.

The definitive list of other rich controls has yet to be decided, but it seems likely that more than these two will be supplied as standard. I know that the ASP+ team would like a Tree control, and some form of Menu control would be nice. But, since the product is still under construction, we'll have to wait and see. In the meantime, read Chapter 7 to see how to create your own controls.

Mobile Controls

For the final release of ASP+ there will be a set of controls for providing WML content to WAP devices. Since one of the ideas of rich controls is their ability to render differently depending upon the browser, you might think that this is an ideal situation – the controls could detect whether a WAP device was browsing them, and render content accordingly. However, the structure of WML means that input pages often have a different structure to standard HTML pages. For this reason, a separate set of controls will be produced.

At the time of writing no details of these have been released, but keep an eye on the supporting Web site and we'll keep you updated.

Custom Controls

One great advantage of the new ASP+ environment is that the controls you use aren't just limited to the supplied controls. As well as there being great potential for a third party control market, it's also possible to author controls yourself. This can be done in one of two ways – as custom controls or as Pagelets.

A custom control is one implemented in one of the supported languages, such as VB or C#. All of the supplied ASP+ controls are implemented in C#, and Microsoft is hoping the source for these will be available in the final release. This will not only help you understand how controls are written, but also help in authoring your own. In fact, the whole of ASP+ was written in C#, so there's no limit to what you can do. Writing your own controls is covered in Chapter 7.

Pagelets are custom controls that are implemented as ASP+ pages. This brings the ability to author controls within the reach of programmers who do not have deep familiarity with the control architecture. Implementation of Pagelets is covered in Chapter 4.

Summary

This chapter has been all about ASP+ Pages and Web Controls - the default set of controls supplied with ASP+. One of the things that should be obvious from reading this chapter is that not only do you get a set of functionally rich controls, but you can bring more consistency to your code. Under ASP when you posted back to the server, there was no way of separating the various parts of code. Under ASP+, with its event handling, it's extremely simple to logically split the code into the event procedures for selected controls.

It's now time to take your look at controls one step further, and delve into the world of handling data in ASP+ pages.

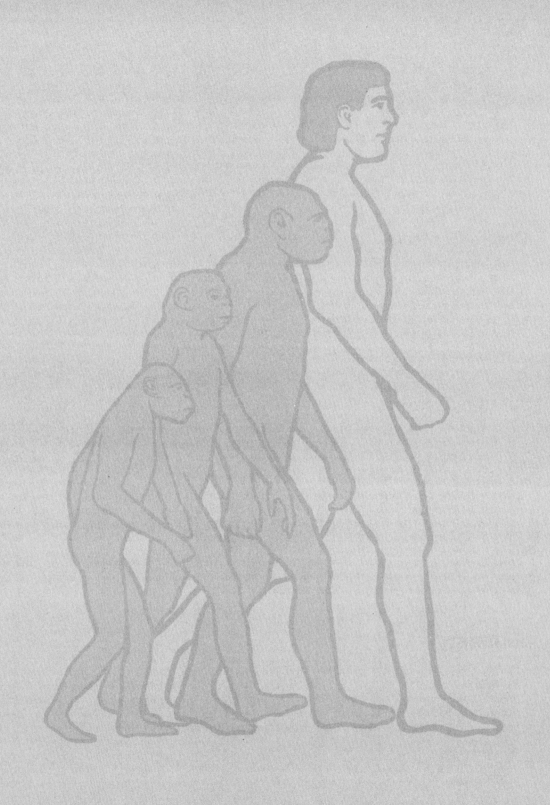

3

Data and Data Binding

One of the reasons for the rapid rise of ASP was its easy access to data stores, and the simple way in which data could be presented. ASP+ has taken this one step further, with the introduction of a new suite of data access technologies, presently called ADO+, offering a rich suite of data handling and binding facilities, to ease the manipulation of all types of data.

In this chapter we'll be looking at how data can be presented in a multitude of ways, and introducing some key concepts of ADO+ as we go along. Specifically we'll be looking at:

- ❑ Why we have a new data access methodology
- ❑ How ADO+ can be used to access data stores
- ❑ How data can be bound to server controls
- ❑ How controls can be bound to non-SQL data
- ❑ How to use the list controls with bound data
- ❑ How to customize the look of your data
- ❑ How data can be updated

Like everything else in ASP+, these new data features are not only very simple to use, but they're also extremely powerful. Data binding is a particular case in point, as it removes a great deal of messy code used to generate output, and provides a greater separation between code and content.

Data binding also works not only against data stores, but also against any COM+ object. And not just those that implement the OLEDB Simple Provider, but any object. This means that you can now bind directly against your business objects, and you do not need to wrap them in order to display their contents.

What is ADO+

This is the bit where you think 'Oh no, not another data access strategy'. Every new version of Visual Studio seems to bring another one, and you may wonder why this is so. There is, in fact, a simple answer – evolution. The Web is evolving, which means that Web applications must evolve too. ASP has grown from a mere baby to a mature development product, so it seems only logical that ADO grows with it.

In the same way that ASP+ is not a replacement for ASP, ADO+ is not a replacement for ADO. Although there is a great deal of overlap between the two versions, they are really targeted at different areas. It was ASP that really pushed the rise of ADO, but there were areas where it really didn't perform the tasks required. To create rich, scalable Web applications, something new is needed.

Data in Web Applications

To understand why ADO+ has been introduced, you have to understand how data is used in Web applications. Remember that the Web is inherently disconnected. For programmers who cut their teeth on single or two tier systems, this is often the hardest thing to grasp, and has particular implications for traditional data access. No longer is it possible to remain connected to the data server while using server based cursors and performing positional updates.

In Web applications we have to think 'disconnected', and in many situations that applies to the data too. When building a Web application you might have to deal with data in any number of places – ASP code on the Web server, a business component, or even the client browser. In some of these you will not be directly connected to the data server; therefore you need to use disconnected data, which allows data manipulation, as well as connection and update back to the server.

ADO+ has been designed to work in this disconnected way, and although it does provide various connected scenarios, there is no support for server-side cursors and positional updates. Data manipulation is intended to be performed without a permanent connection to the server. There are some great reasons for doing this:

❑   **Data Sharing** is promoted, since the disconnected model inherently wraps data with everything it needs. It therefore becomes easy to move data between applications.

❑   **Standardization** is increased, with support for SQL and XML.

❑   **Programmability** is increased, since ADO+ provides a strongly typed environment for the data.

❑   **Performance** is improved, especially where ADO disconnected recordsets are used.

You'll see plenty of other great features as we go through this chapter.

Using ADO+

We're not going to give an exhaustive examination of ADO+ here, since there's too much to cover, but there are some things you'll need to understand, as they'll be utilized in the code through the course of the book. The first thing to get to grips with is code namespaces:

Code Namespace	Contains
System.Data	Base objects and types for ADO+
System.Data.ADO	Managed OLEDB data store objects
System.Data.SQL	SQL Server specific implementations of ADO+ objects.
System.Data.XML	XML objects
System.Data.SQLTypes	SQL data types

What might seem odd is that there is a System.Data.ADO and a System.Data.SQL. As we go through this chapter you'll see that they map pretty much one to one onto each other. The reason is that System.Data provides the code facilities, while System.Data.ADO and System.Data.SQL are the namespaces for the two managed providers.

But why split ADO and SQL, when ADO can talk to SQL? Well, the reason for creating a separate SQL implementation is that it is optimized for SQL Server, and talks directly to SQL Server without going through OLEDB. For those sites that use SQL Server it's a great way to improve the performance of data access.

Using Namespaces

In ASP+ pages you have to tell ASP+ that you wish to use a certain namespace; it's a bit like using the References in a Visual Basic program. To do this you use the Import construct at the top of the page:

```
<%@ Import Namespace="System.Data.ADO" %>
```

This would import the ADO namespace into the ASP+ page, allowing the objects to be used.

Chapter 6 shows you how to include namespaces globally for an application – this is under the Config.Web section, where it discusses assemblies.

The ADO+ Object Model

As you'd expect, ADO+ has a new object model and a host of new objects, some of which will be familiar to existing ADO programmers. The managed provider for ADO consists of:

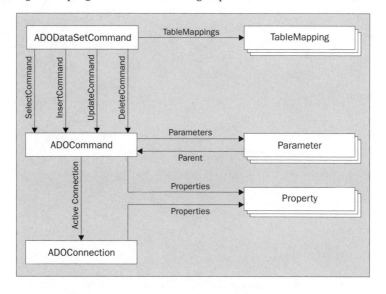

The `ADOConnection`, `ADOCommand`, `Parameter`, and `Property` objects (and the collections of the latter two) are pretty much the same as their ADO equivalents. There are differences, but we don't really need to examine them here. These objects are useful in connected scenarios.

The `ADODataSetCommand` is designed for managing disconnected data, and providing ways to reconcile that data with its data store – that is the standard Create, Read, Update and Delete (CRUD) functionality. Through the four command objects, you can specify the command (most often a SQL statement) that will be used to perform this update. The advantage of this method over the old ADO disconnected recordset is that you have complete control over how data is fetched and updated. The `ADODataSetCommand` also provides impedance, where the names of items in the data store don't have to match the names in the `DataSet`. The `ADODataSetCommand` provides facilities for mapping item names, allowing you to expose a more friendly interface to the data. For example, we may have a column called `A1234` that exists in the table `tblA123`. For the programmer using our business objects, this isn't very intuitive, so ADO+ provides table and column mapping so that we could expose these two objects as `ProductID` and `tblProducts`.

The `TableMapping` object allows the mapping of tables and columns from the data store to the tables and columns in the `DataSet`.

To match these objects, there is also an equivalent set for SQL Server – `SQLConnection`, `SQLCommand` and `SQLDataSetCommand`.

DataSets and DataViews

There are two other objects:

❑ **DataSet**

❑ **Data View**

The **DataSet** is designed to handle the actual data from a data store, and provides access to multiple tables, rows and columns, via the following hierarchy:

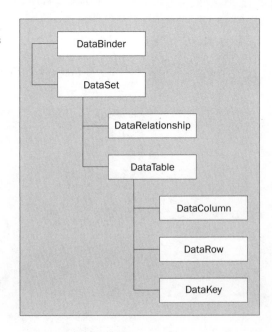

It looks quite complex, but it's not really. Each `DataSet` can contain multiple tables, and maintain the relationship between them. An easy means of understanding this is by thinking of the `DataSet` almost as an offline copy of your data store. The advantage of the `Dataset` is that since it's designed for disconnected data, you can pass multiple tables around the tiers of a Web application in one go, along with the relationships.

The **DataView** is a custom view of a data table, whose prime purpose is to aid in data binding. You can think of the `DataView` as the equivalent of the ADO Recordset, as it contains a single view on top of the table data. Since the DataSet is persisted as XML, it is also easily transported across tiers and applications.

> **The important thing to remember is that a DataSet is not a Recordset. In terms of analogies, then a DataView is more like a Recordset.**

Creating a DataSet

Creating a `DataSet` and a `DataView` of data is simple, as shown in this ASP+ page:

```
<%@ Import Namespace="System.Data" %>
<%@ Import Namespace="System.Data.ADO" %>

<html>
<head>

<script language="VB" runat="server">

  Sub Page_Load(Source As Object, E As EventArgs)

    Dim myConnection As ADOConnection
    Dim myCommand    As ADODataSetCommand
    Dim ds           As New DataSet
    Dim ConnStr      As String
    Dim SQL          As String


      ' set the connection details
    ConnStr = "Provider=SQLOLEDB; Data Source=(local); " & _
              "Initial Catalog=AdvWorks; User ID=sa"
    SQL = "select distinct ProductType from Products"

      ' create the connection
    myConnection = New ADOConnection(ConnStr)

      ' define the command
      ' this fills in the SelectCommand property
    myCommand = New ADODataSetCommand(SQL, myConnection)

      ' run the command and fill the supplied DataSet
      ' The second argument is the table name that the results are
      ' given in the Tables collection
    myCommand.FillDataSet(ds, "Products")
```

```
    ' reset the command to something else
    SQL = "select * from Shipping_Methods"
    myCommand.SelectCommand = new ADOCommand(SQL, myConnection)

    ' and run the new command, giving it a different table name
    myCommand.FillDataSet(ds, "ShippingMethods")

    DataGrid1.DataSource = ds.Tables
    DataGrid1.DataBind()

  End Sub

</script>

<asp:DataGrid id="DataGrid1" runat="server"/>

</html>
```

The output from this page is shown below:

Accessing a DataView

TypedTableName	Namespace	TypedRowName	HasErrors	MinimumCapacity	TableName	DisplayExpression	CaseSensitive
Products		ProductsRow	False	25	Products		False
ShippingMethods		ShippingMethodsRow	False	25	ShippingMethods		False

Let's examine the code in detail to explain how it works. The first two lines import the namespaces for the base data classes and the ADO managed provider.

```
<%@ Import Namespace="System.Data" %>
<%@ Import Namespace="System.Data.ADO" %>
```

The script runs on the Page_Load event, and is the point at which the data is accessed:

```
<html>
<head>

<script language="VB" runat="server">

  Sub Page_Load(Source As Object, E As EventArgs)
```

First come the variable declarations. The ADOConnection will contain the connection details to our data store, and the ADODataSetCommand will provide the management of data between the data store and the client page. This data will be placed in the DataSet.

```
    Dim myConnection As ADOConnection
    Dim myCommand    As ADODataSetCommand
    Dim ds           As New DataSet
    Dim ConnStr      As String
    Dim SQL          As String
```

The next thing to do is set the connection details and the SQL string to be run. Notice that the connection string is a standard OLE DB connection string – that's because we're using the ADO managed provider.

```
ConnStr = "Provider=SQLOLEDB; Data Source=(local); " & _
          "Initial Catalog=AdvWorks; User ID=sa"
SQL = "select distinct ProductType from Products"
```

Now we can create the connection, using the above connection string.

```
myConnection = New ADOConnection(ConnStr)
```

And then we can define the command we wish to run. What's actually happening here is that the SelectCommand property of the ADODataSetCommand is being filled in.

```
myCommand = New ADODataSetCommand(SQL, myConnection)
```

Now we can run the command. The first argument identifies the DataSet, which is to contain the data, and the second argument identifies the table name in that DataSet where the data will be stored. Remember that DataSets can contain multiple tables.

```
myCommand.FillDataSet(ds, "Products")
```

To prove that point, we'll reset the SelectCommand and run another command, putting the data from this into a different table:

```
SQL = "select * from Shipping_Methods"
myCommand.SelectCommand = new ADOCommand(SQL, myConnection)
myCommand.FillDataSet(ds, "ShippingMethods")
```

So now we have a DataSet containing two Tables; we use this as the source of a grid, and bind the data. It is the Tables collection that is, in fact, bound – you don't actually need to understand this – the important point to remember is that a DataSet can contain multiple tables.

```
DataGrid1.DataSource = ds.Tables
DataGrid1.DataBind()

End Sub

</script>

<asp:DataGrid id="DataGrid1" runat="server"/>

</html>
```

We'll be looking at binding in more detail later.

DataViews

To access the actual data held within a DataSet you need to use a DataView. Each Table in the DataSet contains a property called `DefaultView`, which is the default view of the data, containing all rows and columns. So to bind this to a grid we could do this:

```
DataGrid1.DataSource = ds.Tables("ShippingMethods").DefaultView
```

There's much more to DataViews, but that's about all you need to know for the moment.

DataReaders

Like the other ADO objects, the DataReader comes in two flavors – one for SQL and one for ADO. You may have noticed that the ADO+ samples shown so far have been more verbose than some of the ADO code you might be used to, and the DataReader is designed not only to avoid that complexity, but also to provide facilities that the other ADO+ objects don't supply.

Simply put, the DataReader is a forward-only, read-only view on the data set, where the data is accessed a single row at a time. This provides a simple and lightweight way of traversing through data records. For example:

```
Dim myCommand As SQLCommand
Dim myReader  As SQLDataReader
Dim SQL       As String
Dim ConnStr   As String

SQl = "select * from Shipping_Methods"
ConnStr = "server=localhost;uid=sa;pwd=;database=AdvWorks"

myCommand = New SQLCommand(SQL, ConnStr)
myCommand.ActiveConnection.Open()

myCommand.Execute(myReader)

While myReader.Read()
   ShipMethod.Items.Add(New ListItem(myReader.Item("ShippingMethod"), __
                                 myReader.Item("ShippingMethodID")))
End While
```

This is similar to the way a Recordset works in ADO, giving us a way simply to loop through the records.

Future releases of ASP+ will enable an even simpler method, where you'll be able to use a single line to open the DataReader, and then bind directly to the data it holds.

Data Binding

We're going to step away from ADO+ for a moment, and discuss data binding. We'll come back to ADO+ a little later, to look at how you can bind controls to ADO+ data.

Data binding allows the easy transfer of data into ASP+ Server Controls, in a similar way to the IE client-side data binding features. Unlike client side data binding however, server side data binding retains the ease of data display with cross-browser compatibility.

The idea behind data binding is simple – you link Web controls to a source of data, and ASP+ automatically displays the data for you. It's a simple way of producing lists, grids, etc. without actually having to do the legwork.

The syntax for binding is pretty simple, and takes one of two forms, depending upon what type of control you are binding to. We'll look at the first method next and the second method of binding a little later when we see how we customize the look of our data.

The first method is for controls that handle repetition (DataGrid, ListBox, and so on). You set the `DataSource` property of the item you wish to bind, and then call the `DataBind` method. For example:

```
ListBox1.DataSource = prodList
ListBox1.DataBind()
```

You can actually call this `DataBind` method in one of three ways:

❑ On an individual control, in which case just that control is bound.

❑ On a container control (such as a DataGrid), in which case the control and its children are bound.

❑ On its own (with no control), in which case all items on the page are bound.

And, we can use this method to bind to a variety of data sources. These could be:

❑ An array

❑ A simple property

❑ A collection

❑ An expression

❑ The result of a method call

These options need to be examined in more detail. To start off, we'll look at using the ListBox for our data binding.

Arrays

Using arrays is the simplest form of data binding and is easy to achieve. For example, suppose you wanted a list of product names in a list box:

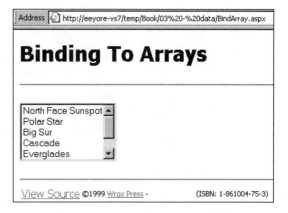

We could use the following ASP+ code to generate this list:

```
<html>
<script language="VB" runat="server">

   Sub Page_Load (Sender As Object, E As EventArgs)

      Dim catList As new ArrayList

      catList.Add ("North Face Sunspot")
      catList.Add ("Polar Star")
      catList.Add ("Big Sur")
      catList.Add ("Cascade")
      catList.Add ("Everglades")
      catList.Add ("Parka")
      catList.Add ("Sierra")

      ' now bind the listbox to the array
      Categories.DataSource = catList
      Categories.DataBind()
   End Sub

</script>

<form runat="server">

   <asp:ListBox id="Categories" runat="server" />

</form>
</html>
```

This code simply creates a new `ArrayList` and fills it using the `Add` method. Then it sets the `DataSource` of the ListBox to the array, and calls the `DataBind` method. These are the two key points – setting the `DataSource` of the control identifies where the data is to come from, and calling `DataBind` actually binds the data to the control.

Bound Data and PostBack

One thing that's worth looking at is what happens to this data when we post back to the server. For example, what happens if we change the contents of our server side form to this:

```
<asp:ListBox id="Categories" autopostback="true" runat="server" />
<p>
  <asp:Label id="SelectedValue" runat="server" />
</p>
```

The `autopostback` property, when set to `true`, means that selecting a value from the list will automatically post back to the server. This is great, but remember that the Page_Load event is run every time the page is loaded, and we are creating our array and binding to the list every time. So, any values selected in the list would be lost.

The solution is to use the `IsPostback` property of the page, to identify whether we are in a postback situation or not. So the `Page_Load` should now look like:

```
Sub Page_Load (Sender As Object, E As EventArgs)

    If Not IsPostBack Then
      Dim catList As new ArrayList

      catList.add ("North Face Sunspot")
      catList.add ("Polar Star")
      catList.add ("Big Sur")
      catList.add ("Cascade")
      catList.add ("Everglades")
      catList.add ("Parka")
      catList.add ("Sierra")

      Categories.DataSource = catList
      Categories.DataBind()
    Else
      SelectedValue.Text = "You selected " & Categories.SelectedItem.Text
    End If

End Sub
```

Now, we only create the array and bind if we haven't posted back – that is, if it's the first load for a page. If we have posted back, then we display the selected value of the list.

Note that you don't have to use the `AutoPostBack` feature – you could just as easily put a command button on the form and then handle the display of the selected value in the button's `onclick` event. However, you'd still only want to perform the binding on the first page load.

Extending the Binding

Binding to an array is simple, but you can extend this idea by creating an array of classes and binding to that. This example is in C#, and has comments explaining each section:

```csharp
<script language="c#" runat="server">
  // create the class, simply containing two properties
  public class Product
  {
      private int    _productID;
      private string _productName;

      public Product (int ID, string Name)
      {
        this._productID = ID;
        this._productName = Name;
      }

      public int ProductID
      {
        get { return _productID; }
      }
```

```
        public string ProductName
        {
          get { return _productName; }
        }
    }

    // Now, when the page loads,  we can fill the
    // array with instances of the class.
    void Page_Load(Object Src, EventArgs E )
    {
        // create a new array
        ArrayList prodList = new ArrayList();

        // add a new item to the array
        // each item is a new instance of the class
        prodList.Add (new Product(1, "North Face Sunspot"));
        prodList.Add (new Product(2, "Polar Star"));
        prodList.Add (new Product(3, "Big Sur"));
        prodList.Add (new Product(4, "Cascade"));
        prodList.Add (new Product(5, "Everglades"));
        prodList.Add (new Product(6, "Rockies"));
        prodList.Add (new Product(7, "Sierra"));

        // bind to the array
        Categories.DataSource = prodList;
        Categories.DataBind();
    }

</script>
```

Because we have bound a complex item to the ListBox, we need to define more explicitly where the data for the list box comes from. For this we use the `DataTextField` and `DataValueField` properties:

```
<form runat="server">

  <asp:ListBox id="Categories"
       DataTextField="ProductName"
       DataValueField="ProductID"
       runat="server" />

</form>
```

The `DataTextField` identifies the field in the underlying structure (i.e. the class) where the data to be displayed is held, and `DataValueField` identifies the value to be held by that item. The actual HTML created is:

```
<select name="Categories" id="Categories" size="5">
  <option value="1">North Face Sunspot</option>
  <option value="2">Polar Star</option>
  <option value="3">Big Sur</option>
  <option value="4">Cascade</option>
  <option value="5">Everglades</option>
  <option value="6">Rockies</option>
  <option value="7">Sierra</option>
</select>
```

We could just as easily have used the `DropDownList` control, which would show only one item.

Binding to XML Data

Since XML is a big part of ASP+, there's also an easy way to bind elements to XML data. For example, consider the Adventure Works products in an XML file:

```xml
<root>
<schema id="DocumentElement" targetNamespace=""
xmlns="http://www.w3.org/1999/XMLSchema" xmlns:msdata="urn:schemas-microsoft-
com:xml-msdata">
    <element name="Products">
        <complexType content="elementOnly">
            <element name="ProductID" type="int"></element>
            <element name="ProductCode" minOccurs="0"
                        type="string"></element>
            <element name="ProductType" minOccurs="0"
                        type="string"></element>
            <element name="ProductIntroductionDate" minOccurs="0"
                        type="timeInstant"></element>
            <element name="ProductName" minOccurs="0"
                        type="string"></element>
            <element name="ProductDescription" minOccurs="0"
                        type="string"></element>
            <element name="ProductSize" minOccurs="0"
                        type="string"></element>
            <element name="ProductImageURL" minOccurs="0"
                        type="string"></element>
            <element name="UnitPrice" minOccurs="0"
                        type="double"></element>
            <element name="OnSale" type="int"></element>
        </complexType>
    </element>
</schema>
<DocumentElement>
    <Products>
        <ProductID>1</ProductID>
        <ProductCode>AW390-12</ProductCode>
        <ProductType>SleepingBag</ProductType>
        <ProductIntroductionDate>1996-04-30T23:00:00</ProductIntroductionDate>
        <ProductName>North Face Sunspot</ProductName>
        <ProductDescription>windproof, water-resistant, even heat distribution,
storage sack included, red (re)</ProductDescription>
        <ProductImageURL>/advworks/images/Dsleepingbags25.gif</ProductImageURL>
        <UnitPrice>390</UnitPrice>
        <OnSale>0</OnSale>
    </Products>
    <Products>
        <ProductID>2</ProductID>
```

To load the XML, we use the following C# code:

```csharp
<%@ Import Namespace="System.Data" %>
<%@ Import Namespace="System.IO" %>

<script language="C#" runat="server">
```

```
    void Page_Load(Object Source, EventArgs E)
    {
      DataSet      ds = new DataSet();
      FileStream   fs;
      StreamReader xmlStream;

      fs = new FileStream(Server.MapPath("products.xml"),
                          FileMode.Open, FileAccess.Read);
      xmlStream = new StreamReader(fs);

      ds.ReadXml(xmlStream);

      fs.Close();

      DataGrid1.DataSource = ds.Tables[0].DefaultView;
      DataGrid1.DataBind();
    }

</script>

<asp:DataGrid id="DataGrid1" runat="server" />
```

This code uses the `FileStream` object to read the XML into the `DataSet`, and shows some important points. Let's look at some of the code in more detail:

Firstly we use the `FileStream` as a method of accessing the XML file. A `FileStream` object allows us to interact with the file system – a bit like the old `Open #` in Visual Basic. Here we just want to open the file in read-only mode.

```
      fs = new FileStream(Server.MapPath("products.xml"),
                          FileMode.Open, FileAccess.Read);
```

Next we use a `StreamReader`, which provides a way of reading the contents of a file stream.

```
      xmlStream = new StreamReader(fs);
```

Now, here's the really cool bit. We use the `ReadXml` method of the DataSet to read from the `StreamReader` into the `DataSet`. This gives us an easy way to read XML data into DataSets, and thus into DataViews and the binding framework.

```
      ds.ReadXml(xmlStream);
      fs.Close();
```

Once the data has been read into it, the repeated elements in the XML become the columns in the data set, and so can be bound in the normal way. We'll be looking at the `DataGrid` later in the chapter.

The DataSet also has a `WriteXml` method, to allow sets of data to be written out to XML files.

Binding to Database Data

All of the above data binding scenarios are great, but what you really need to do is bind to data from a data store, so let's go back to ADO+ and see how this can be done. We'll start with a simple ListBox:

```
<%@ Import Namespace="System.Data" %>
<%@ Import Namespace="System.Data.ADO" %>

<script language="VB" runat="server">

  Sub Page_Load(Source As Object, E As EventArgs)

    Dim myConnection As ADOConnection
    Dim myCommand    As ADODataSetCommand
    Dim ConnStr      As String
    Dim CmdStr       As String
    Dim ds           As New DataSet

    ConnStr = "Provider=SQLOLEDB; Data Source=(local); " & _
              "Initial Catalog=AdvWorks; User ID=sa"
    CmdStr = "select * from Products"

    myConnection = New ADOConnection(ConnStr)
    myCommand = New ADODataSetCommand(CmdStr, myConnection)

    myCommand.FillDataSet(ds, "Products")

    ListBox1.DataSource = ds.Tables("Products").DefaultView
    ListBox1.DataBind()

  End Sub

</script>

<asp:ListBox id="ListBox1" runat="server"
   DataTextField="ProductName" DataValueField="ProductID"/>
```

Building the DataSet is exactly the same as we saw earlier in the chapter, as is setting the DataSource and calling DataBind, only this time we bind to the DefaultView of the table in the DataSet. Since a DataSet contains multiple columns, we have to use the DataTextField and DataValueField to identify which columns are bound to the Text and Value properties of each <OPTION> element in the list.

Binding Radio and Check Buttons

Lists of checkboxes or radio buttons are useful for selection options, and following the same data binding principles:

```
<%@ Import Namespace="System.Data" %>
<%@ Import Namespace="System.Data.ADO" %>

<html>
<head>
```

```
<script language="VB" runat="server">

  Sub Page_Load(Source As Object, E As EventArgs)

    If Not IsPostBack Then

      Dim myConnection As ADOConnection
      Dim myCommand    As ADODataSetCommand
      Dim ds           As New DataSet
      Dim ConnStr      As String
      Dim SQL          As String

      ConnStr = "Provider=SQLOLEDB; Data Source=(local); " & _
                "Initial Catalog=AdvWorks; User ID=sa"
      SQL = "select distinct ProductType from Products"

      myConnection = New ADOConnection(ConnStr)
      myCommand = New ADODataSetCommand(SQL, myConnection)

      myCommand.FillDataSet(ds, "Products")

      SQL = "select * from Shipping_Methods"
      myCommand.SelectCommand = new ADOCommand(SQL, myConnection)
      myCommand.FillDataSet(ds, "ShippingMethods")

      Categories.DataSource = ds.Tables("Products").DefaultView
      ShippingMethod.DataSource = ds.Tables("ShippingMethods").DefaultView

      Page.DataBind()

    End If

  End Sub

  Sub SendMeInfoBtn_Click(Source As Object, E As EventArgs)

    Dim item         As ListItem
    Dim selectedItems As String

    For Each item In Categories.Items
      If item.Selected Then
        selectedItems &= item.Text & ", "
      End If
    Next

    Confirmation.Text = "Information on " & selectedItems & _
                        " will be sent to you via " & _
                        ShippingMethod.SelectedItem.Text + "."


  End Sub

</script>
```

```
<form runat="server">

  <table border="0" width="100%">
   <tr>
    <td>
      <asp:CheckBoxList id="Categories" RepeatLayout="Flow"
          DataTextField="ProductType"
          DataValueField="ProductType"
          runat="server" />
    </td>
    <td valign="top">
      <asp:RadioButtonList id="ShippingMethod" RepeatLayout="Flow"
          DataTextField="ShippingMethod"
          DataValueField="ShippingMethodID"
          runat="server" />
    </td>
   </tr>
  </table>

  <br/>

  <asp:Button id="DoSomethingBtn"
       Text="Send me information on these items"
       onclick="SendMeInfoBtn_Click"
       runat="server"/>

  <br/>

  <asp:Label id="Confirmation" runat="server"/>

</form>
</html>
```

This example shows several points. The first is that a `DataSet` can contain more than one table. Here we've run two queries (one for the product types and one for the shipping methods) and added each one to the `DataSet`. The `DefaultView` of each table is then used to bind to either a `CheckBoxList` or a `RadioButtonList`. Both of these controls set the `RepeatLayout` attribute to flow the elements down the page.

The second point to note is that we only bind on the first access to the page – that is, when not posting back. The state of controls is kept so you don't lose the values, as shown below, where I've selected some values and clicked the button:

Binding Radio buttons and Check boxes

☐ Backpack   ○ Speedy Express
☐ Boot   ● Federal Shipping
☑ Carabiner   ○ Mail Company
☐ Crampon   ○ Slow Shipping
☐ Harness
☐ Pants
☑ Parka
☐ RockShoes
☐ Shirt
☑ SleepingBag
☐ Supplies
☐ Tent

Send me information on these items

Information on Carabiner, Parka, SleepingBag, will be sent to you via Federal Shipping.

You can clearly see that despite the fact we've posted back to the server, none of the values in the lists changed. The state management takes care of that for us.

The DataGrid Control

The DataGrid control is designed to produce HTML output that represents a spreadsheet-like grid of cells from bound data. This wasn't too difficult in the past, but it's now extremely simple, and very flexible. At it's simplest, you just bind the DataGrid to a source of data:

```
<%@ Import Namespace="System.Data" %>
<%@ Import Namespace="System.Data.ADO" %>

<script language="VB" runat="server">

  Sub Page_Load(Source As Object, E As EventArgs)

    Dim myConnection As ADOConnection
    Dim myCommand    As ADODataSetCommand
    Dim ConnStr      As String
    Dim CmdStr       As String
    Dim ds           As New DataSet

    ConnStr = "Provider=SQLOLEDB; Data Source=(local); " & _
              "Initial Catalog=AdvWorks; User ID=sa"
    CmdStr = "select * from Products"

    myConnection = New ADOConnection(ConnStr)
    myCommand = New ADODataSetCommand(CmdStr, myConnection)

    myCommand.FillDataSet(ds, "Products")

    DataGrid1.DataSource = ds.Tables("Products").DefaultView
    DataGrid1.DataBind()

  End Sub

</script>

<asp:DataGrid id="DataGrid1" runat="server" />
```

By default a bordered table is produced, with the first row taking the column names from the data.

Binding a DataGrid

ProductID	ProductCode	ProductType	ProductIntroductionDate	ProductName	
1	AW390-12	SleepingBag	05/01/1996 00:00:00	North Face Sunspot	
2	AW310-12	SleepingBag	01/16/1996 00:00:00	Polar Star	

Customizing the look

While this is extremely simple, it's a little dull, so we need to customize how it looks. There are several ways to do this; the first is by changing some styles of the various parts of the table:

```
<asp:DataGrid id="DataGrid1"
    GridLines="None"
    HeaderStyle-BackColor="Tan"
    ItemStyle-BackColor="Bisque"
    runat="server"/>
```

Here we've turned off the grid lines, and set the `BackColor` attribute for the header and each item.

The second method of customization is achieved by selecting which columns are displayed, and what heading names they should have:

```
<asp:DataGrid id="DataGrid1" AutoGenerateColumns="false"
    GridLines="None"
    HeaderStyle-BackColor="Tan"
    ItemStyle-BackColor="Bisque"
    runat="server">
  <property name="Columns">
  <asp:BoundColumn HeaderText="Product Code"
          DataField="ProductCode" />
  <asp:BoundColumn HeaderText="Name"
          DataField="ProductName" />
  <asp:BoundColumn HeaderText="Price"
          DataField="UnitPrice" />
  <asp:BoundColumn HeaderText="Description"
          DataField="ProductDescription" />
  </property>
</asp:DataGrid>
```

To ensure that the complete set of columns isn't automatically generated, we turn off the `AutoGenerateColumns` attribute. Then we use the `Columns` property of the grid to add some `BoundColumn` elements, which identify only the columns we want to see.

With both of these additional modifications you get a grid that looks quite good, and you've only had to do minimal changes to your code:

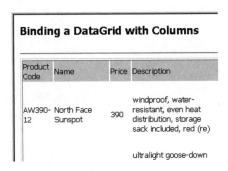

Templating the Columns

To take this one step further we can add a template to a column, which allows us to specify not only the contents, but also the column's appearance. Many ASP+ controls provide their own look, but this isn't always what the user (or programmer) requires. Templates are a way for users to supply an alternative look to the output of a control. When a control supports templates, you add the ASP+ template elements, and then within the template you insert the elements and controls that you want shown. For example:

```
<asp:TemplateColumn HeaderText="Picture">

 <template name="ItemTemplate">

  <asp:Image
      ImageURL='<%# Container.DataItem("ProductImageURL") %>'
      runat="server" />

 </template>

</asp:TemplateColumn>
```

So, instead of a bound column we now have a `TemplateColumn`. This means that we must supply the look of the column by using an Image control (the `template` element is covered under the Using Templates section).

Within the template you can see the second form of data binding, which we mentioned earlier. Here we have to identify the actual source of the data item. With a `BoundColumn` this would be supplied automatically, but because we have templated the column, we have to specify where the data is coming from.

The syntax is quite simple – you just specify the item within an inline code block, placing a # sign after the code block opens:

```
<% #   item to bind to goes here %>
```

To bind an image control we need to specify the URL, which is contained in the `ProductImageURL` column in the DataSet. To extract this we have to know a little about how the data is stored when we bind it to a DataGrid. For list controls, the current row of data is held in the DataItem, but we can't extract it directly, because the image is a child control. Instead we have to use a `Container` to say 'the control that contains me'.

With this templating we now have a page that looks a little better:

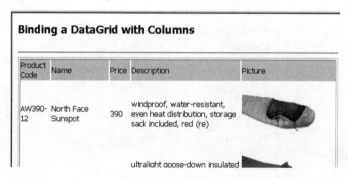

Binding a DataGrid with Columns

Product Code	Name	Price	Description	Picture
AW390-12	North Face Sunspot	390	windproof, water-resistant, even heat distribution, storage sack included, red (re)	
			ultralight goose-down insulated	

Other DataGrid Options

The DataGrid is quite flexible and has a host of other features, but there are too many of them to cover here. Among them are properties to allow:

- ❏ Selection of styles for the header, footer, item, and alternating items

- ❏ Application of different styles when a row is selected

- ❏ Automated deletion of rows

- ❏ Automated sorting of data columns

- ❏ Paging of data

It's also likely that the DataGrid will be enhanced in the future to give rich client side functionality when an up-level browser, such as Internet Explorer, is being used.

Using Templates

Although this looks OK, we could do better. The grid reminds us too much of a traditional datagrid, and it doesn't really look like an interesting page of details. To spruce it up we'll use some templates, and gain complete control over how the page turns out. There are five types of template we can use with the grid:

- ❏ The **HeaderTemplate**, which is for the first line of our output.

- ❏ The **ItemTemplate**, which is for each line of our output, or each odd numbered line if the **AlternatingItemTemplate** is also used.

- ❏ The **AlternatingItemTemplate**, for every other item in our output.

- ❏ The **SeparatorItemTemplate**, to separate the items in the output.

- ❏ The **FooterTemplate**, for the last line of our output.

These templates are used with the Repeater and DataList controls. The DataGrid control doesn't use these templates directly – you have to template the columns.

Individual controls have the option of exposing whatever templates they want. The grid exposes those detailed above, but when authoring controls you can decide what those templates are. You'll see how this can be done in Chapter 7.

The Repeater Control

The Repeater control is designed to provide data binding to a list of items, but without supplying any visual output at all. To get the look we have to provide it via templates. So, to display the catalogue details, we could replace the data grid with a Repeater:

```
<asp:Repeater id="DataGrid1" runat="server">

  <template name="HeaderTemplate">
  <table>
  </template>
```

```
    <template name="ItemTemplate">
     <tr>
       <td>
       <asp:Image ImageURL='<%#
           Container.DataItem("ProductImageURL") %>'
         runat="server" />
       </td>
       <td>
       <%# Container.DataItem("ProductName") %><br/>
       <%# Container.DataItem("ProductCode") %><br/>
       <%# Container.DataItem("ProductDescription") %>
       </td>
     </tr>
     </template>

     <template name="FooterTemplate">
     </table>
     </template>

  </asp:Repeater>
```

So, for the `HeaderTemplate`, we start the HTML Table, and finish it in the `FooterTemplate`. Each row is constructed in the `ItemTemplate`. This gives us the following output:

Binding using the Repeater

 North Face Sunspot
AW390-12
windproof, water-resistant, even heat distri

 Polar Star
AW310-12
ultralight goose-down insulated alpinist's b
included, green (gn)

You could add an `AlternatingItem` template to highlight every other line:

```
    <template name="AlternatingItemTemplate">
     <tr>
       <td>
       <asp:Image ImageURL='<%#
           Container.DataItem("ProductImageURL") %>'
         runat="server" />
       </td>
       <td style="background-color: silver">
       <%# Container.DataItem("ProductName") %><br/>
       <%# Container.DataItem("ProductCode") %><br/>
       <%# Container.DataItem("ProductDescription") %>
       </td>
     </tr>
     </template>
```

Now, every other line has the item details shaded:

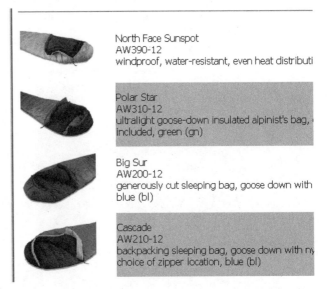

So, the templates have allowed us to change the look of our page with a few simple lines on the server. Trying to do this in existing ASP would be rather tricky.

The DataList Control

This still isn't a great look, so let's use the `DataList` control to customize this even further. One advantage that this control has over the Repeater is that the elements can flow horizontally or vertically. This allows us to have columns of items, to give a look like this:

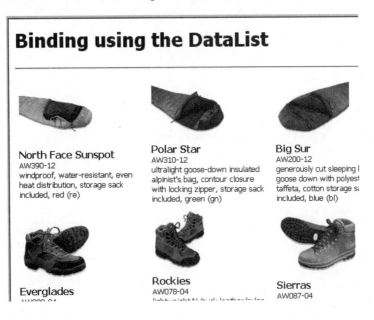

The code for this is simple, again just replacing the actual control to display the data:

```
<asp:DataList id="DataGrid1" border="0"
    RepeatDirection="Horizontal" RepeatColumns="4"
    runat="server">

  <template name="ItemTemplate">
  <table>
    <tr>
     <td>
     <asp:Image ImageURL='<%#
          Container.DataItem("ProductImageURL") %>'
        runat="server" />
     </td>
    </tr>
    <tr>
     <td>
     <b><%# Container.DataItem("ProductName") %><br></b>
     <font size="-1">
        <%# Container.DataItem("ProductCode") %><br>
        $<%# Container.DataItem("UnitPrice") %>
     </font>
     </td>
    </tr>
  </table>
  </template>

</asp:DataList>
```

This example uses the RepeatDirection property to say that the items should flow horizontally across the page, and the RepeatColumns property to specify how many columns there should be. This gives the greatest flexibility in layout.

Editing Data

This fancy layout stuff is all very well, but what happens if you want to edit data? Well, the DataList and the DataGrid both support editing of data, by way of some special event handlers and commands. It's fairly easy to set up; you just have to follow a few steps:

1. Add the command event handlers to the grid.

2. Add the command column to the grid.

3. Template the columns of the grid, adding controls for the ItemTemplate (such as label controls for viewing the data), and the EditItemtemplate (such as text boxes for editing the data).

4. Create the event handler to update the data.

The full source for this is in the EditGridColumns.aspx file, available for download from www.wrox.com, but we'll just consider the most important points here. Let's look at this in detail, starting with the event handlers to the grid:

```
<ASP:DataGrid id="ProductGrid" runat="server"
   OnEditCommand="ProductGrid_Edit"
   OnCancelCommand="ProductGrid_Cancel"
   OnUpdateCommand="ProductGrid_Update"
   DataKeyField="ProductID"
   AutoGenerateColumns="false">
```

The DataKeyField identifies the unique key in the DataView that the grid is bound to. Setting this means that the DataKeys collection of the grid is filled with the selected field, allowing us to extract the key for a particular row. In our particular case we are showing this column, but the idea of the DataKeys collection is to allow you to hold the ID field without necessarily showing it.

Inside the grid, you customize the columns by modifying the Columns collection, and the first column you add is a special one, to add commands for the selected event handlers:

```
<property name="Columns">
<asp:EditCommandColumn EditText="Edit"
   CancelText="Cancel" UpdateText="Update" />
```

The three properties we are setting here correspond to the On...Command properties we set on the grid itself. This is how we link up the EditCommandColumn to our code.

Now you need to template the columns – we'll just show one here to demonstrate:

```
<asp:TemplateColumn HeaderText="Code"
   SortField="ProductCode">
 <template name="ItemTemplate">
 <asp:Label
    Text='<%# Container.DataItem("ProductCode") %>'
    runat="server"/>
 </template>

 <template name="EditItemTemplate">
 <asp:TextBox id="edit_@ProductCode"
    Text='<%# Container.DataItem("ProductCode") %>'
    runat="server"/>
 </template>
</asp:TemplateColumn>
```

The idea is that for the initial, read-only view, the data is shown in labels. These don't allow the user to edit the data. But, for the EditItemTemplate, we show the data in text boxes. You can use any type of input field here, such as list boxes, radio buttons, and so on. We'll explain the odd looking ID on the text box a little later.

Now you need to hook up the event handlers, starting with the Edit one:

```
Sub ProductGrid_Edit(Sender As Object, _
          E As DataGridCommandEventArgs)
  ProductGrid.EditItemIndex = E.Item.ItemIndex
  BindGrid()
End Sub
```

The `EditItemIndex` property of the grid identifies the row that is to be edited. This information comes from the argument of the event handler itself, where the `ItemIndex` property is supplied by the event system. It knows which row you've selected and passes this information to the event handler. `BindGrid` is a procedure that just runs a command against the database to extract the Product information, and then binds the grid to a DataView.

> *You might wonder why we have to do this, since much of the data binding in this chapter has shown that the state information is saved between postbacks. The simple reason is that the grid could contain a large amount of data, and keeping all of it in the viewstate could lead to unnecessarily large pages. Consequently, the grid doesn't maintain it's state, and so we have to supply it every time.*

What happens now is that the grid is redrawn, and the row being edited now has an **Update** and a **Cancel** link, and the template for the row is changed to the `EditItemTemplate`:

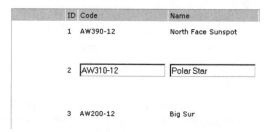

When the **Cancel** link is clicked, the following event procedure is run:

```
Sub ProductGrid_Cancel(Sender As Object, _
            E As DataGridCommandEventArgs)
   ProductGrid.EditItemIndex = -1
   BindGrid()
End Sub
```

This just resets the `EditItemIndex` property, and the template reverts back to the `ItemTemplate`.

The code for the Update link is more complex, so we'll take it in stages:

```
Sub ProductGrid_Update(Sender As Object, _
            E As DataGridCommandEventArgs)

   Dim updateCmd     As String
   Dim myCommand     As ADOCommand
   Dim myConnection AS ADOConnection
   Dim myParam       AS ADOParameter
   Dim myTextBox     As TextBox
   Dim connState     As Integer
   Dim paramNumber   As Integer
```

The first thing to do is define the SQL statement that will be used to update the data:

```
updateCmd = "UPDATE Products " & _
            "SET ProductCode = @ProductCode, " & _
            "ProductName = @ProductName, " & _
            "ProductDescription = @ProductDescription " & _
            "WHERE ProductID = @ProductID"
```

This is a standard SQL UPDATE command, and the variables starting with @ become the parameters of the command.

Next we open a connection to the database, and create a new `ADOCommand`, using this SQL statement and the same connection details we used to populate the grid:

```
myConnection = New ADOConnection(ConnStr)
myConnection.Open()
myCommand = New ADOCommand(updateCmd, myConnection)
```

Then we can create the parameters for the command:

```
myCmd.Parameters.Add(new ADOParameter("@ProductID", _
                                      ADODBType.Integer, 4))
myCmd.Parameters.Add(new ADOParameter("@ProductCode", _
                                      ADODBType.VarChar, 10))
myCmd.Parameters.Add(new ADOParameter("@ProductName", _
                                      ADODBType.VarChar, 50))
myCmd.Parameters.Add(new ADOParameter("@ProductDesc", _
                                      ADODBType.VarChar, 255))
```

This is the point where the `DataKeyField` property comes into play. It was defined on the DataGrid control, to fill the `DataKeys` collection. To make sure we update the correct row in the data store, we extract this key field from the selected item. Remember that this column is read-only, so is treated differently from the other columns.

```
myCmd.Parameters.Item("@ProductID").Value = _
      ProductGrid.DataKeys.Item(E.Item.ItemIndex)
```

And now that strange ID field on the text boxes comes in. To fill the parameters of the command, we need to extract the data from the text boxes in the grid. Since each text box has a unique name, we can use the `FindControl` method to find it. To make this easy, we've given the text boxes an ID that is `edit_` followed by the parameter name. So, we can loop through the parameters (skipping the first one, since it's the ID field), and extract the value from the `TextBox` control.

```
For paramNumber = 1 to myCmd.Parameters.Count - 1
  myParam = myCmd.Parameters.Item(paramNumber)
  myTextBox = E.Item.FindControl("edit_" & _
                  myParam.ParameterName)

  myParam.Value = myTextBox.Text
Next
```

All that's left to do is open the connection, execute the command, and close the connection. The data store will then be updated.

```
myCommand.Execute()
```

To tidy up, we clear the EditItemIndex, so no rows are in update mode, and then redisplay the grid.

```
    MyDataGrid.EditItemIndex = -1
    BindGrid()

End Sub
```

The great thing about this approach is its structured nature. If you want to add editing capabilities you just add the edit command and handle the event. The code you produce will naturally be much cleaner. The templating makes it easy to dynamically change style for items that are being edited. In fact, there's no reason why you have to use an initial display that's non-editable – you can always display text boxes in the ItemTemplate, and then just handle the update command.

The sample file has got a little extra code, to cope with error handling, but otherwise that's all there is to it. Producing an editable set of data is simply a matter of setting the templates and wiring in the event procedures. It's far easier than any method in traditional ASP.

There is also a delete method and associated event, for handling deletes to the database. The method used is pretty much the same as for the update; you would only need to alter your SQL statement accordingly.

Advanced Data Binding

As we saw earlier, when a control is bound to a data source, the binding details usually look like this:

```
    Text = '<%# Container.DataItem.ProductName %>'
```

Here the ProductName would be a column in the data source. There is, though, no reason why you have to use this, and you can place any inline code within the binding section. This allows you to bind to methods, properties or expressions, as the following code demonstrates:

```
<script language="vb" runat="server">

  Dim String1 As String = "ASP+"
  Dim String2 As String = "It's great stuff"

  Public Sub Page_Load (Sender As Object, E As EventArgs)
    Page.DataBind()
  End Sub

  ReadOnly Property ProductName As String
    Get
      ProductName = "The Wrox Wonder Book"
    End Get
  End Property

  Function AddTwoNumbers(NumberOne As Integer, _
                         NumberTwo As Integer) As Integer
    AddTwoNumbers = NumberOne + NumberTwo
  End Function
```

```
</script>

Here is the value of our property:
<asp:Label id="Label1" Text='<%# ProductName %>'
    runat="server"/>
<p>

Here is the return value from our method:
<%# AddTwoNumbers(14, 335) %>
<p>

And here is the value of a bound expression:
<%# String1 + " : " + String2 %>
```

Here we've created a read-only property on the page, and used that as the source of data. Note that we are not binding to the `DataSource` attribute, because that requires a collection of items (such as an array). Since the property `ProductName` only returns a single value, we are using a different control and just setting the `Text` attribute.

This is in fact, just some inline code. We've created a property for the page, and in other code (such as a function) we could just refer to the property by its name. That's exactly what we are doing here – just entering the name as the source for the Text property of the label. The latter two examples make this clearer, since they include a function and an expression.

The difference between normal code and code within data binding constructs, is that code within the binding constructs is executed when the `DataBind()` method is called. You must therefore be aware of what this code does, especially if it relies upon global variables or property values that might not have been set.

Controls

Another technique is to bind one control to the contents of another, which is particularly useful for taking values from list boxes or drop down lists. The code is fairly simple to follow:

```
<script language="vb" runat="server">

  Sub Page_Load (Sender As Object, E As EventArgs)

    If Not IsPostBack Then
      Dim catList As new ArrayList

      catList.add ("North Face Sunspot")
      catList.add ("Polar Star")
      catList.add ("Big Sur")
      catList.add ("Cascade")
      catList.add ("Everglades")
      catList.add ("Parka")
      catList.add ("Sierra")

      Categories.DataSource = catList
    End If
```

```
      Page.DataBind()

   End Sub

</script>

<form runat="server">

  <asp:DropDownList id="Categories" autopostback="true"
       runat="server" />
  <p>
    You selected:
    <asp:Label id="SelectedValue"
         Text='<%# Categories.SelectedItem.Text %>'
         runat="server" />
  </p>

</form>
```

There are a couple of points to note here. The first is the use of the `autopostback` attribute on the `DropDownList`, which means that whenever an item is selected, the post back to the server is automatically performed. The second is the way the binding is done – here we are binding the `Text` attribute of the Label to the `SelectedItem` of the `Categories` list. Since the page load does a `DataBind` for all elements, this is automatically bound to the selected list item.

Summary

This chapter has been a quick look at the new data handling features in ASP+, and how the list controls can utilize these to easily produce great looking pages. As these controls encapsulate all that's needed for displaying data, development time should be reduced, and code should be cleaner.

It's only the tip of the iceberg, and we haven't had time to mention some of the other features, such as:

- ❏ Automatic sorting of columns
- ❏ The paging of data within tables
- ❏ Applying styles to different parts of a grid
- ❏ Adding custom command buttons
- ❏ How to handle errors from the data store

There are also areas to look forward to in future releases of the product, such as the ability to use external templates for customizing the look of your pages. This allows not only the code to be split from the content, but also the content to be split from the look, to provide further modularization of your pages.

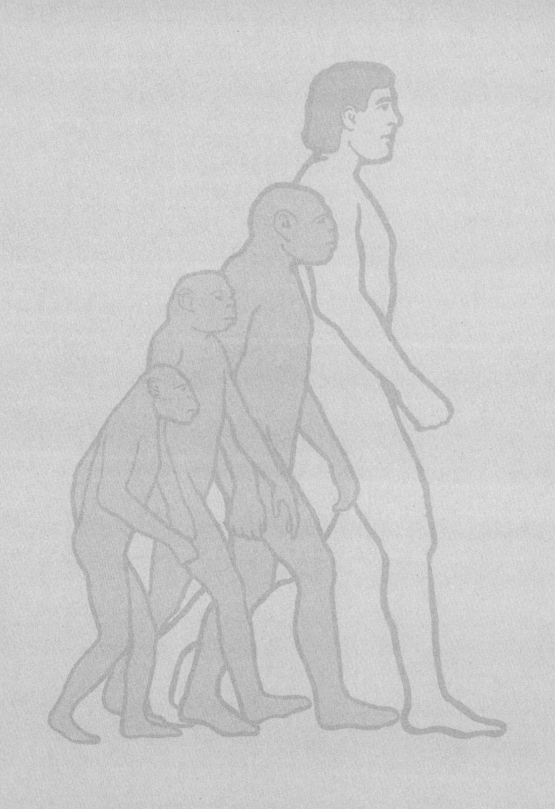

Advanced ASP+ Page Techniques

In the previous chapters, we've looked at the basics of using ASP+ to create dynamic pages. We've seen how much easier it is to accomplish the common tasks that are required, and how ASP+ saves you, the developer, from the need to write repetitive code for these tasks.

In this chapter, we have some 'loose ends' to tie up. We'll see how some of the other features of ASP+, which we haven't covered in earlier chapters, can be used to provide dynamic pages that will work on all the common Web browsers. This includes the usually time-consuming task of validating user input, building reusable code modules, output caching, and managing errors that arise in your pages.

The topics we'll be covering are:

- ❑ Input validation with the new ASP+ controls
- ❑ Creating separate code sections with 'Code Behind'
- ❑ Creating reusable sections of code with 'Pagelets'
- ❑ Managing caching of the page output
- ❑ Error handling, tracing, and debugging techniques

We start with a look at the new validation controls that are provided with ASP+.

Input Validation Techniques

One of the most time-consuming tasks when building Web pages that take input from users is the need to validate their inputs before carrying out any processing on them. For example, if a text box on the order page of your e-commerce site asks for the user's e-mail address, it makes sense to see if they entered it – and if it is in the correct format – before trying to send them an e-mail confirmation message.

In fact, it's a good idea to validate all inputs from your users. It's common for users to click the Submit button more than once, while they are waiting for the first request to produce some visible result. Alternatively they may simply click it by accident, when instead they just wanted to go to another page. Presenting them with some cryptic error message because your database update routine can't cope with invalid values is not a good plan.

However, validation has traditionally been an area where many sites have skimped on the implementation. This is often because validation is not universally simple to do. Internet Explorer 4 and higher provide an 'enhanced forms' capability, which allows you to disable controls and change the page content easily while the page is loaded using Dynamic HTML client-side scripting techniques. Some of the same effects can be achieved in Navigator, but in a different way. And other browsers don't allow any such interaction client-side.

So, do you carry out validation on the client, saving on round trips to the server? Or do you do it on the server to gain compatibility with all browsers, but at the same time cause extra round trips to validate the page each time? The ideal situation would be to do it client-side in appropriate browsers, and server-side in others. But then you have to determine the browser first, and code both scenarios yourself each time.

Overview of the ASP+ Validation Controls

ASP+ is designed to make validation much easier, by carrying out all the arduous parts of the task automatically. It has six **validation controls** that take care of this:

- ❑ The **RequiredFieldValidator** control, which checks that a value has been entered into a control.

- ❑ The **CompareValidator** control, which checks that the control contains a specific value, or matches it with the contents of another control.

- ❑ The **RangeValidator** control, which checks that the value entered into a control falls within a particular range of values.

- ❑ The **RegularExpressionValidator** control, which checks that the value entered matches a specific regular expression.

- ❑ The **CustomValidator** control, which passes the value that a user enters into a control to a specified client-side or server-side function for custom validation.

- ❑ The **ValidationSummary** control, which collects all the validation errors and places them in a list within the page.

Each of the controls can be linked to one (or more in the case of the **CompareValidator**) HTML or ASP+ form control elements, such as text boxes, list boxes, password boxes, file upload boxes and the **ASP:RadioButtonList** control (*support for other controls will come in later releases of ASP+*). You can also link more than one validation control to each control element on a form.

Automatic Client-side or Server-side Implementation

Each control uses the browser type (UserAgent) string to detect the browser type, and generates the appropriate code for the validation routines required – either client-side in Internet Explorer 4 and above, or server-side in all other browsers. This means that performing validation is simply a matter of inserting the validation control into the page and setting the properties to the required values.

Preventing Spoofing with Invalid Values

One of the dangers with using client-side validation is that the user could create a page of their own that doesn't perform validation. When they submit this to your server, it could provide invalid values. To prevent this, the validation controls that are supplied with ASP+ automatically perform validation of posted values on the server, even when the original validation was done on the client.

You can control where the validation is carried out with a Page directive. This overrides the automatic browser-sniffing process. The directive:

```
<%@ Page ClientTarget="DownLevel" %>
```

forces the validation controls to only do validation on the server, while the directive:

```
<%@ Page ClientTarget="UpLevel" %>
```

forces the controls to use client-side validation as well as the server-side validation of posted values. Note that the "UpLevel" directive will force the client to attempt to use client-side script for the validation – even if it doesn't support this technique.

Multiple Validation Criteria

As we mentioned earlier, you can attach more than one validation control to a form control element to perform more complex validation. For example, you can specify that one text box must contain a value between x and y, and that another text box must then contain a value that is greater than, less than, equal to, or not equal to the first text box.

Intuitive 'Invalid Value' Reporting

One of the aims of the validation controls is to allow as much freedom as possible in page design and layout, while still allowing the controls to be easy to program. Each of the validation controls can automatically generate programmer-specific output in the page at the place where the control is inserted into the page – they don't have to be physically located next to the controls that they are validating. This output can include HTML as well as text, so that it's easy to create complex but attractive tables containing the form controls and the validation output.

The way that the validation errors are displayed is completely unrestrained by the controls. For example, we can specify that the text "Error – invalid characters(s)" is to be displayed when a validation error occurs for a particular control:

The **ValidationSummary** control is a different kind of control that aggregates the error messages from all the other validation controls on the page, and can be used to provide a summary of all the validation errors discovered when the page is submitted to the server. This makes forms even more intuitive for the user, while saving huge amounts of coding on the programmer's part.

For example, the **ValidationSummary** control can provide a bulleted list of validation errors at any point you wish within the page, like this:

> - The user name must be 8 alpha-numeric characters
> - Your password and password confirmation do not match

Finally, the base classes from which the controls are built are also available so that you can use them to build your own validation controls if required, perhaps a Zip Code validator, a Telephone Number validator, or a Country validator. However, the default selection provided with ASP+ should generally satisfy all your needs.

The ASP+ Validation Control Summary

The standard code to insert the validation controls is:

```
<asp:type_of_validator id="validator_id" runat="server"
    controlToValidate="control_id"
    errorMessage="error_message_for_summary"
    ... other control-specific property settings go here ...
    display="static|dynamic|none">

    ... text to display inline when a validation error occurs ...

</asp:type_of_validator>
```

Each control type has one or more specific properties that define how it should behave. For example the **RegularExpressionValidator** control has a property validationExpression, which specifies the regular expression against which the value of the form control is matched. We'll summarize the specific details of each validation control next, then see an example of all of them in use.

The RequiredFieldValidator Control

The **RequiredFieldValidator** control is used where a value must be supplied. For example, in the following code, the txtName text box is a required value on a form. The controlToValidate is the id of the text box control, and the initialValue is the value that is in the control when it is first displayed. This is used to detect whether the user has changed the value – if there is no default text in the text box, then this property can be omitted:

```
<input type="text" id="txtName" value="Enter your name" runat="server" />
...
<asp:RequiredFieldValidator id="validator1" runat="server"
    controlToValidate="txtName"
    errorMessage="You must enter your name"
    initialValue="Enter your name"
    display="static">
    *-Error-*
</asp:RequiredFieldValidator>
```

The Display Property

The display property indicates how the validation control's output will be rendered in the page. The value "static" tells the control to reserve (i.e. take up) sufficient space in the page for the text content (in this case the string "*-Error-*") so that the page layout doesn't change when this content is displayed.

The value "dynamic" means that the control will only take up space in the page when the error text string is displayed, meaning that the layout of the page might change. However, this is useful when you have more than one validation control attached to a control on the form. The value "none" tells the control that no inline output will be displayed, even if the input value is invalid. Instead, the **ValidationSummary** control (or the Page.IsValid method that we discuss later) can be used to detect if there was an error, and display the contents of the errorMessage property elsewhere in the page.

The CompareValidator Control

The **CompareValidator** control, as the name suggests, can be used to compare the value in one form control with the value in a different form control, or with a specific value. There are properties you set to indicate the data type of the values (i.e. how the comparison should be made) and the operator to be used for the comparison:

```
<input type="password" id="pwdPassword" runat="server" />
<input type="password" id="pwdConfirm" runat="server" />
...
<asp:CompareValidator id="validator2" runat="server"
    controlToValidate="pwdConfirm"
    errorMessage="The password and confirmation values do not match"
    controlToCompare="pwdPassword"
    type="String"
    operator="Equal"
    display="static">
    *****
</asp:CompareValidator>
```

In this example, we are comparing the values in two controls, and to be valid the controls must have the same String-type value. The options available for the type and operator properties are shown in the following table:

type property Enumeration	operator property Enumeration
String	Equal
Integer	NotEqual
Double	GreaterThan
DateTime	GreaterThanEqual
Currency	LessThan
	LessThanEqual
	DataTypeCheck

The value `DataTypeCheck` for the `operator` property simply checks that the entry is of the data type specified in the `type` property, without performing any value comparison. In all cases, if the value in a control cannot be legally converted into the type specified by the `type` property, the validation will fail. To compare the values in two controls, as in our example above, we specify the `id` of the 'other' control in the `controlToCompare` property. If we want to compare to a specific value, rather than to the value in another control, we use the `valueToCompare` property instead.

The RangeValidator Control

The **RangeValidator** control is useful where you want to ensure that a value falls within a specific range, for example, checking if the user entered a value between 18 and 90 for their age:

```
<input type="text" id="txtAge" runat="server" />
...
<asp:RangeValidator id="validAgeRange" runat="server"
  controlToValidate="txtAge"
  type="Integer"
  minimumValue="18"
  maximumValue="90"
  errorMessage="Applications can only be accepted for ages between 18 and 90"
  display="dynamic">
  *
</asp:RangeValidator>
```

In this case, we have two properties named `maximumValue` and `minimumValue` that are used to specify the range of acceptable values. And, as in the **CompareValidator** control, there is a `type` property that specifies how the comparison should be made. Alternatively, you can compare the value in the form control (to which this validation control is attached) to the values in other controls on the page. To do this, you specify the `id` values of these controls using the `maximumControl` and `minimumControl` properties instead. You can also mix these if required, perhaps using just the `minimumValue` and `maximumControl` properties.

The Regular Expression Validator Control

The **RegularExpressionValidator** control is probably the most versatile of the validation controls. It performs a match between the attached form control's value and a regular expression that you specify. If you aren't familiar with the regular expression syntax, it's worth learning it just to benefit from using this validation control:

```
<input type="password" id="pwdPassword" runat="server" />
...
<asp:RegularExpressionValidator id="validator3" runat="server"
  controlToValidate="pwdPassword"
  validationExpression=".*\d.*[A-Z].*|.*[A-Z].*\d.*"
  errorMessage="Your password must contain a number and an uppercase letter"
  display="none">
</asp:RegularExpressionValidator>
```

In this example, we've used the regular expression `".*\d.*[A-Z].*|.*[A-Z].*\d.*"`. This specifies that the value can either match `".*\d.*[A-Z].*"` or `".*[A-Z].*\d.*"` (the two parts of the expression are separated by a 'pipe' or vertical bar character). In each expression, the `'.'` period character signifies any character, and the `'*'` asterisk means any number of the preceding character. `'\d'` means a digit from 0 to 9, and `[A-Z]` means any upper-case letter.

So this first part of the regular expression specifies that the value can contain any mix of characters followed by a number, any other characters, an upper-case letter, and any other characters. The second part allows the same thing, but with an upper-case letter followed by a number.

> *You'll find the full description of the syntax for regular expressions in the Windows SDK, or online at http://msdn.microsoft.com/scripting/jscript/doc/jsregexpsyntax.htm. Note that you should only use the syntax that is supported for JavaScript 1.0 for the most browser-compatible results, as the test may be carried out on the client.*

The Custom Validator Control

There will always be some cases where comparisons, range-checking or regular expressions can't provide the complex validation that you need. In these cases, the **CustomValidator** control can be used. It allows you to create a custom client-side or server-side function (in any supported language) that performs the validation and returns either `True` or `False`. For example:

```
<input type="text" id="txtCardNumber" runat="server" />
...
<asp:CustomValidator id="validCCard" runat="server"
  controlToValidate="txtCardNumber"
  onServerValidationFunction="ValidateCreditCardNumber"
  errorMessage="The credit card number you entered is not valid"
  display="dynamic">
  *
</asp:CustomValidator>
...
<!-- custom validation function -->
<script language="VB" runat="server">
Function ValidateCreditCardNumber(objSource As Object, _
                                  strISBN As String) As Boolean
  ...
  If {.. some test condition ..} Then
    ValidateCreditCardNumber = True
  Else
    ValidateCreditCardNumber = False
  End If
End Function
</script>
```

Here, we've used a server-side function written in Visual Basic, which would perform some calculation required to validate a credit card number. The function name is specified in the `onServerValidationFunction` property of the control. This function could be some mathematics using the checksum in the card number, or it could even go out to a credit-card processing agency to check if this user actually has funds available. All our function then has to do is return either `True` or `False`.

To perform client-side validation, you use the `ClientValidationFunction` property instead, and specify the name of a function that is written in the client-side page (i.e. in a script section that **does not** have the `runat="server"` attribute). For maximum browser compatibility, you probably want to use JavaScript 1.0 syntax for this function, as it will be executed on the client. Remember to include a server-side validation routine as well (specified in the `onServerValidationFunction` property) to prevent spoofing of values.

The ValidationSummary Control

Once a page containing validation controls has been compiled, all the validation controls are available within the context of the Page object. While you shouldn't need to access them this way, it does allow the final validation control to perform its magic. The **ValidationSummary** control collects the values from the errorMessage property of each control where the validation test failed, and can present these messages to the user within the page.

We can insert the **ValidationSummary** control anywhere in a page like this:

```
<asp:ValidationSummary id="validSummary1" runat="server"
   headerText="The following errors were found:"
   showSummary="True"
   displayMode="List" />
```

This creates a simple list containing the error messages specified for each validation control elsewhere in the page where the validation test failed. The contents of the headerText property are placed above the list, and the displayMode property specifies how the list is displayed. The options are "List" to produce a list of values separated by HTML <br> characters, "BulletList" (the default) to place the messages in <li> elements within an unordered HTML <ul> list, and "SingleParagraph" to display the messages un-delimited with a single paragraph.

Notice that there is a showSummary property, which defaults to True. If you set it to False, only the content of the headerText property is displayed – useful for a generic error message when any error is encountered and you don't want to provide individual error messages.

> There is also a property named **showMessageBox**, which causes the **ValidationSummary** control to display the list of error messages in a pop-up **alert** dialog on the client. Note that this only works when the client is Internet Explorer 4 or above.

The Page.IsValid Property

As the Page object maintains a list of all the validation controls, and the results of each validation test, it can expose these results to code running on the server. The validation controls can be accessed through the Page.Validators collection if required though there is rarely any need to do so.

However, more useful, is the IsValid property of the Page object. This can be accessed from within any server-side code, and returns True if all the validation tests succeeded, or False if any of them failed. So, it's possible to place a message in the page to indicate this. Here, we're checking the IsValid property when a 'Submit' button on the page is clicked:

```
...
<script language="VB" runat="server">
 Sub SubmitButton_Click(objSource As Object, objArgs As EventArgs)
   If Page.IsValid Then  'there were no validation errors, so...
     'pass the values on to the page that processes them
     Server.Transfer("show_valid_values.aspx")
   Else     'one or more validation tests failed, so...
     'display a message in a <span> element named spnErrorMessage
     strErrMsg = "Sorry, your values could not be validated."
```

```
        spnErrorMessage.innerHTML = strErrMsg
    End If
  End Sub
</script>
...
```

Using the ASP+ Validation Controls

We've created an example page that uses all the validation controls. It is called `validation.aspx`, and can be found in the `Chapter04` subdirectory of the samples that you can download from http://www.wrox.com/. This is what the page looks like after we've provided some suitable values for the controls:

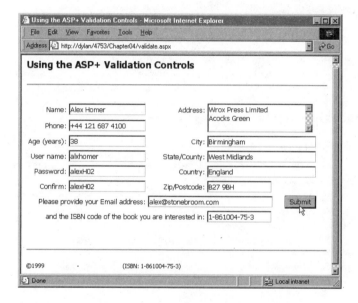

Note that we've used a normal textbox control for the password and confirm password, simply to make it easier to see what's going on. Normally you would use an `<input type="password">` control here, and the validation controls will work just the same way.

The code to create this contains a complex HTML table, with the `rowspan` and `colspan` attributes used to create the separate sections of the table for the various controls. You can examine the source of the page to see the HTML. What we're interested in here is the way that the ASP+ validation controls are used to validate user input before passing the values to another page.

The Code for the Validation Example Page

We want the Name control in our page to be validated as a required value, so we use the **RequiredFieldValidator** for this. It's placed in a separate table cell, next to the text box, and attached to it via the `controlToValidate` property. The cell containing this validation control has the style class "error" assigned to it.

This style class, defined elsewhere in the page, specifies that the content should be displayed in red:

```
...
<td align="right">Name:</td>
<td>
 <input type="text" id="txtName" size="20" runat="server" />
</td>
<td class="error">
  <asp:RequiredFieldValidator id="validName" runat="server"
    controlToValidate="txtName"
    errorMessage="You must enter your name"
    display="static">
    *
  </asp:RequiredFieldValidator>
</td>
...
```

So, if the validation fails, the content of the validation control element, a single asterisk, will be displayed in this table cell. By setting the display property to "static", we force the control to take up space in the cell even when the validation succeeds, thus maintaining the layout of the table. Note that ASP+ only implements this at the client for Internet Explorer 4 and higher, where the contents of an element can be dynamically shown and hidden using Dynamic HTML.

Validating the 'Phone' Field

The Phone field is optional in our form, but if a value is supplied we check that it contains only legal characters using the RegularExpressionValidator control. The regular expression we use indicates that the value can start with a 'plus' sign, and then can only contain spaces, digits, hyphens and parentheses:

```
...
<input type="text" id="txtPhone" size="20" runat="server" />
...
<asp:RegularExpressionValidator id="validPhone" runat="server"
  validationExpression="^\+?[\ \d-\(\)]*"
  controlToValidate="txtPhone"
  errorMessage="The phone number you provided contains invalid characters"
  display="static">
  *
</asp:RegularExpressionValidator>
...
```

Validating the 'Age' Field

For the Age field, we insist on a value being provided, and that it must be between 18 and 90. This is achieved by using two validation controls – a **RequiredFieldValidator** and a **RangeValidator**:

```
...
<input type="text" id="txtAge" size="20" runat="server" />
...
<asp:RequiredFieldValidator id="validAge" runat="server"
 controlToValidate="txtAge"
 errorMessage="You have to tell us how old you are for insurance purposes"
 display="dynamic">
 *
```

```
    </asp:RequiredFieldValidator>
    <asp:RangeValidator id="validAgeRange" runat="server"
     controlToValidate="txtAge"
     type="Integer" minimumValue="18" maximumValue="90"
     errorMessage="We can only accept your application if you are aged 18 to 90"
     display="dynamic">
     *
    </asp:RangeValidator>
    ...
```

Notice that the display property of each is set to "dynamic" in this case. We know that the Name control will force the column to be set to the appropriate width for one asterisk, so it doesn't matter about reserving space for this control's output. And, more to the point, if we had set both to "static" we would be reserving room for two asterisks. If the first was not displayed and the second was, it would not be adjacent to the textbox as we require.

Note that, other than the **RequiredFieldValidator** (and the **CompareValidator** when comparing to the value in another control), the validation controls assume that no entry is required and so will not indicate an error if the user leaves the control empty. So in this case, only one of the validation tests can fail at any one time – and only one asterisk will ever be displayed.

Validating the 'User Name' Field

In the case of the User Name field, we again use two validation controls. A **RequiredFieldValidator** specifies that this value is mandatory, and a **RegularExpressionValidator** is used to validate the value that the user supplies. We will allow any combination of eight alpha-numeric characters, so we use the regular expression "\w{8}" for the validationExpression property.

Validating the 'Password' and 'Confirm' Fields

We saw earlier how we can compare the values in two controls, and this is what we do with the Password and Confirm text boxes (we used text boxes rather than input type="password" controls to make it easier to see the values while experimenting).

The validationExpression property for the Password text box validation control is ".*\d.*[A-Z].*|.*[A-Z].*\d.*", which specifies that the value must contain at least one upper-case letter and at least one number. The Confirm text box then only needs to use the **CompareValidator** control to ensure that the password and confirmation values match.

Validating the 'Email' Field

We've specified that the user must provide an e-mail address, and so we attach a **RequiredFieldValidator** to this control. However, we also want to check that the format of the password is correct, and we do this by attaching a **RegularExpressionValidator** to the Email text box as well.

In this case, the validationExpression property is set to ".*@.*\..*". This specifies that the value must be some characters ('.*') followed by an '@' character, followed by some more characters then a period ('\' indicates the literal value of the next character in the expression, so '\.' indicates a period), followed by some more characters.

Validating the 'ISBN' Field

There is no way that we can validate an ISBN (International Standard Book Number) other than with some custom code. ISBN numbers use modulo 11 arithmetic to check that that value is valid – the final character is the checksum and can be a number from 0 to 9 or 'X' (which has the value 10).

So, in this case, we use a **RequiredFieldValidator** to ensure that the user enters a value, and then a **CustomValidator** to check that value:

```
...
<input type="text" id="txtISBN" size="16" runat="server" />
...
<asp:RequiredFieldValidator id="validISBN" runat="server"
  controlToValidate="txtISBN"
  errorMessage="You must provide an ISBN code for the book"
  display="dynamic">
  *
</asp:RequiredFieldValidator>
<asp:CustomValidator id="validISBNChars" runat="server"
  controlToValidate="txtISBN"
  onServerValidationFunction="ValidateISBN"
  errorMessage="The ISBN code you have entered is not valid"
  display="dynamic">
  *
</asp:CustomValidator>
```

The Custom Funtion to Validate the 'ISBN' Field

The Visual Basic function that performs validation of the ISBN is shown next. It's in a `<script>` section within this page, and returns `True` if the ISBN is valid, or `False` if it isn't:

```
<!-- custom validation function -->
<script language="VB" runat="server">
Function ValidateISBN(ByVal objSource As Object, _
                      ByVal strISBN As String) _
                      As Boolean
  Dim lngTotal As Long = 0          'weighted mod 11 total of digits
  Dim arrDigits(11) As Integer      'array of ISBN digits
  Dim strChar As String             'string to hold single digits
  Dim intLoop As Integer            'generic loop counter
  Dim intDigits As Integer = 0      'number of digits found

  'parse out any non digits except for X (which means 10)
  For intLoop = 1 To Len(strISBN)
    strChar = UCase(Mid(strISBN, intLoop, 1))
    If (strChar >= "0" And strChar <= "9") Or (strChar = "X") Then
      intDigits = intDigits + 1
      If intDigits < 11 Then
        'save first 10 values in array
        If strChar = "X" Then
          arrDigits(intDigits) = 10
        Else
          arrDigits(intDigits) = CInt(strChar)
        End If
      End If
    End If
  Next

  'should have found 10 digits
  If intDigits = 10 Then
```

```
    'add up the weighted values
    For intLoop = 0 To 9
       lngTotal = lngTotal + (arrDigits(intLoop + 1) * (10 - intLoop))
    Next

    'use Modulo 11 and check if it's exactly divisible
    If (lngTotal Mod 11) = 0 Then
       ValidateISBN = True     'OK
    Else
       ValidateISBN = False    'invalid
    End If

  Else  'not 10 digits
       ValidateISBN = False    'invalid
  End If

End Function
</script>
```

Custom Validation on the Client

As we've specified the name of our function in the `onServerValidationFunction` property, it will always be executed on the server. An alternative would be to use a function that is sent to the browser as part of the page, written in JavaScript (probably 1.0 for maximum browser compatibility). Then we could specify the name of this function in the `ClientValidationFunction` property, and have the validation performed without a server round-trip. However, this won't work in browsers that don't support the script we use.

To cope with this, we could detect the browser type in our ASP+ page and set the properties of the validation control dynamically, depending on whether the browser will support client-side script. If the browser supports script, we would set the `ClientValidationFunction` property and include the function code in the client page. If not, we would set the `onServerValidationFunction` property and omit the client-side script from the page we send to the client.

Displaying the Validation Summary

At the end of the page, we want to display a summary of the validation errors. This is easy enough to do – we just insert a **ValidationSummary** control into the page at the point where we want the summary to appear. In our example, we've accepted the default values for `displayMode` (`BulletList`) and `showSummary` (`True`), and we don't use any `headerText`:

```
    . . .
    <asp:ValidationSummary id="validSummary" runat="server" />
    . . .
```

Viewing the Results of the Example Page

So, what happens when we provide some invalid values for the controls? The next screenshot shows the results of entering some invalid values when using Internet Explorer 5.5:

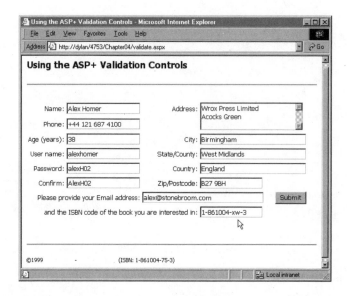

You can see that each control (except the ISBN control) is validated immediately that the text cursor is moved from it, i.e. when it loses the input focus. This is because ASP+ has detected that this is an **'uplevel'** client, and the validation code is included in the page as client-side script. When a value fails the validation test, the text within that validation control (in our case, an asterisk character) is made visible in the page with no round trip to the server required.

However, the validation for the ISBN control is only done server-side, so no asterisk appears to indicate that the value for this control is invalid until the page is submitted.

How the Client-side Validation Works

If you view the source of the page in the browser, you can see how this works. For the User Name control, this section of HTML is created and sent to the client by ASP+:

```
...
<td align="right">User name:</td>
<td>
 <input name="txtUserName" id="txtUserName" type="text" size="20">
</td>
<td class="error">
  <span id="validUserName" ControlToValidate="txtUserName"
        ErrorMessage="You must enter your network user name"
        Display="Dynamic" style="color:Red;display:none;">
  *
</span>
<span id="validUserChars" ControlToValidate="txtUserName"
        ErrorMessage="The user name must be 8 alpha-numeric characters"
        ValidationExpression="\w{8}"
        Display="Dynamic" style="color:Red;display:none;">
  *
</span>
...
```

Notice that the style attributes for the `<span>` elements that hold the text content (the asterisks) and the error message include display:none, so that they aren't visible when the page first loads. ASP+ also adds the following line to the page, which loads a JavaScript source file from the server that contains the functions used in the validation – and makes them available on the client:

```
<script language="javascript" src="/_aspx/v1beta1/script/WebUIValidation.js">
</script>
```

Among these functions are the ones that show and hide the text content of each validation control:

```
function ValidatorHide(Validator) {
    Validator.IsValid = true;
    if (typeof(Validator.Display) == "string") {
        if (Validator.Display == "None") {
            return;
        }
        if (Validator.Display == "Dynamic") {
            Validator.style.display="none";
            return;
        }
    }
    Validator.style.visibility="hidden";
}

function ValidatorShow(Validator) {
    Validator.IsValid = false;
    if (typeof(Validator.Display) == "string") {
        if (Validator.Display == "None") {
            return;
        }
        if (Validator.Display == "Dynamic") {
            Validator.style.display="inline";
            return;
        }
    }
    Validator.style.visibility="visible";
}
```

The `<form>` element in the page also has an onsubmit attribute added, which executes a section of JavaScript code when the form is submitted:

```
<form {other attributes} language="javascript" onsubmit="ValidatorOnSubmit();">
...
function ValidatorOnSubmit() {
    if (Page_ValidationActive) {
        ValidatorCommon_onsubmit();
    }
}
```

This calls routines in the WebUIValidation.js script that validate the control values client-side, then submit the form if all the checks succeed. If they don't, the page is not submitted. However, the **ValidationSummary** control executes at this point and displays a summary of the errors automatically:

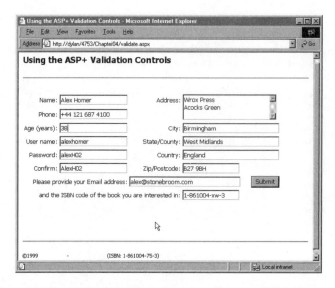

So, as we saw earlier, entering an invalid value when using Internet Explorer 4 or above provides immediate indication of all errors, without a round trip to the server. However, an invalid value in the ISBN control does not automatically trigger the appearance of the asterisk – as you can see in the previous screenshot. An invalid value error message is not included in the validation summary either. This is because this control only validates the value server-side, and the form has not yet been submitted to the server.

The Server-side Validation for the ISBN Control

So, if we correct the other errors that prevent the page from being submitted, we can click the Submit button to send the values to the server. Now, the custom server-side validation function for the ISBN executes, and checks that the entry is valid. If not, as in this case, the page is reloaded with all the values present and the asterisk error indication for the ISBN control. The appropriate error message is also included in the summary at the foot of the page:

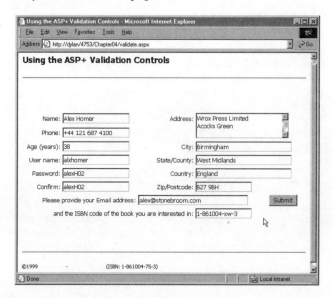

You can also see that there is an error message added to the top of the page. This is because we included an event handler for the `Page_Load` event in our page. It inserts the generic error message into a `<span>` element named `spnErrorMessage` that we included in the HTML definition of the page:

```
<span id="spnErrorMessage" runat="server" class="error"></span>
...
<script language="VB" runat="server">
 Sub Page_Load(ByVal objSource As Object, ByVal objArgs As EventArgs)
   If IsPostBack Then
     If Page.IsValid Then
       Server.Transfer("show_valid_values.aspx")
     Else
       strErrMsg = "Sorry, your values could not be validated " _
               & "- see the notes at the bottom of the page"
       spnErrorMessage.innerHTML = strErrMsg
     End If
   End If
 End Sub
</script>
```

And if, after all this experimentation, you do manage to satisfy all the validation criteria and submit the page, you'll be rewarded with a simple list of the values that were submitted.

ASP+ Validation in Other Browsers

So far, we've only looked at how the validation controls behave in Internet Explorer. This is classed as an **'uplevel'** client, because it allows functionality to be transferred 'up' to the client. Microsoft (perhaps rather condescendingly) classes all other browsers as **'downlevel'** clients, and the validation controls behave differently in these types of client.

In fact, the reason is more to do with the client-side hooks that the validation controls require, such as the ability to change the contents of HTML elements on the page while it is displayed. It's quite possible that the controls will take advantage of some of the features in newer browsers such as Netscape 6 in the future.

So, in 'downlevel' clients, all the work is done on the server instead of being transferred to the client. This means that each validation check requires a round-trip to the server, and so the dynamic error indicators (i.e. our red asterisks) cannot be displayed as the user is filling in the values in the controls. They are only displayed when the form is submitted.

The good news, however, is that it works in almost all browsers. For example, the same page after submitting some invalid values using Netscape Navigator 6 is shown overleaf:

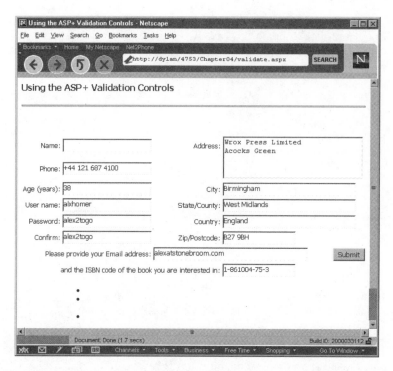

Next, here it is in Opera – which, like Navigator, supports client-side JavaScript. However, again, it doesn't support the dynamic page update features required for fully client-side validation so the page requires a round-trip to the server each time. And, because of this round trip, the error summary also includes the incorrect ISBN as well:

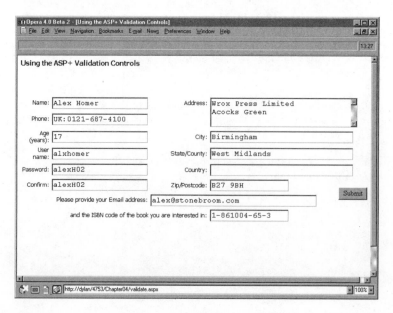

And finally, a browser that doesn't support any scripting at all. This is the result in the W3C reference browser named **Amaya**:

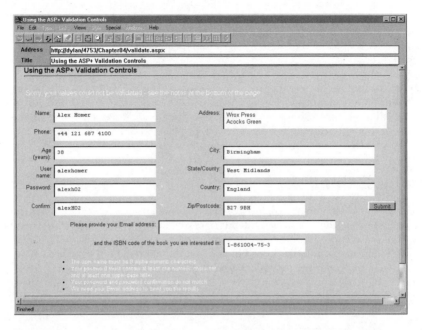

So, the validation controls are a really useful way to cut down the amount of repetitive code you have to write, while still providing high performance and good user interaction on the client. They are also a very good example of the way that the ASP+ rich controls can take advantage of 'uplevel' client functionality.

Programming with 'Code Behind'

One of the problems facing Web programmers and Web page designers is that the increasing complexity required in pages makes it difficult to separate different parts of the development process. Server-side code and HTML are often intermixed in the page, and it's hard to separate them in a sensible and intuitive way so that each member of the development team can work on their own parts without disturbing the work of others.

ASP+ provides two new ways to accomplish this task without having to resort to using the #include directive, as is common in earlier versions of ASP. The first of these techniques is to separate the code content of a page completely from the HTML and other text, layout or graphical information by placing it in a separate file.

This technique is called '**code behind**' (or 'code behind forms'), and takes advantage of the fact that the ASP+ runtime framework compiles each part of the page into a COM+ object and from these creates an execution 'tree'. The file containing the code is just another component of the page, and it exposes the routines it contains like any other COM+ object.

What is actually happening is that we are creating a **base class** that the compiled .aspx page will inherit from. And when we declare variables of the correct control type with the correct name (i.e. that matches the name of the class in the 'code behind' template) these variables will be correctly initialized to refer to the control that the page instantiates.

'Code Behind' in Development Tools

This separation of code and content also makes it easier for development tools to help programmers build ASP+ pages. Visual Studio 7 is likely to take this approach when it appears, and it is in some ways similar to the technique we saw in Visual Basic 6 for creating 'Web Classes'. The result is a development environment that is familiar to traditional programmers; an editor for creating the interface 'form' and a separate code editor.

It also means that other HTML development tools can be used to build the visible interface part of a Web application. As long as the tool doesn't 'mess with' the HTML elements and ASP+ control definitions (i.e. it leaves the attributes it doesn't recognize alone), it will all work together properly afterwards. So, you might prefer to use a tool like FrontPage or similar to create the forms for your Web application, then build the code in the new Visual Basic editor (or even Windows Notepad) afterwards.

Using 'Code Behind'

Using the 'code behind' technique is relatively simple, though there are some pitfalls you have to be aware of. First you create the HTML for the interface. Then you create a separate **class** file in any of the supported languages that provides the functionality required for the interface 'form' page. In outline, this class file is identical to any other class file that you might create in your chosen language, for example in Visual Basic a normal (not a 'code-behind') class file looks like this:

```
Public Class class_name

  Public variable_name As variable_type

  Public Function function_name(parameters) As return_type
     ... function implementation here ...
  End Function

  Public Sub subroutine_name(parameters)
     ... subroutine implementation here ...
  End Sub

End Class
```

Creating a 'Code Behind' Class in Visual Basic

Next, you must inherit the objects from the ASP+ environment that you need to use in the class. By default, ASP+ provides automatic inheritance for the common objects in an .aspx page, but not in a class file. For example, you will need to import at least the System and the Web library – depending on what functions you use in your class file.

Finally, your class must inherit from the ASP+ Page class so that it can be integrated into the ASP+ page in which it's used. This is done with the Inherits statement in Visual Basic:

```
Imports System
Imports System.Web
System.Web.UI
System.Web.UI.WebControls
System.Web.UI.HtmlControls
```

```
Public Class class_name
Inherits System.Web.UI.Page
 ...
End Class
```

Creating a Code Behind Class in C#

In C#, you add the system objects by simply defining the inheritance of the Page class when you create your new class:

```
using System;
using System.Web;
using System.Web.UI;
using System.Web.UI.WebControls;
using System.Web.UI.HtmlControls;

public class class_name : Page {
  ...
}
```

Inheriting the Class File in an ASP+ Page

To connect the class file containing the code implementation to your ASP+ page, you add an Inherits entry to the <%@Page...%> directive, and specify the location of the 'code behind' file:

```
<%@Page Inherits="class_name" Src="path_to_class_file" %>
```

For example, to inherit from a Visual Basic class named ValidateClass that is implemented in a file named validateclass.vb in the same directory as the page, we would use:

```
<%@Page Inherits="ValidateClass" Src="validateclass.vb" %>
```

The Src attribute is optional, and if omitted ASP+ will expect to find a compiled class file in the /bin directory of the application.

> Note that it is important to use the correct file extension for your class files – .vb for Visual Basic files, .js for JScript files and .cs for C# files. This ensures that they are passed to the correct compiler when the page is first executed.

A CodeBehind Example

As an example of using the 'code behind' programming technique, we've separated out the validation code from our previous example into a file named validateclass.vb. It simply contains the ValidateISBN function we used inline in our earlier example. We named the class ValidateClass, and so we can insert it into the page using the directive we saw earlier:

```
<%@Page Language="VB" Inherits="ValidateClass" Src="validateclass.vb" %>
```

The sample page is named `validate_codebehind.aspx`, and is in the `Chapter04` directory of the samples that are available from our Web site at http://www.wrox.com/. When you run it, it looks just the same as the previous inline example. You can also use this technique to inherit from compiled DLLs if required – see the ASP+ SDK for more information.

There is one minor change required to the code for the class file. To use the VB string handling functions, you need to ensure that the code-behind class imports the Visual Basic namespace. This is done by adding the line:

```
Imports Microsoft.VisualBasic
```

However, we took this opportunity to change our function so that it uses the runtime framework `System.Text` functions rather than the intrinsic VB string functions. This involves adding the appropriate `Imports` statement to the class file:

```
Imports System.Text
```

Now, we can use the `StringBuilder` object to create a string that we want to work on. Then, instead of the `UCase` and `Mid` functions provided by VB, we use the `Append` and `Chars` methods of the `StringBuilder` object to manipulate the string. The code that implements the class, and the changes to the original function code, are highlighted in the next listing:

```
Imports System
Imports System.Text

Public Class ValidateClass
Inherits System.Web.UI.Page
Public Function ValidateISBN(objSource As Object, _
                        strArgs As String) As Boolean
  Dim strISBN As New StringBuilder    'the ISBN as entered by the user
  Dim lngTotal As Long = 0            'weighted mod 11 total of digits
  Dim arrDigits(11) As Integer        'array of ISBN digits
  Dim strChar As String               'string to hold single digits
  Dim intLoop As Integer              'generic loop counter
  Dim intDigits As Integer = 0        'number of digits found

  strISBN.Append(strArgs)
  'parse out any non digits except for X (which means 10)
  For intLoop = 0 To strISBN.Length - 1
    strChar = strISBN.Chars(intLoop)
    If (strChar >= "0" And strChar <= "9") Or (strChar = "x") Or _
                                              (strChar = "X") Then
        intDigits = intDigits + 1
        If intDigits < 11 Then
          'save first 10 values in array
          If (strChar = "x") Or (strChar = "X") Then
            arrDigits(intDigits) = 10
          Else
            arrDigits(intDigits) = CInt(strChar)
          End If
        End If
    End If
  Next
```

```
...
... remainder of function code unchanged ...
...
End Function
End Class
```

Creating Reusable Controls with Pagelets

The second new technique for creating reusable code, and separating code from content, is through the use of **pagelets**. While this rather quaint name could well change in the final release version of ASP+, the fundamentals are sure to remain.

The idea behind pagelets is that you can create reusable sections of code or content as separate ASP+ **custom controls**, and use these controls in other pages in just the same way as you would the intrinsic ASP+ controls. You don't have to be aware of how the pagelet code works. And while 'code behind' techniques are primarily aimed at just inheriting code classes into a page, pagelets allow you to generate parts of the user interface as well. You can use them as a way of encapsulating other controls and code into a reusable 'package'.

This brings several advantages – especially when compared to the previous technique with ASP of using the #include directive to insert or include the contents of a file that create sections of the page:

❑ Pagelets are self-contained. They provide a separate variable namespace, which that means no methods or variables conflict with existing ones in the hosting page that uses the same name.

❑ Pagelets can be parameterized, which means users can set arguments on them using attributes on the element that inserts the pagelet into the main hosting page.

❑ Pagelets can be used more than once within a hosting page without having to worry about variable and method conflicts (as each one lives inside its own namespace).

❑ Pagelets can be written in a different language from the main hosting page.

Building a Pagelet Control

As an example of using a pagelet, we have taken the validation page we used in the first section of this chapter and used it as a pagelet in another ASP+ page. We removed all the peripheral 'stuff' from the page, leaving only the <form> section that contains the HTML controls and validation controls, and the code for the custom ValidateISBN function. This file is then saved with the .aspc 'component' file extension.

*Note that a pagelet should **not** include the <html> or <body> elements, as these are already likely to be present in the page that hosts it. One other point to watch out for if you include a <form> in your pagelet (as we've done in our example) is that this pagelet cannot then be used inside another <form> on the main page.*

Next, we need to register the pagelet with the main page that will use it. This is done using the <%Register...%> directive:

```
<%@ Register TagPrefix="ch04" TagName="InputForm" src="validate_pagelet.aspc" %>
```

Here, we've specified that we'll use the page named `validate_pagelet.aspc` (our original `validate.aspx` file with the peripheral content removed), and that it should be registered with ASP+ as an element named `<ch04:InputForm>`. When the main page is loaded, the runtime framework will compile the pagelet file (if it's not already cached in compiled form), and make it available to this page.

A Pagelet Example

Here's the code for the example page, named `pagelet.aspx`, which uses our new validation pagelet. It's in the `Chapter04` subdirectory of the sample files available for this book from http://www.wrox.com/. The page contains the style information for the entire page (including the pagelet, which will inherit the styles). For the time being, ignore the inline ASP code at the end of the page (in the final `<div>` element) – we'll come back to this later:

```
<%@Page Language="VB"%>

<%@ Register TagPrefix="ch04" TagName="InputForm" src="validate_pagelet.aspc" %>

<html>
<head>
<title>Re-using An ASP+ Page as a 'Pagelet'</title>
<style>
 body,td,th,input,textarea  {font-family:Tahoma,Arial,sans-serif; font-size:10pt}
 .error     {font-family:Tahoma,Arial,sans-serif; font-size:12pt; color:red}
</style>
</head>
<body>

... <script> section goes here...

<div style="font-family:Comic Sans MS; font-size:26pt; font-weight:bold;
            color:darkred; background-color:gainsboro">
  <img src="wrox.gif" width="82" height="76" alt="Wrox Press"
       align="middle" vspace="10" hspace="10">
  The Wrox Book Query Page<br clear="all" />
</div>

<div style="width:100%;background-color:lightblue"><br />
    Enter your details and click <b>Submit</b>
  to get more details about our books<br /> 
</div>

<!-- insert the validation form pagelet here -->
<ch04:InputForm id="Pagelet" runat="server" />

<div style="width:100%;background-color:lightgreen"><br />
  <%
  If IsPostBack Then
    strFooter = "  <b>" & Pagelet.ValidationResult & "</b>"
  Else
    strFooter = "  A service brought to you by " _
              & "<b>Wrox Web Design</b> - we do it in ASP+"
  End If
  Response.Write(strFooter)
  %>
```

```
      <br /> 
   </div>

   </body>
   </html>
```

Viewing the Example Page

The next screenshot shows what the final page looks like. You can clearly see the validation form that we created for the example in the earlier sections of this chapter. The HTML in the `<body>` of the previous listing just adds a decorative header and footer to the page:

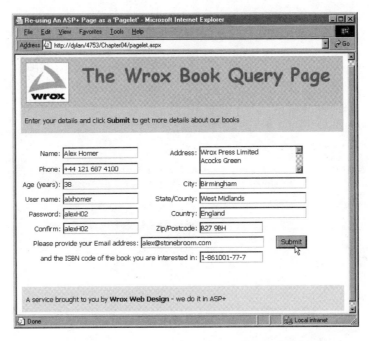

And, like the earlier example, providing an invalid ISBN number produces an error message when the form is submitted:

Using the Values that are Submitted

Once the user enters a valid ISBN (as well as valid values for the other controls) we can do something with these values. In our example page, we use some code in the `Page_Load` event handler (in the `pagelet.aspx` file) that redirects them to a page on the main Wrox Web site containing details about that book:

```
...
<script language="VB" runat="server">
 Sub Page_Load(objSource As Object, objArgs As EventArgs)
   Dim strISBN As String
   'get value of ISBN text box via a custom property of the Pagelet
   strISBN = Pagelet.IsbnValue
   If Len(strISBN) > 0 Then
    'parse out any non digits except for X (which means 10)
    Dim strDigitsOnly As String
    Dim strChar As String
    Dim strQuery As String
    For intLoop = 1 To Len(strISBN)
      strChar = UCase(Mid(strISBN, intLoop, 1))
      If (strChar >= "0" And strChar <= "9") Or (strChar = "X") Then
        strDigitsOnly = strDigitsOnly & strChar
      End If
    Next
    'create the correct URL and query string for the specified book
    strQuery = "http://www.wrox.com/Consumer/Store/Details.asp?isbn=" _
           & strDigitsOnly
    Page.Navigate(strQuery)
   End If
 End Sub
</script>
...
```

Note that we collect the ISBN value from a **custom property** named `IsbnValue` that the pagelet exposes. We'll look at this topic shortly. Meantime, here's the result when the user submits the form after correcting the ISBN code:

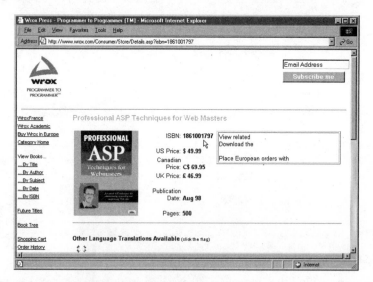

Exposing Custom Properties and Functions

A pagelet can expose custom properties and custom functions for use in the parent 'container' page. As well as the HTML to create the form controls and validation controls, and the custom `ValidateISBN` function, the pagelet we've provided also exposes both a custom property and a custom function.

The pagelet file, named `validate_pagelet.aspc`, contains this script section:

```vb
...
<script langauge="VB" runat="server">

Public Property IsbnValue As String
  Get
    'return the value of the txtISBN textbox
    IsbnValue = txtISBN.Value
  End Get
  Set
    'set the value of the txtISBN textbox
    txtISBN.Value = IsbnValue
  End Set
End Property

Public Function ValidationResult() As String
  If Page.IsValid Then
    ValidationResult = "The values you provided have been accepted"
  Else
    ValidationResult = "There is a problem with the values you provided"
  End If
End Function
</script>
...
```

This code creates a custom `String`-type read-write property named `IsbnValue` that returns or sets the value of the `txtISBN` textbox, and a custom function named `ValidationResult` that returns a string indicating the result of the validation checks carried out within the pagelet.

The `IsbnValue` property is implemented as a read-write property simply to show how it can be done. We don't actually write to the property in our example. To make it read-only, we just omit the `Set...End Set` part of the code.

Using the IsbnValue Property

We used the custom `IsbnValue` property of the `Pagelet` class in our code in the main page like this:

```vb
...
'get the value of the ISBN text box via a custom property
strISBN = Pagelet.IsbnValue
...
```

Note that if you do provide properties that can be written to, you can then use them as attributes in your page. For example, we could preset the value of the ISBN textbox when we insert the pagelet into our main page like this:

```
<ch04:InputForm id="Pagelet" IsbnValue="1-861004-75-3" runat="server" />
```

Using the ValidationResult Function

We also used the custom function named `ValidationResult` in our main page, by simply calling this function. Again, it is part of the `Pagelet` class, and so we used this code at the bottom of the main page:

```
...
<%
If IsPostBack Then
   'call the custom function in the pagelet to get any error message
   strFooter = "  <b>" & Pagelet.ValidationResult & "</b>"
Else
   strFooter = "  A service brought to you by " _
            & "<b>Wrox Web Design</b> - we do it in ASP+"
End If
Response.Write(strFooter)
%>
...
```

So, when this page is loaded in response to a postback (i.e. when the form is submitted) the value returned by our custom `ValidationResult` function will be displayed:

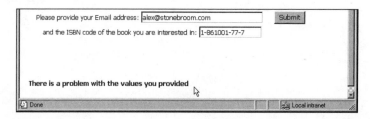

Alternatively, if the validation is successful, the page will display the message "The values you provided have been accepted". However, as it stands, we are redirecting the user to another site if the validation succeeds, so this part of the page is never executed. If you want to see the message, simply comment out the `Page.Navigate` statement in the `Page_OnLoad` event handler then submit a set of valid values.

Other Pagelet Techniques

There are other techniques that you can take advantage of with pagelets. If you examine the samples that we provide, you'll see that many use pagelets to create the header and footer for each page, and to allow you to view the ASP+ source code for the page. You can also load pagelets dynamically at runtime using the `LoadControl` method of the `Page` object, rather than statically as we did with the `<%@Register...%>` directive in the example you've seen here.

This works because the pagelet becomes just another control within the page, and so the same techniques that you use with the intrinsic ASP+ controls work with pagelets. You can load specific pagelets on demand, perhaps in response to client requests, resize them, add scroll bars – the list goes on and on.

Using the ASP+ Cache and the Output Cache

ASP+ implements caching at several levels. As we discussed in Chapter 1, the intermediate-level code that the language compilers create is automatically cached to improve performance when pages are executed repeatedly. However, there are two other caches that are implemented by ASP+, and which can be used by developers to increase the performance of their pages.

The two caches that we're interested in here are:

❑ The **output cache**, which can be configured to improve performance for dynamic pages that are the same for different users.

❑ The **ASP+ cache** that the developer can use within their pages to improve the efficiency of code or pass values between pages.

The Output Cache

One of the criticisms of dynamic page creation techniques is that they are less scalable and require more server resources than just sending static HTML files to clients. A solution that many sites have adopted is batch processing the pages and saving the results to disk as static HTML files. However, this can only work if the content is not directly dependent on the client each time – in other words the page is the same for all requests. This is the case for things like product catalogues and reports, and the update process only needs to be run when the data required for building the page changes.

ASP+ includes a new feature called dynamic output caching that can provide the same kind of effect automatically, without the need to write the pages to disk. Instead, it can cache the dynamically created output (i.e. the content that the client receives), and use this cached copy for subsequent requests. This is better than writing the content to a disk file, as it removes the need for disk access each time.

Of course, this will only be of any use where the page content is the same for all requests for a particular page. If a different page has to be generated for each user, then the cached page cannot be reused. However, ASP+ is clever: it can detect the contents of the **query string** appended to a URL and it will only use the cached copy if the values in the query string are exactly the same (and in the same order within the query string).

So pages that change depending on the contents of the query string will be served correctly – if the contents of the query string are different from those used when the cached copy was created, a new copy is created instead. This new copy is also cached, and is then available for use by clients that provide matching query string values. In the release version of ASP+, it is hoped to extend this feature to the contents of a <form> that is POSTed to the server as well. The output cache also exposes an interface that the developer can use to tailor the way it works for specific ASP+ applications, and with the standard HTTP 1.1 caching techniques.

An Output Caching Example

To see output caching in action, try the sample page named output_cache.aspx that we provide in the Chapter04 subdirectory of the samples for this book. It creates a simple page containing a <form> section with the method set to GET, so that the values are submitted to the server in the query string:

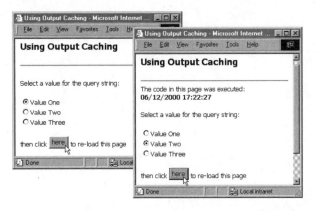

When you click the button to submit the page, it is reloaded showing the time that the page was executed by ASP+. Now select a different value for the radio buttons and submit the page again. The time is updated to the present time. However, if you now select the first option and reload the page, you should see that the original execution time is still shown – the page was delivered from the output cache rather than being re-executed by ASP+.

Experiment with the various options, watching the time each time you submit the page. You should see that the output page for each option is cached for 15 seconds. Requests for that page after 15 seconds result in it being re-executed and the new time displayed.

How Does it Work?

All this happens because we've added an `OutputCache` directive to the page that receives the query string:

```
<%@OutputCache Duration="15"%>
```

This tells ASP+ to cache the dynamic output for 15 seconds, and reuse the cached copy for requests that have the same query string values as the cached copy. This is the main body of the page – you can see that the method of the `<form>` is set to `"get"` because we need the values to be submitted in the query string for output caching to work in current versions of ASP+:

```
<!-- div to display the contents of the cache -->
<div id="divExecutedTime" runat="server" />

<form method="get" runat="server">
  Select a value for the query string:<p />
  <input type="radio" value="1" name="queryvalue"
         id="chkValue1" runat="server" />Value One<br />
  <input type="radio" value="2" name="queryvalue"
         id="chkValue2" runat="server" />Value Two<br />
  <input type="radio" value="3" name="queryvalue"
         id="chkValue3" runat="server" />Value Three<br />
  <p />then click
  <input type="submit" id="cmdExec" value="here" runat="server"
         onserverclick="cmdExec_Click" /> to re-load this page
</form>
```

Displaying the Code Execution Time

When the 'submit' button is clicked, the form values are added to the URL as a query string and sent to the server with the request for the same page. Also in this page is the following `<script>` section:

```
<script language="VB" runat="server">

Sub Page_Load(objSender As Object, objArgs As EventArgs)
  If Not IsPostback Then chkValue1.Checked = True
End Sub

Sub cmdExec_Click(objSender As Object, objArgs As EventArgs)
  strMessage = "The code in this page was executed:" _
             & "<br /><b>" & CStr(Now) & "</b><p />"
  divExecutedTime.innerHTML = strMessage
End Sub

</script>
```

The `Page_Load` event handler is there just so that the first of the three option buttons is selected when the page is first loaded – i.e. when there are no values being sent from the `<form>`. The `cmdExec_Click` event handler runs when the 'submit' button is clicked, and just updates the `<div>` element on the page with the current time – i.e. the time that the page was last executed.

To disable output caching for a page, we can use:

```
<%@OutputCache Duration="0"%>
```

This is the default if we don't provide a different value, or when we omit the directive altogether.

The ASP+ Cache

The ASP+ cache can be used to store our own objects and values that we reuse in our pages, allowing performance improvements. And, because the cache is global to the ASP+ application, it also provides a neat way to pass values between pages within the same application. The cache access methods are thread-safe; they implement automatic locking and so it is safe for them to be accessed concurrently from more than one page. Just remember that another page may change the values that you place in the cache – it isn't 'per user' like the `Session` object.

Adding, Updating, Extracting, and Removing Cached Items

Using the cache is just like using the ASP `Application` or `Session` objects. We add or update values in the cache by specifying the **key** or name of the item:

```
'add a value to the ASP+ cache
Cache("MyKey") = "MyValue"
```

To extract the value of an item with a specified key, we use this syntax:

```
'extract a value from the ASP+ cache
strValue = Cache("MyKey")
```

And to remove items from the cache, we execute the `Remove` method, specifying the key of the item to remove:

```
'remove a value from the ASP+ cache
Cache.Remove("MyKey")
```

There is an alternative syntax for inserting items into the cache, using the `Insert` method:

```
Cache.Insert("MyKey", "MyValue")
```

There are many ways that you can use caching in your applications, and the interface that is available provides far more control than we've had scope to discuss here. For example you can create dependencies between objects that are cached, or dependencies on disk files, so that when one item is invalidated and flushed from the cache (or when the disk file changes), the dependent items are also removed.

There are also optional parameters for the `Insert` method that allow you to specify expiration of cached items, their 'decay' priority, and even an event handler that will be called when this item is removed from the cache. And, to see what's in the cache at any time, there are methods to enumerate the contents.

An ASP+ Cache Example

For a simple demonstration of the ASP+ cache in action, try the sample page named `aspplus_cache.aspx`. This contains a `<form>` with two text boxes and a 'submit' button that posts the values to the same page again:

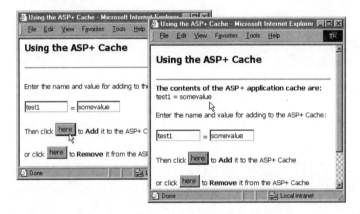

When the page reloads, as shown in the screenshot, the values stored in the ASP+ cache are displayed – you can see the value we entered there. The code for the page includes a `<div>` element where the contents of the cache are displayed, and a `<form>` that contains the two text boxes and the 'submit' button:

```
<!-- div to display the contents of the cache -->
<div id="divCacheContents" runat="server" />

<form runat="server">
  Enter the name and value for adding to the ASP+ Cache:
  <p />
  <input type="text" id="txtName" size="10" runat="server" />
  =
  <input type="text" id="txtValue" size="10" runat="server" />
  <p />
  Then click
  <input type="submit" id="cmdAdd" value="here" runat="server"
         onserverclick="cmdAdd_Click" />
  to <b>Add</b> it to the ASP+ Cache<p /> or click
  <input type="submit" id="cmdRemove" value="here" runat="server"
         onserverclick="cmdRemove_Click" />
  to <b>Remove</b> it from the ASP+ Cache<p />
</form>
```

Displaying the Cache Contents

The remainder of the page is a `<script>` section that performs the caching and displays the cached contents. To display the contents of the ASP+ cache, we can simply iterate through the `Cache` object's collection of cached items using a `For Each...Next` loop:

```
...
Sub ShowCacheContents()
  'display all the items in the ASP+ cache
  strContents = "<b>The contents of the ASP+ application " _
             & "cache are:</b><br />"
  For Each objItem In Cache
    strName = objItem.Key
    If Left(strName, 7) <> "System." Then
      strContents = strContents & strName & " = " & Cache(strName) & "<br />"
    End If
  Next
  'display the contents in the <div> element
  divCacheContents.InnerHTML = strContents
End Sub
...
```

Notice that we specifically exclude any items that have a name starting with "System". The ASP+ cache is also used by the runtime to cache intrinsic objects that are created as the page executes, and these all belong to the System namespace. We don't want to include these in our page (though you can comment out the If and End If statements if you want to see them).

Adding an Item to the ASP+ Cache

To add the values from the form controls to the cache, we simply include an event handler in the page that is called when the 'Add' button is clicked:

```
...
Sub cmdAdd_Click(objSender As Object, objArgs As EventArgs)
  If txtName.Value <> "" Then
    'add this item to the cache
    Cache(txtName.Value) = txtValue.Value
  End If
  ShowCacheContents
End Sub
...
```

Removing an Item from the ASP+ Cache

And to remove an item from the cache, we use an event handler that is called when the 'Remove' button is clicked:

```
...
Sub cmdRemove_Click(objSender As Object, objArgs As EventArgs)
  If txtName.Value <> "" Then
    'remove this item from the cache
    Cache.Remove(txtName.Value)
  End If
  ShowCacheContents
End Sub
...
```

Here's the result of removing a value that we previously added with the key "test2":

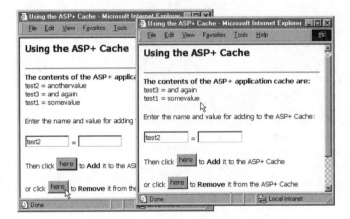

Error Handling, Tracing, and Debugging

New techniques have been added to ASP+ for managing errors, seeing what's happening in an ASP+ page, and for helping to find runtime errors that cause incorrect results. We don't have room in this book to devote lengthy discussion to these topics, and, moreover, they are still evolving in the preview release of ASP+. However, the following section will give you some ideas on how you might use these new techniques.

Custom Error Pages

As it says in some of the Microsoft documentation – "*Errors happen. Deal with it*". In previous versions of ASP, the concept of custom error pages was introduced. By changing the setting in the Internet Service Manager utility, you can specify the page that is sent to the client in response to specific errors detected in any folder of your Web site. ASP+ now makes this even easier to achieve, and provides more flexibility.

Specifying a Custom Error Page

First you must specify a default error page for your ASP+ application or Web site by editing the config.web file in the application root or WWWRoot directory:

```
<configuration>
  ...
  <customerrors defaultredirect="http://hostname/errorpage.aspx" mode="on" />
  ...
</configuration>
```

The mode attribute specifies when the custom error page should be displayed. The value "on" means that is will always be displayed when an error occurs. The value "off" (the default) means that it will never be displayed, and the value "remoteonly" means that local users (http://localhost/ or http://127.0.0.1/) will still see the default ASP error page while all other users will see the custom error page. This last setting is useful, as the very detailed default ASP error page provides helpful debugging information for the developer or administrator.

You can also specify different pages for each error, which can be ASP+ pages or just plain HTML pages:

```
<configuration>
  ...
  <customerrors   defaultredirect="http://hostname/errorpage.aspx"
                  mode="remoteonly">
    <error statuscode="500" redirect="/errorpages/callsupport.html" />
    <error statuscode="404" redirect="/errorpages/adminmessage.html" />
    <error statuscode="403" redirect="/errorpages/noaccess.html" />
  </customerrors>
  ...
</configuration>
```

For more details about using the `config.web` *file, see the discussion of the ASP+ Application Framework in Chapter 6.*

Now the `defaultredirect` error page (or one of the other specified error pages) will handle errors that occur in this ASP+ application. This error page is loaded when a 'Not Found' or 'Access Forbidden' response is generated, or an 'Internal Server Error' (caused by an ASP code or object error) occurs while loading, parsing, compiling or processing the page.

Once you have enabled default error pages, you can optionally over-ride the values in the `config.web` file for specific pages by adding the `ErrorPage` attribute to the `Page` directive in that page:

```
<%@Page ErrorPage="my_custom_error_page.aspx"%>
```

We've provided a simple example page named `error_handling.aspx` that demonstrates the use of custom error pages. It's in the `Chapter04` subdirectory of the samples that are available for this book from our Web site at http://www.wrox.com/. You'll need to copy the `config.web` file into your `WWWRoot` directory first, then edit the value for `defaultredirect` depending on the location of the custom error page on your server.

Using the Error Information in ASP+

Using an ASP+ custom error page means that you can access information about the error. This information is available in the error page from the `Form` collection:

```
...
<%
'collect the error information
Dim strErrCode As String     'it will be of the form "ASPxxxx"
Dim strErrTitle As String    'the error message text
Dim strErrSource As String   'the page where the error occurred

strErrCode = Request.Form.Item("ErrorCode")
strErrTitle = Request.Form.Item("ErrorTitle")
strErrSource = Request.Form.Item("ErrorPage")
%>

<b>There was an error in the page <% = strErrorSource %></b><p />
ASP+ reports the error code: <b><% = strErrorCode %></b><br />
<% = strErrorTitle %>
...
```

If there is an error while executing your custom error page, ASP+ will just display a blank page instead.

Of course, if you prefer, you can still use the `Server.GetLastError` method and the `ASPError` object to retrieve the ASP error object and display its properties. This was introduced in ASP 3.0. However, it is not available in the preview version of ASP+, though it will be implemented in later beta releases and the final version of ASP+.

Page-level Tracing

A useful way of finding out what's going on in your code is to enable **tracing**. If you discount the use of the odd `Response.Write` statement that you inject into your code to track variable values, this feature hasn't been available in ASP before. ASP+ now provides a proper trace facility, which is enabled by adding the `Trace` attribute to the `Page` directive:

```
<%@Page Language="language" Trace="True" %>
```

Now, when the page is executed, a table containing information about the processing is added to the foot of the page. You can see this in the `show_trace.aspx` page that we provide with the rest of the samples for this book:

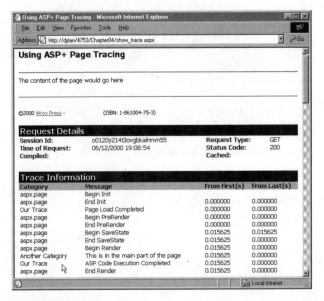

Writing to the Trace Object

You'll see in the previous screenshot that the trace information contains two entries in the category 'Our Trace' and one in the category 'Another Category'. The trace object is exposed to your code, and you can write to it in any page to track the processing, check the intermediate values, or discover any bottlenecks in your code. To add the first of the entries that appear in the screenshot above, we used this code in the `Page_Load` event handler of the `show_trace.aspx` page:

```
...
'in the Page_Load event handler:
Trace.Write("Our Trace", "Page Load Completed")
...
```

Elsewhere in the main body of the page, we included this code:

```
<%
Trace.Write("Another Category", "This is in the main part of the page")
%>
```

and to create the third of our custom entries, we added this to the page, after the HTML:

```
'at the end of the page:
Trace.Write("Our Trace", "ASP Code Execution Completed")
```

Displaying the Values of Variables

To output the value of a variable, you simply replace the text string with that variable – making sure that you convert (or cast) it to a `String` type first:

```
'write the value of an Integer variable to the Trace object:
Trace.Write("Value of MyInteger", CStr(MyInteger))
```

You can even get the output displayed in Red in the trace results by using `Trace.Warn` instead.

The great thing with the new tracing feature is that you can add as many of these `Trace.Write` statements as you like. Once you've finished debugging, you just remove the `Trace="True"` attribute from the `Page` directive, and the statements are ignored. This contrasts with the technique of using `Response.Write` statements, which not only scatter the output all over the final page, but also have to be removed once you've finished debugging.

What Does the Trace Output Contain?

In the previous example, you can see how the `Trace` object automatically inserts useful information into a series of tables at the end of the page. The screenshot above shows the session ID and the time that the request was processed. It also contains the times taken for each part of the processing of the page to occur. This is really useful if you are looking for a section of inefficient code that might be slowing your page down, or if you are wondering which part of the process is taking up all the processing time.

However there is much more useful information in the `Trace` output than that. By scrolling down through the sample page, you'll see that there are sections for:

❑ The **Control Tree**, which displays a list of all of the controls that have been instantiated in your page, showing the size of each one and the ways that they are nested:

Control Id	Type	Render Size (including children)	Viewstate Size (excluding children)
Page	ASP3.show_trace_aspx	1913	0
ctrl0	ASP0.Heading_aspc	456	0
ctrl0:lblTitle	System.Web.UI.HtmlControls.HtmlGenericControl	58	36
ctrl0:ctrl2	System.Web.UI.LiteralControl	23	0
ctrl0:ctrl0	System.Web.UI.LiteralControl	337	0
ctrl0:lblHeading	System.Web.UI.HtmlControls.HtmlGenericControl	54	36
ctrl0:ctrl3	System.Web.UI.LiteralControl	23	0
ctrl0:ctrl1	System.Web.UI.LiteralControl	7	0
ctrl1	ASP1.Footing_aspc	422	0

❑ The contents of all the members of the **Cookies collection**:

Cookies Collection		
Name	**Value**	**Size**
AspSessionId	h3xsdbeshkflzzqucwer4045	---

❑ A summary of all the **HTTP Headers** sent from the client with the request:

Headers Collection	
Name	**Value**
Connection	Keep-Alive
Accept	application/msword, application/vnd.ms-excel, application/vnd.ms-powerpoint, image/gif, image/x-xbitmap, image/jpeg, image/pjpeg, application/x-comet, */*
Accept-Encoding	gzip, deflate
Accept-Language	en-gb
Host	dylan
Referer	http://dylan/4753/Chapter04/
User-Agent	Mozilla/4.0 (compatible; MSIE 5.01; Windows 98)

❑ The contents of all the members of the **ServerVariables collection** (only a few are displayed here):

Server Variables	
Name	**Value**
ALL_HTTP	HTTP_CONNECTION: Keep-Alive HTTP_ACCEPT: application/msword, application/vnd.ms-excel, application/vnd.ms-powerpoint, image/gif, image/x-xbitmap, image/jpeg, image/pjpeg, application/x-comet, */* HTTP_ACCEPT_ENCODING: gzip, deflate HTTP_ACCEPT_LANGUAGE: en-gb HTTP_HOST: dylan HTTP_REFERER: http://dylan/4753/Chapter04/ HTTP_USER_AGENT: Mozilla/4.0 (compatible; MSIE 5.01; Windows 98)
ALL_RAW	Connection: Keep-Alive Accept: application/msword, application/vnd.ms-excel, application/vnd.ms-powerpoint, image/gif, image/x-xbitmap, image/jpeg, image/pjpeg, application/x-comet, */* Accept-Encoding: gzip, deflate Accept-Language: en-gb Host: dylan Referer: http://dylan/4753/Chapter04/ User-Agent: Mozilla/4.0 (compatible; MSIE 5.01; Windows 98)
APPL_MD_PATH	/LM/W3SVC/1/ROOT
APPL_PHYSICAL_PATH	e:\inetpub\wwwroot\
AUTH_TYPE	
AUTH_USER	
AUTH_PASSWORD	
LOGON_USER	
REMOTE_USER	
CERT_COOKIE	

Application-level Tracing

As well as enabling tracing for specific pages in the `<%@Page...%>` directive, you can also enable it for complete applications by adding a section to the `config.web` file for that particular application. This provides a great way to trace and monitor performance in your ASP+ applications.

All that's required is the `trace` configuration setting in `config.web` for the application or Web site:

```
<configuration>
   ...
   <trace enabled="true" pageoutput="false"
          requestlimit="20" outputmode="time" />
   ...
</configuration>
```

The `pageoutput` attribute specifies whether the table of trace values should be displayed in the page or not. When set to `false` (the default if omitted), the trace information is still logged but not displayed in the pages. However, the trace log can be examined afterwards by using a special utility (see below). The `requestlimit` attribute specifies how many trace requests should be stored on the server. The default if omitted is 15.

The trace.axd Utility

The `trace.axd` utility is accessed through a special **HttpHandler** named `trace.axd`. You simply add the instruction to the `config.web` file:

```
<configuration>
  ...
  <httphandlers>
    <add verb="*" path="trace.axd"
         type="System.Web.InternalSamples.TraceHandler" />
  <httphandlers>
  ...
</configuration>
```

This defines the HTTP handler that will be used instead of the default ASP+ Page handler when requests for the resource `trace.axd` are received. This HTTP handler is responsible for reading the trace log information and displaying it.

For more details about using the `config.web` file, see the discussion of the ASP+ Application Framework in Chapter 6.

To view the trace log, simply reference the path to your application with the resource name 'trace.axd' appended to it, for example: http://localhost/myapplication/trace.axd.

We added the application-level trace instruction to the `config.web` file in our server's WWWRoot directory to collect trace information for all ASP+ pages that we execute within that directory and all its subdirectories. This is the result after a few pages have been loaded:

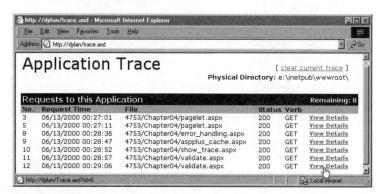

Each entry in the trace log provides a hyperlink where we can view more information about that page's execution. What we get from these links is the same information that we saw when we looked at the trace output in the earlier example – the only real difference is that here we can compare the results for several pages, or for the same page over different executions.

Tracing works for all requested files within our application domain, including Web services. However, note that you will get some performance degradation when tracing is turned on. You should not really be using tracing on a live site, only on your test platforms.

The ASP+ Debugger

ASP+ is supplied with a full-featured debugging tool, optimized for use with ASP+, and providing support for local and remote machine debugging – including the setting of breakpoints and the ability to single-step through code.

Enabling Debugging

To use the ASP+ debugger, you have to enable debugging for the ASP+ application by adding a specific entry to the config.web file:

```
<configuration>
   ...
   <compilation debugmode="true"/>
   ...
</configuration>
```

For more information about debugging, check out the dedicated Web site for this book at http://www.wrox.com/beta.

Summary

In this chapter, we've covered several unrelated topics that are not discussed in the previous chapters. In particular, the new **validation controls** that are included with ASP+ will make your life much easier when building forms that collect information from users. As well as seeing them in use in 'uplevel' clients like Internet Explorer 4 and above, we also saw how they work great in all other browsers as well.

We also examined some techniques for separating code from content when building more complex ASP+ pages. You can use the '**code behind**' techniques to separate the code easily and quickly from the presentation information and content. Alternatively, you can use ASP+ '**pagelets**' to build reusable controls that encapsulate both code and presentation information – or just code functions that are called from the main page.

We also considered how the ASP+ dynamic output cache can improve scalability and efficiency, and at the same time reduce the overhead on your server. It can also be used to store your own values or objects in applications and while processing pages.

Finally, we looked very briefly at the new error handling, tracing and debugging features of ASP+. These include the ability to specify individual custom error pages to handle errors in any ASP+ page, and to create trace information automatically – even writing your own values to the trace object. There is also an updated debugger provided with ASP+ for use with your pages and applications.

Overall, the topics we covered were:

- ❑ Input validation with the new ASP+ controls
- ❑ Creating separate code sections with 'Code Behind'
- ❑ Creating reusable sections of code with 'Pagelets'
- ❑ Managing caching of the page output
- ❑ Error handling, tracing and debugging techniques

In the next chapter, you'll see another technique that separates code from presentation information, but this time using a new feature of the runtime framework called **Web Services**. As you'll see, however, Web Services are more than just that – they can be used to build all kinds of new features into your applications.

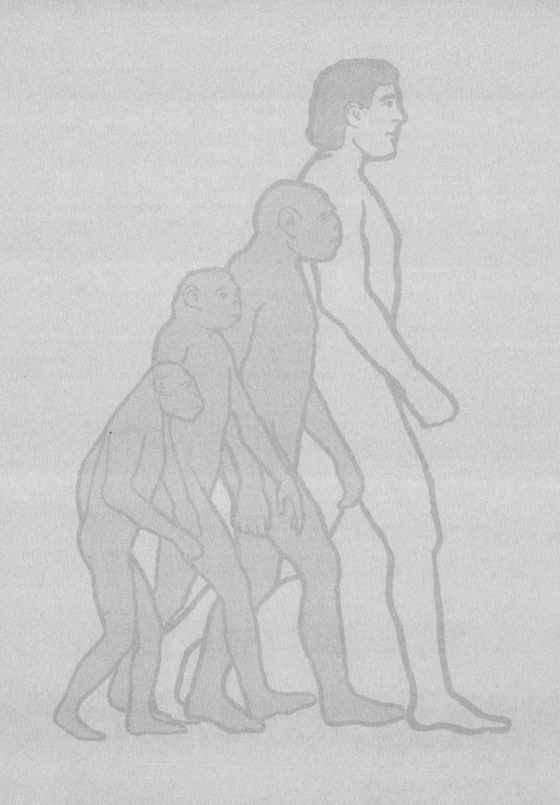

5

Web Services

Historically, most application development work has been targeted towards building rich local application services. Examples of this include: products such as Microsoft Office, Intuit Quicken, or the plethora of third party applications, components, and tools you can purchase for your PC or workstation.

With the advent of the Internet and HTTP/HTML we have seen a migration of such applications to the Web. These applications have been made globally available through a Web server, and defined their UI with HTML. For example, we have sites such as Quicken.com and Investor.com to replace our traditional desktop financial applications.

However, Web applications have done a poor job of taking advantage of the Internet to make this application logic available to a variety of clients. A good example of this is reusing services traditionally provided by institutions such as Fidelity or Merrill Lynch, and making this data consumable by your financial Web site. Each site is its own island of information, and end-users must learn a plethora of user IDs and UI to navigate through the massive amount of information.

The future will be the ability for both rich local applications and Web applications to take advantage of the Internet to offer a common set of services to a variety of clients. Microsoft Web services will enable this.

In this chapter, we will cover:

- ❑ What is a Web service?
- ❑ Creating an ASP+ Web Service
- ❑ Web service protocols and data types
- ❑ Describing Web services
- ❑ Programmatically accessing our service

What is a Web Service?

A Web service is application logic that is programmatically available, and can be exposed using the Internet. Just as applications have targeted the rich services of the platform in the past, Web applications of the future will take advantage of Web services for programmability and feature enhancement.

For example, we use application logic on the Internet on a daily basis. We interact with services through a browser for requests such as stock quote data:

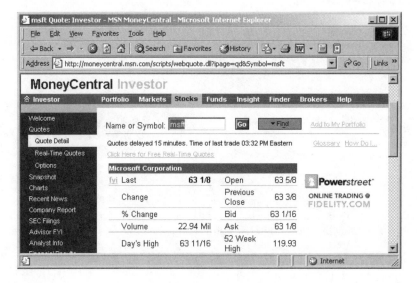

In the above screen shot from Microsoft's moneycentral.com Web site, application logic is used to perform a look-up for a stock symbol (MSFT) and return the related information formatted in HTML to the browser. The application logic is tied to the browser's UI and the end user is limited to the usage of this information in the context in which it is presented. Technologies such as personalization and membership have been made available on some sites, but at most this is simply a filter to determine what data the server believes is relevant for consumption by the end user.

We can, of course, obtain this data from MoneyCentral.com and use it for our own application:

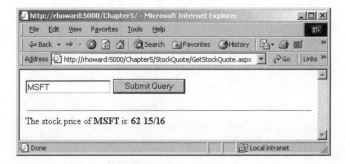

As seen in the above screenshot, I've written code to screen-scrape MoneyCentral.com. In some ways, this allows us to use the business logic that MoneyCentral.com provides, but it's somewhat of a hack since we're parsing the entire HTML document to simply find the price of our quote.

One of the driving forces behind Microsoft's Web Services efforts is further separation of application logic from presentation, to enable the Web such that developers can build new and interesting solutions without being tied strictly to the browser.

For example, rather than screen-scraping, we would much rather have MoneyCentral's application logic programmatically available. What we really want is a `StockQuote` component with a `string GetQuote(string strSymbol)` method. Rather than parsing an HTML document for one piece of data, we simply use moneycentral.com's `GetQuote()` method remotely. This is what Web services enables.

Now that we have an idea of what a Web service is, let's look at how a Web service is built.

Architecture

When we think of the architecture of Web services, there are several considerations we must make as it relates to both design and coding of our system. In the introduction to this chapter, we briefly mentioned that building Web services today requires the developer to write the plumbing code to enable Web services.

Writing Plumbing Code

Plumbing code includes the facilities to discover, describe, access, and interpret services. The diagram below illustrates the use of Web services between a consumer of a service and the provider of a service:

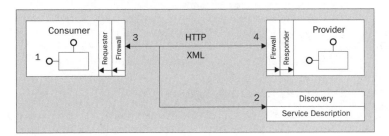

Here's what's happening in our diagram (which we'll revisit throughout the chapter):

Discovery and Description of the Service

A consumer that wishes to use a Web service writes code (1) that makes use of a provider's Web service. The provider's service, however, must first be discoverable, or known (2), and a contract (service description) must exist between the consumer and provider.

This contract outlines what services the provider exposes, and the semantics used by the calling consumer. For example, in this chapter we'll look at a Math class that exposes an `Add()` routine to consumers.

Requesting the Service

After the client has both the contract and location of the provider of the service, it may make a request (3). The contract is necessary so that the client knows how to use the service. The location of the service is relative since the service and contract can exist together or separately.

The client needs some rules to properly encode (XML) and transmit (HTTP) the request to the provider. Once the provider receives the request (4) it must decode the XML and assemble the transport (HTTP) packets in the correct order, and do any other necessary work to remotely invoke the logic that makes up the service.

Responding to the Request

This process is then reversed, as the provider encodes and transports the response back the consumer, where the consumer must then decode and assemble the message.

Let's explain some of these aspects in more detail.

Message Based

Web services are based on Internet protocols for a reason. Internet protocols are extremely efficient for handling large volumes of user requests without getting overloaded. We also already know that the message-based model of request/response semantics used by browsers to servers can scale very well. Web services will scale just as well as dynamic Web applications, because services are based on the same request/response paradigm Web applications along with the same protocols.

Synchronous and Asynchronous Messages

Although the request/response model of browser-to-server is synchronous, message based systems inherently support an asynchronous model as well (though this is not always implemented). In a synchronous design, we would make a request for a Web service from our application and wait (blocking other resources) until we received a response.

This is similar in fashion to how a browser works in that we make a request and wait for the response. However, Web services support the asynchronous model of requesting (sending) the resource and later checking back to see if our results are available, in the mean time continuing about our other work.

XML as the Data Description Language

Web services send data back and forth in XML. And, although XML is not always the best solution for the data exchange problem (as it is quite verbose) it does solve the problem of system interoperability.

Approachable

XML is very approachable from a user or developer point of view. Not only does XML make our system human readable and human writeable, but it makes debugging much easier as we can see what is being sent back and forth – (have you ever opened up a RMI or DCOM packet to see what was being sent? – good luck).

Standards Based Data Exchange Format

XML is platform independent. This is a huge step in the right direction to ensure that systems can interoperate, as we no longer need to concern ourselves with system-to-system integration but with protocol standards.

However, there has to be a common language of XML used to exchange information. Already there are several different implementations of XML encoding to solve Web services problems provided by a variety of vendors. The key to Microsoft's Web services strategy is not that it is XML and HTTP based (that's easy), but that Microsoft, along with IBM, is supporting the W3C submitted proposal for Simple Object Access Protocol (SOAP). We'll discuss SOAP later in the chapter.

The bottom line for solving the cross platform issue is: as long as both systems can understand the XML grammar used and can agree upon serialization order of data (protocol), they can interoperate through Web services via XML data exchanges.

Now that you've got an idea of what is involved with creating Web services, let's begin our discussion of the Web services features in ASP+.

Creating an ASP+ Web Service

The goal for Web Services in ASP+ is to provide a programming abstraction that allows developers to easily expose programmatic functionality to the Web, without the developers requiring knowledge of HTTP, COM, or data marshaling. Rather, developers author Web services by simply creating classes and exposing methods and properties as Web-callable (in the sense of making the application logic available as a Web service). We'll come back to the programmatic definition of Web-callable a little later.

Business Logic

Reviewing our Web services consumer/provider diagram, the Web services provider exposes Web callable business logic:

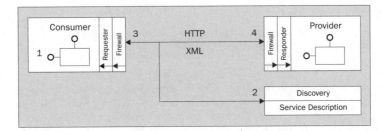

We say business logic since the service can be written in any tool (ASP, ASP+, ISAPI, PERL, Java, etc.) that allows us to access the request/response features of a Web server. ASP+, of course, supports a programming abstraction to make this very easy.

The programming abstraction that ASP+ Web Services builds upon is that of component-based development. Therefore, our ASP+ Web service is an NGWS Runtime object.

Simple Class

Let's start our discussion of ASP+ Web services by looking at a simple business logic class we wish to expose as a service: a Math class with an Add() routine.

The Math class allows us to focus on the ASP+ technology that drives services rather than the logic of the application and we'll use this simple class throughout this chapter. Here's an example implementation of an Add() method in a Math class provided in both C# and VB7:

C# Math Class

```
class Math {
  public int Add(int a, int b) {
    return a + b;
  }
}
```

Visual Basic 7 Math Class

```
Class Math
  public Function Add(a As Integer, b As Integer) As Integer
    Add = a + b
  End Function
End Class
```

Both examples accept two `ints` (a and b) and return the sum of these two values.

So, given an existing class with existing methods, what do we need to do to expose it as a Web service? In ASP+ we create an `.asmx` file.

Authoring an .asmx file

Defined, an `.asmx` file is simply a declarative text file that contains:

❑ **Processing Directives** – Processing directives instruct the complier how the compile the given resource.

❑ **Class Attributes** – Used to 'decorate' classes and specify additional behaviors. These behaviors are applied or ignored based on the processing directives used.

❑ **NGWS Runtime Objects and Application Code** – Defined either declaratively in the `.asmx` file, or in pre-complied class.

> As we'll learn in the next chapter, files with the extension: `.asmx` are mapped to a NGWS object in the ASP+ application configuration file (config.web). This class is known as an `HttpHandler` and it is responsible for handling ASP+ Web Service requests.

Similar to ASP+ pages, ASP+ Web service files are also complied upon the first request, and cached across subsequent requests.

Math Class

Given our Math class with its `Add()` method from above, here's one way these classes could appear as ASP+ Web Service files:

C# Class as an .asmx File

```
<%@ WebServices Language="C#" %>

using System.Web.Services;

class Math {
  [WebMethod]
  public int Add(int a, int b) {
    return a + b;
  }
}
```

Visual Basic 7 Class as an .asmx File

```
<%@ WebService Language="VB" Class="Math" %>

Imports System.Web.Services

Class Math
    public Function <WebMethod()>Add(a As Integer, b As Integer) As Integer
        Add = a + b
    End Function
End Class
```

The above code sample looks like a mix of an NGWS Runtime class and an ASP+ page. We see similar concepts to pages through the use of directives `<%@ Directive Name="Value"%>`, and the fact that the file is declarative and not compiled. However, code is not declared in `<script runat=server> </script>` blocks, which is definitely something we would expect to find in an ASP+ page.

Now that we've created an `.asmx` file, how do we test it? Lucky for us, we don't need to build any special utilities or tools to test out our service, as ASP+ allows us to use a Web browser. ASP+ also provides us with the necessary tools to allow clients to easily access our service programmatically (which we'll look at later).

Testing Through a Web Browser

When we access a Web service file on our Web server through a browser it introspects (the programmatic term is reflection) on the compiled class, and returns an HTML view of the Web service:

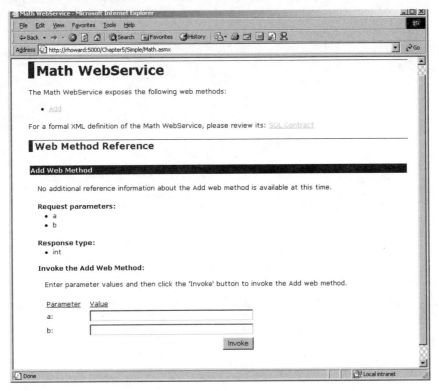

The file used to display this HTML view is in fact an ASP+ page (used as a template for the Web service) named **DefaultSdlHelpGenerator.aspx,** and can be found in **\winnt\complus\ v2000.14.1809** (number will vary).

We'll learn about a file known as config.web *in the next chapter. This file lets us set application settings for our Web application. In* config.web *we specify the template page for Web services to use.*

Using DefaultSdlHelpGenerator.aspx

Looking through this HTML page we will see several links as well as an HTML form. We can use this HTML form to invoke the service.

> **We'll be coming back to SDL contract link a little later in the chapter.**

Invoking the Web Service

The ASP+ DefaultSdlHelpGenerator.aspx template provides us with HTML forms whose inputs correspond to the parameters of our Add() method in our Math.asmx file:

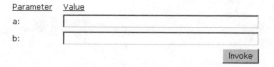

This form allows us to invoke the Add() method of our Math class through the browser for testing purposes. The a and b parameters list, with their associated text boxes, map to the Add() method's int a and int b in parameters:

```
public int Add(int a, int b) { ... }
```

Typing in values such as 3 and 4 and pressing the Invoke button submits the form via HTTP Get and opens a new HTML browser with a URL of: .../Math.asmx/Add?a=3&b=4 and a display of:

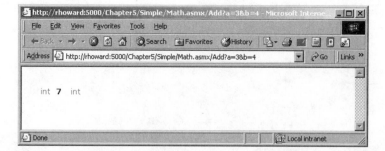

Now that we've built a Web service, let's discuss the .asmx file syntax in more detail, and learn what we need to do to use this service programmatically.

.asmx File Syntax

Both of these Web services discussed above contain processing directives: `<%@ WebSevices Language="C#"%>`, the `[WebMethod]` attribute, and the `Math` class with application code. Similar to ASP+ pages, Web services have both directives and attributes have various settings that we can use.

Processing Directives

The processing directive `<%@ directive {attribute="value"}%>` allows us to specify behaviors that the compiled ASP+ Web service should adhere to. These include setting parameters such as the language, and the NGWS Runtime object containing the application logic.

Language

The `language` attribute, which we've already seen `<%@ WebSevices Language="C#"%>` allows us to specify the language in which the `.asmx` file is written in. Any ASP+ supported language is available for use, such as: C#, VB7, and JavaScript.

Class

The `class` attribute, which we'll look at later in the chapter, allows us to name a NGWS Runtime object rather than declaring our Web Service code in an `.asmx` file. This declared class must then contain methods or properties that have the `WebMethod` attribute.

WebMethod Attribute

The `[WebMethod]` in C# or `<WebMethod()>` in VB7 is known as a programming attribute. When Web service files are compiled (either on the first request, or with a command line utility available post beta 1) and `WebMethod` attributes on methods or properties are encountered, Web Services are enabled only for those methods and properties. Those methods and properties without the `WebMethod` attribute are not enabled for Web services. We can think of `WebMethod` as being a class accessor that marks the method or property as 'Web-callable'.

Not Everything is Public

The purpose of defining methods as Web-callable, rather than simply allowing any public method to be accessible, is to prevent over exposure. For example, every NGWS Runtime object derives from `Object`. Thus, every class supports a base set of public methods (such as `ToString()`), however these methods don't need to be made available as Web-callable.

In addition to marking a method as Web-callable, the `WebMethod` compiler directive has properties that we can define.

Description

The `description` property `description="[string]"` allows us to add a brief description or comment when we declare the `WebMethod` compiler directive:

```
[WebMethod(description="Expose Add method as web callable")]
```

At compile time the description property is ignored.

Transaction

Similar to ASP+ pages, ASP+ Web Services supports code execution within the context of a Microsoft Transaction Server (MTS) transaction. This ensures that all interactions with MTS aware resources – SQL Servers, MSMQ Servers, Oracle Servers, SNA Servers, etc. – maintain the ACID (Atomic, Consistent, Isolated, Durable) properties required to run robust distributed applications.

To enable support for transactions we must specify this property on `WebMethod`:

```
[WebMethod(Transaction=Transaction.Required)]
```

It is important to note that a transaction will only be created if the first `WebMethod` called is marked with the `Transaction` attribute. A `WebMethod` not marked with the `Transaction` attribute that calls a `WebMethod` with the `Transaction` attribute will not execute within the context of an MTS transaction.

EnableSessionState

Session state is available by default to all Web service classes. Web service developers may optionally disable session state on individual `WebMethods` if they know that session state will not be accessed during that request, and they do not wish to pay the performance penalty required to fetch and load it. Developers disable session state for a `WebMethod` using a `Boolean` property: `EnableSessionState`; on the `WebMethod` attribute:

```
[WebMethod(EnableSessionState=False)]
```

In addition to supporting sessions and transactions, ASP+ Web services supports all of the application services we would expect to find in an ASP+ page, such as application state.

Application Services

Just as we can use session state in our ASP+ Web service, we also can use all of the application services found in ASP+ pages: security, application state, caching, etc. Although security and caching in Web services are not implemented fully in beta 1, support for application state is.

ASP+ Application State

Similar to ASP 3.0, ASP+ Application State provides a dictionary-like API that enables Web developers to store and share values across an entire Web application. ASP+ developers can utilize application state within ASP+ pages, application files (`global.asax`), and Web services.

For example, here's how we could implement a simple `HitCounter` using application state in our Math class:

```
<%@ WebServices Language="C#" %>

using System.Web.Services;

class Math {
  [WebMethod]
    public int Add(int a, int b) {
```

```
    if (Application["HitCounter"] == null) {
      Application["HitCounter"] = 0;
    }
    else {
      Application["HitCounter"] = ((int) Application["HitCounter"]) + 1;
    }

    return a + b;
  }

[WebMethod]
public int HitCounter() {
  get{
    return (int) Application["HitCouter"]
  }
}

}
```

Now that we've looked at how to author an ASP+ Web service using .asmx files, along with the file syntax, let's look at the protocols we use to enable access to the Web service.

Web Service Protocols

Protocols define rules that specify the format and transmission of data. We use different classes of protocols when using the Internet: TCP/IP, HTTP, SMTP, etc. Some protocols such as TCP/IP provide rules for transporting other protocols such as HTTP and SMTP. Each protocol has different behaviors and defines different rules, but all carry some type of data.

Web services also need protocols to format and transmit data between endpoints. In our Web Services diagram, the protocol is what is used to enable the consumer and provider to communicate in a known format:

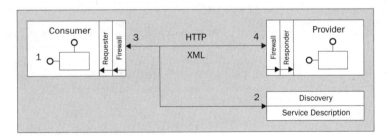

ASP+ Supported Protocols

ASP+ supports three types of protocols we can use for Web Services, all of which return XML in the body of an HTTP message:

❑   **HTTP-GET** – Support for the HTTP Get verb for encoding and passing of parameters, along with request semantics.

❑   **HTTP-POST** – Support for the HTTP Post verb for encoding and passing of parameters, along with request semantics.

❑   **SOAP** – Simple Object Access Protocol (SOAP) W3C submitted document that describes a platform neutral contract for serialization and transport of data using XML and HTTP.

Let's start by looking at HTTP-Get.

HTTP-Get

The HTTP-Get Web service protocol uses the HTTP Get verb to send data to the server: http://rhoward:5000/Chapter5/Simple/Math.asmx/Add?a=12&b=12. Name value pairs are UUencoded (a process of encoding data in a format suitable for transmission) and sent as an extension to the requested URL as ?[name=value]&[name=value]. These querystring values are not matched to methods parameters in ordinal position, but by matching the name value to the method's parameter name, e.g. a = a.

Data is returned as an XML document in the form:

```
<?XML version="1.0"?>
<[data type]>[value]<[data type]>
```

If the method being called returns an int, the XML document would be: <int>[value]</int>.

The HTTP-Get protocol allows us to simply call Web services by specifying a URL and setting the values.

HTTP-Post

Unlike HTTP-Get, HTTP-Post sends the data to the server in the body of the message. It too UUencodes its data, and returns its results in an identical format to HTTP-Get:

```
<?XML version="1.0"?>
<[data type]>[value]<[data type]>
```

If the method being called returns an int, the XML document would contain <int>[value]</int>.

Simple Object Access Protocol (SOAP)

SOAP is an open specification (at version 1.1 at time of writing) submitted to W3C, authored by Microsoft, IBM/Lotus, Developmentor, and UserLand (to name a few). The specification defines a contract for request and response semantics that, if both consumer and provider adhere to, allows for a powerful platform-neutral data exchange model. SOAP defines a serialization format for request/response semantics using XML and common transport protocols such as HTTP.

We won't be discussing SOAP in great detail in this book.

SOAP supports passing classes, structs and datasets as parameters to a Web method (as it goes beyond simple support of name/value pairs of Http-Get/Post). However, the data transmitted is substantially larger than that transmitted by HTTP Get/Post, as the full XML grammar is transmitted with each message.

A SOAP message consists of three parts:

❑ **Envelope** – An extensible XML framework that describes the message being sent.

❑ **Encoding Rules** – Specify how the data transmitted is to be serialized.

❑ **Remote Procedure Calls** – Supports the description of RPCs and their responses.

At a technical level SOAP is merely data marshaled into a string as XML and transported in the body of an HTTP message via POST. It is the semantics of the XML string that makes SOAP powerful. Simply agreeing upon the ordering of the data wrapped by XML tags allows consumers to intelligently unwrap a SOAP message and understand its meaning.

Here's what a sample SOAP message might look like for our `Add()` method of our Math class:

```
POST /Chapter5/Simple/Math.asmx HTTP/1.1
Host: rhoward:5000
Content-Type: text/xml; charset="utf-8"
Content-Length: nnnn

<SOAP-ENV:Envelope
   xmlns:SOAP-ENV="http://schemas.xmlsoap.org/soap/envelope/"
   SOAP-ENV:encodingStyle="http://schemas.xmlsoap.org/soap/encoding/">
    <SOAP-ENV:Body>
        <m:Add xmlns:m="Some-URI">
            <a>3</a>
            <b>4</b>
        </m:Add>
    </SOAP-ENV:Body>
</SOAP-ENV:Envelope>
```

In the above SOAP request, we first see the HTTP headers that specify the action (POST) with the location and host. Next, we see the content type that is being sent, `text/xml`, as well as the content length. Following these HTTP headers we encounter the body of our SOAP message sent to the server.

We start with the SOAP `<Envelope>` that wraps the `<Body>` of the message. Inside of the `<Body>` we find the method that is being called (`Add`) along with its parameters and values: `<a>` and `<b>`.

And here is what we would expect the response to look like:

```
HTTP/1.1 200 OK
Content-Type: text/xml; charset="utf-8"
Content-Length: nnnn

<SOAP-ENV:Envelope
   xmlns:SOAP-ENV="http://schemas.xmlsoap.org/soap/envelope/"
   SOAP-ENV:encodingStyle="http://schemas.xmlsoap.org/soap/encoding/"/>
    <SOAP-ENV:Body>
        <m:AddResponse xmlns:m="Some-URI">
            <result>7</result>
        </m:AddResponse>
    </SOAP-ENV:Body>
</SOAP-ENV:Envelope>
```

As you can clearly see, SOAP is quite verbose compared with the same calls with HTTP `Get` or `Post`. The benefit of SOAP becomes clearer as the transmitted data becomes more complex. SOAP is the protocol of choice for ASP+ Web services. Later we'll look at a tool to generate client proxies for Web services, the proxy will use the SOAP protocol to communicate with the service.

Although XML allows us to exchange information, as the developer you still have to write the application logic for the Web service you wish to expose and work within the boundaries of XML serialization mechanisms. That means understanding the data types we can encode in XML and transport, i.e., marshal.

Data Types

ASP+ Web Services supports a fairly complete set of data types that can be encoded as XML and sent between consumers and providers of Web services. However you should still pay close attention to the types that are used in Web-callable methods, as use of unsupported types will result in bugs.

We'll simply list the supported types for the various protocols in this section, and in the Advanced Web Services section at the end of the book we'll cover some examples of the more complex data types.

Types supported for SOAP

SOAP supports a more complete set of data types than does HTTP-Get or HTTP-Post. Using Get or Post only allows us to send and receive name/value pairs of data. Using the rich XML grammar of SOAP we can better serialize more complex structures, such as classes and the new DataSet covered in Chapter 3:

Type	Description
Primitive Types	Standard primitive types. The complete list of supported primitives is String, Int32, Byte, Boolean, Int16, Int64, Single, Double, Decimal, DateTime, and XmlQualifiedName.
Enum Types	Enumeration types, e.g. "public enum color { red=1, blue=2 }".
Arrays of Primitives, Enums	Arrays of the above primitives, such as string[] and int[].
Classes and Structs	Class and struct types with public fields or properties. The public properties and fields are serialized.
Arrays of Classes (Structs)	Arrays of the above.
DataSet	ADO+ DataSet Types. DataSets can also appear as fields in structs or classes.
Arrays of DataSet	Arrays of the above.
XmlNode	XmlNode is an in-memory representation of an XML fragment (like a lightweight XML document object model). For example, "<comment>This ispretty neat</comment>" could be stored in an XmlNode. You can pass XmlNodes as parameters, and they are added to the rest of the XML being passed to the Web Service (the other parameters) in a SOAP-compliant manner. The same is true for return values. This allows you to pass or return XML whose structure changes from call to call, or where you may not know all the types being passed. XmlNode can also appear as fields in structs or classes.
Arrays of XmlNode	Arrays of above.

Types supported for HTTP Get and Post

HTTP `Get` and `Post` support a more limited set of data types, since each respective type must be marshaled into a form of name/value string:

Type	Description
Primitive Types (limited)	Most standard primitive types. The complete list of supported primitives is Int32, String, Int16, Int64, Boolean, Single, Double, Decimal, DateTime, TimeSpan, UInt16, UInt32, UInt64, and Currency. From the client's perspective, all these types turn into string.
Enum Types	Enumeration types, e.g. "public enum color { red=1, blue=2 }". From the client's perspective, enums become classes with a static const string for each value.
Arrays of Primitives, Enums	Arrays of the above primitives, such as string[] and int[].

Now that we understand the various protocols and types that our consumer and provider may use to communicate, we still need a contract for our Web service. A contract describes the method and property prototypes (parameters and return values) that our service supports. We need this data so that our consumer knows how to properly format a request, choose which protocol to invoke the request in, and receive a response.

Describing Web Services

Clients that use services need a contract that defines what the service is providing, so that clients can know the available methods, properties, and prototypes, and call them correctly. A good example here is that just as we needed Interface Definition Language (IDL) to describe the interfaces, methods, and properties in the COM world, we need a similar description language for Web services.

Having a description language also provides us with the other benefits:

- **Early binding** – Early bind to services since we know their data types before we use them.

- **Development Features** – Take advantage of intelli-sense code completion in our Visual Studio development environment.

Service Description Langauge (SDL)

With the public announcement of NGWS, Microsoft has also announced Service Description Language (SDL). SDL is the public "contract" for our Web service; it is an XML document that describes:

- **Service Transports** – The protocols, e.g. HTTP GET, used to access a Web service and their respective end-points, e.g. http://rhoward:5000/Chapter5/Simple/Math.asmx.

- **Invocation Semantics** – Defines how requests are made to the service, e.g. agreed XML serialization format, and how the service responds, e.g. agreed XML serialization format such as SOAP.

- **Call Order** – Defines the semantics of how a client and server communicate for a request.

> These are all wire level details, meaning that the SDL does not care about the implementation details of the service. We could, for example, use SDL to describe the available services generated by a PERL script on Linux.

Below is a snippet of SDL that describes the service transport (`httpget`), and the invocation semantics (nested in `<request>` and `<response>`). This section of our SDL contract is what was used to respond to our browser's HTTP Get request from the HTML form:

```
...
<httpget xmlns="urn:schemas-xmlsoap-org:get-sdl-2000-01-25">
 <service>
  <requestResponse name="Add"
                   href="http://rhoward:5000/Chapter5/Simple/Math.asmx/Add">
   <request>
    <param name="a" />
    <param name="b" />
   </request>
   <response>
    <xmlMime ref="s0:int" />
   </response>
  </requestResponse>
 </service>
</httpget>
...
```

In the above example `<request>` encloses the semantics of the two parameters that are accepted: a and b, and the `<response>` `<xmlMime ref="s0:int"/>` which refers to a schema (s0) that defines an `int`.

Creating an SDL Document

There are several different ways we can code an SDL document.

- ❑ **Create it ourselves** – We can code the SDL document ourselves.

- ❑ **Use a utility** – Use a command line utility named WebServiceUtil.exe (we'll look at this later in the chapter).

- ❑ **Self Generate** – Allow the `.asmx` file to generate it for us.

Creating SDL Ourselves

Writing out the SDL by hand would be an enormously time consuming task; believe me, I've done it! Although the file is XML and is therefore human-readable and human-writeable, XML is also very verbose, and thus we would write a lot of XML to describe a few simple tasks... and that's just for our simple Math class!

Autogenerating SDL

ASP+ Web Services take the mundane SDL creation complexity into account, and provide us with a simple means of accessing the service's SDL.

We can request an ASP+ Web Service's SDL, by performing an HTTP Get request with `?SDL` appended on the end. For example, when we perform this request against our `Math.asmx` file:

```
http://rhoward:5000/Chapter5/Simple/Math.asmx?sdl
```

We get the following:

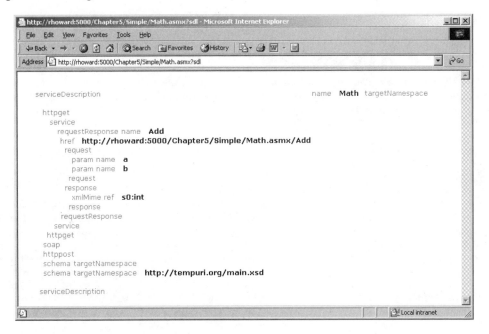

Note: sections of the SDL have been collapsed.

In the above SDL we see the sample code shown earlier, but, rather than us coding this ourselves, ASP+ has generated it for us.

Programmatically Accessing Our Service

So far we've created an ASP+ service and have solved half of the problem with using XML and common Web transports, such as HTTP, for Web services. Revisiting our Web service diagram, this would include creating the Web service provider, (4) exposing the provider via XML and HTTP, and (2) describing the provider's service with SDL:

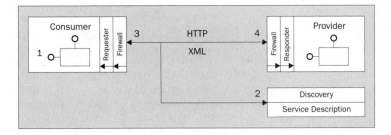

The problem that we haven't solved is how we use a Web service from a consumer. This includes how that consumer makes use of SDL to understand what WebMethods the provider is providing, and how we call them.

What we need is a proxy class or stub that our consumer can use for accessing the service. This proxy class needs to understand the SDL document and use it to give us a simple programming framework for consumer service use.

Again, ASP+ has made this very simple.

Creating a Proxy Class

A proxy class (or stub) is code that looks exactly like the class it is meant to represent, but does not contain any of the application logic. Instead a proxy class contains marshaling (how we order the data into a manner that allows it to be sent) and transport logic. Clients use the proxy, and treat it as if it is the class it is meant to represent.

Let's put this in more concrete terms with our Math class.

Math Proxy Class Example

We have a Math class that is accessible in an ASP+ Web service file. We can access this class using standard Web protocols and XML. We've accessed the class through a browser, and we could access it from applications where we provide the marshaling/serialization and transport logic.

However, writing our own plumbing code is no fun, and all we want is to create an instance of the Math class and use its Add() method.

With a proxy class, we get the client behavior of creating an instance of the Math class and use its Add() method just as we would if the class was local.

Both ASP+ and Visual Studio 7 provide tools for creating proxy classes for Web services. We won't be looking at the Visual Studio 7 tools in this book, but we will look at the ASP+ tool: WebServiceUtil.exe.

WebServiceUtil.exe

WebServiceUtil.exe is a command line utility that creates a stub or proxy class from an SDL document. We can then compile this class and use it to call Web Services without needing to write any network or marshaling code.

> *Although we need this tool for generating the NGWS Runtime proxy class, Visual Studio 7 will eventually do this work for us.*

We have three uses for WebServiceUtil.exe, each supporting additional switches:

❑ WebServiceUtil /c:proxy /pa [/l] [/n] [/o] [[/x] [...]] – The /c:proxy switch is what we will use to create proxy classes for a given SDL document.

❑ WebServiceUtil /c:template /pa [/l] [/n] [/o] [[/x] [...]] – Given an SDL document, WebServiceUtil.exe will output the class that the SDL represents. For example, if we specified /c:template and gave WebServiceUtil.exe the SDL from our Math class, we would get back a method prototype for Add() that we could then define:

```
public abstract int Add(int a, int b);
```

❑ `WebServiceUtil /c:SDL /u /a [/o]` – We use the `/c:SDL` switch to create an SDL file from a given NGWS Runtime component.

Here are the various switches that `WebServiceUtil.exe` supports:

Switch	Description
`/a[ssembly]`	The name of an NGWS Assembly component containing Web services. This switch is applicable to the SDL creation scenario when we want to generate an SDL document without using HTTP Get `[path]?sdl` option.
`/c[ommand]`	The command option allows us to specify the usage scenario we want to use `WebServiceUtil.exe` for: `proxy`, `template`, or `SDL`.
`/l[anguage]`	The language to generate the code in. Choose from C#, VB, and JS. The default language is C#.
`/n[amespace]`	The namespace to generate the code in. The default namespace is the global namespace.
`/o[ut]`	The location to create files. The default output directory is the current directory.
`/pa[th]`	A local path to a service description file, or a URI that the service description file was retrieved from.
`/u[ri]`	The URI of a directory containing Web services.
`/x[sd]`	A local path to an xml schema file (filename must end in `.xsd`).

Using WebServiceUtil.exe

Given that we poses the the URL endpoint for our `Math.asmx` Web Service, we can easily create a proxy class source file using this command line utility:

```
webserviceutil /c:proxy /pa:http://rhoward:5000/Chapter5/Simple/Math.asmx?sdl
               /l:CSharp /n:myMath
```

In the above line we specify that we want to create a client class (`/c:proxy`) for the Web Service existing at `http://rhoward:5000/Chapter5/Simple/Math.asmx?sdl`. Next, we specify the language as CSharp (`/l:CSharp`), and finally the class's namespace: `myMath`.

The resulting source code is output as `Math.cs` (or .vb for VB and .js for JScript):

Let's take a look at the resulting source code for our proxy classes, both in C# and VB:

C# Proxy Class Source Code: Math.cs

```
namespace myMath {
...
   public class Math : SoapClientProtocol {
      public Math() {
         this.Path = "http://rhoward:5000/Chapter5/Simple/Math.asmx";
      }
      [SoapMethod("http://tempuri.org/Add")]
      public int Add(int a, int b) {
         object[] results = Invoke("Add", new object[] {a, b});
         return (int)results[0];
      }
   ...
   }
}
```

VB Proxy Class Source Code: Math.vb

```
   ...
   Namespace myMath
      Public Class Math
         Inherits System.Web.Services.Protocols.SoapClientProtocol

         Public Sub New()
            MyBase.New
            Me.Path = "http://rhoward:5000/Chapter5/Simple/Math.asmx"
         End Sub

         Public Function <System.Web.Services.Protocols.SoapMethodAttribute
                     ("http://tempuri.org/Add")>
                     Add(ByVal a As Integer, ByVal b As Integer) As Integer
            Dim results() As Object = Me.Invoke("Add", New Object() {a, b})
            Add = results(0)
            Exit Function
         End Function
      ...
      End Class
   End Namespace
```

We've cut some of the proxy code out, namely two methods that start as BeginAdd() and EndAdd(). These methods contain the definitions that allow us to call our Add() routine asynchronously and are outside the scope of this book.

The important code to note in both the C# and VB code examples (highlighted) is that clients will create an instance of a class called Math, and will invoke its Add() method. The invocation of the method is identical to that of the Math class in our Math.asmx file.

In each instance of the generated proxy class, the constructor (called every time a Math class is created) sets a property called Path. The Path property is the URI of our Math Web Service, the value of which indicates where the Math implementation exists.

Compiling the Proxy Class

Finally, we need to compile the proxy class to begin using it. We'll cover the command line compilers of VB7 and C# in more detail in the next chapter, but for now there are `make_c#.bat` and `make_vb.bat` files provided with the source of this book, available from www.wrox.com:

The resulting compiled class is `Math.dll`. In order to use this DLL, we must publish it to our application's `\bin` directory. We will discuss the `\bin` directory in Chapter 6, but for now all you need to know is that this is where compiled URT Runtime objects are published and that `\bin` lives at the root of the Web virtual site or root in IIS:

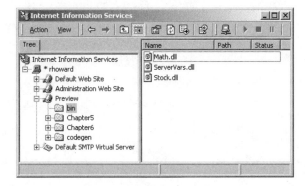

Now that the proxy class is compiled and deployed in our `\bin` directory, let's use it.

Calling the Math Web Service from an ASP+ Page

Once a NGWS Runtime component has been deployed to the `\bin` directory, it is available for us to use in our ASP+ Web application. For example, we can write the following ASP+ page that uses the `myMath.Math` NGWS component:

```
<script language="c#" runat=server>

  public void Page_Load(Object Sender, EventArgs e)
  {
    // Create an instance of the proxy object
    myMath.Math mathProxy = new myMath.Math();

    Text1.InnerHtml = mathProxy.Add(500, 30).ToString();
  }
</script>
<FONT face=arial size=2>
<FONT size=4><B>Web Service Proxy Example</B></FONT>
<HR size=1>
The value of the web service is: <SPAN id=Text1 runat=server/>
</FONT>
```

In the above code sample we are invoking the proxy class `Math.dll` that we added to our `\bin` directory passing in the values of 500 and 30, resulting in: 530:

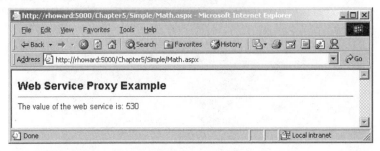

Now that we've looked at using the Web service, let's take a quick look at what ASP+ Web services send over the wire (keep in mind that this can be secured with SSL).

Wire Transmissions

As we stated earlier the proxy class generated by `WebServiceUtil.exe` uses SOAP as the protocol to communicate with the ASP+ Web service. If you're like me, you probably want to look at the network traffic to see just what is really going back and forth in these network transmissions.

I installed Microsoft's Network Monitor along with the Math class's proxy NGWS Runtime object and `Math.aspx` page on my server: `Lestat`. I then monitored the traffic between the consumer (`Lestat`) and the provider (`RHoward`) to view the network traffic.

A total of five exchanges took place for me to use the Math class's `Add()` method remotely.

SOAP Request

When a request is made for the URL `http://lestat/.../math.aspx`, the math proxy class sends an HTTP Post notification to the Web service provider `RHoward`. If the `RHoward` server is available it will reply with HTTP/1.1 100 Continue, and Lestat will then send the body of the POST. These exchanges take place in frames 4, 5, and 6 of the screen shot below. Frame 6 is where we first see the SOAP payload:

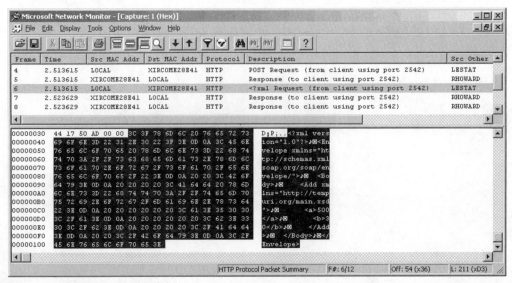

Inside frame 6 we find the contents of the SOAP request. We can see by examining the contents of this message that we have sent a request for the addition of 500 and 30:

```xml
<?xml version="1.0"?>
<Envelope xmlns="http://schemas.xmlsoap.org/soap/envelope/">
  <Body>
    <Add xmlns="http://tempuri.org/main.xsd">
      <a>500</a>
      <b>30</b>
    </Add>
  </Body>
</Envelope>
```

Once RHoward receives this SOAP message, it invokes the Web service's Add() method and returns the result, also formatted as a SOAP message.

SOAP Response

Frame 7 of our exchange represents RHoward sending the HTTP headers back to Lestat, followed by frame 8 which is the SOAP response:

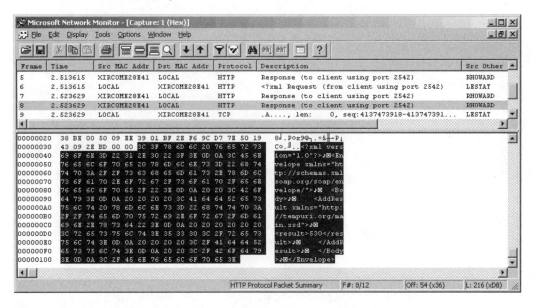

Again, inspecting this SOAP message we learn that we have successfully retrieved the result of calling the Add() method on our ASP+ Web service:

```xml
<?xml version="1.0"?>
<Envelope xmlns="http://schemas.xmlsoap.org/soap/envelope/">
  <Body>
    <AddResult xmlns="http://tempuri.org/main.xsd">
      <result>530</result>
    </AddResult>
  </Body>
</Envelope>
```

As you can clearly see, ASP+ fully supports SOAP and sends XML from server to server.

Summary

In this chapter we've introduced the powerful new programming paradigm of Web services, and how Microsoft has made Web service development nearly trivial with ASP+.

We started the chapter with a discussion of what a Web service is, and with an overview of the plumbing need to create Web services. After the overview, we examined how we can take a NGWS Runtime object and easily expose it as an ASP+ Web service. In this section we also covered the file syntax of .asmx files, and delved into one of the application services available in beta 1.

Next, we discussed how we access Web services both through a browser and through a generated proxy class, and finally we looked at the network traffic sent from server to server.

If you are interested in learning more about SOAP, I would suggest the following two sites:

http://msdn.microsoft.com/xml/default.asp
http://www.develop.com/soap

In review, here are the sections we covered in this chapter:

❑   What is a Web service?

❑   Creating an ASP+ Web Service

❑   Web service protocols and data types

❑   Describing Web services

❑   Programmatically accessing our service

There is a ton of opportunity in the Web Services market-space. Although browser based endpoints/portals, such as Yahoo are well known, who will be the endpoint or portal for Web Services?

In the next chapter we're going to look at two of the files used to compose an ASP+ application: global.asax and config.web. In addition we'll examine HTML forms based security as well as application deployment.

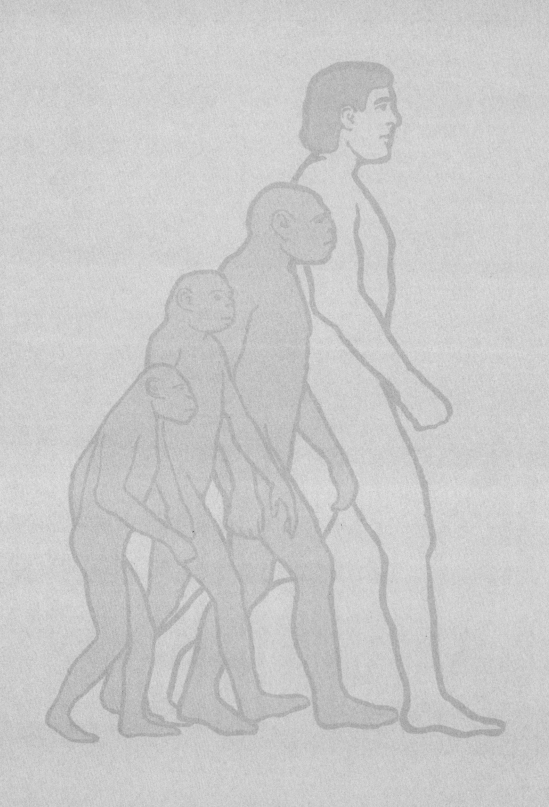

6

Application Framework and Services

Just like the Active Server Pages development model you know and love, ASP+ supports the concept of a Web application along with application specific settings and services. The product documentation defines an ASP+ Application as:

> ...[the] sum of all [resources] that can be invoked or run in the scope of a given [Internet Information Server] virtual directory (and its subdirectories) on a Web application server.

An ASP+ Web application consists of pages, Web services, global application files, configuration files, assemblies, application services, and other resources. We've already looked at pages (Chapter 2), and Web services (Chapter 5), but what we haven't seen are: global application files (`global.asax`), configuration files (`config.web`), application services (such as security), or how we deploy our Web application.

In this chapter we'll explore some of the files used for building Web applications, along with one of the services, HTML Forms Authentication. We'll also look at how we deploy our application, and write a custom HttpHandler, the ASP+ replacement for ISAPI.

Here's a look at what we'll be covering:

- ❑ Using the global application file: `global.asax`
- ❑ Application Configuration
- ❑ Authentication and Authorization Services
- ❑ Deploying the Application
- ❑ Writing a Custom HttpHandler

Let's start this chapter with a discussion of global.asax, the file used for application events and state.

Using the Global Application File: global.asax

Similar to ASP, ASP+ supports a global declarative file per application for application events and state. Events are code sections that we can participate in and are called at certain points during request and application processing. State is the collection of variable instances and data unique to the application or browser sessions scoped within it.

What Does it Look Like?

Global.asax looks remarkably similar to ASP's global.asa, with the exception of directives and new events. For example, the following code should look familiar if you've worked with global.asa:

```
<script language="VB" runat=server>
    Sub Session_OnStart()
        ' Code goes here
    End Sub

    Sub Session_OnEnd()
        ' Code goes here
    End Sub
</script>
```

In this example we've shown the OnStart and OnEnd events for Session. This is a 'carryover' from ASP, and we've only shown this brief example to re-affirm to you that the programming model you are familiar with is still available.

> *Though not shown, global.asax supports the <script src="[location]">
> attribute/value pair to point to a different location for source.*

Event Driven

Application code is only callable within events. Any application code that we want run, for example when a new session instance is created, must be run within an event; in this case the Session_OnStart() event.

Where Does global.asax Live?

The global.asax application file lives in an Internet Information Server virtual root or directory, which signifies an application in IIS. If a global.asax file exists in a directory that is not marked as an application it is ignored.

Opposite is a screen shot from the **Internet Services Manager** in Windows 2000 Server:

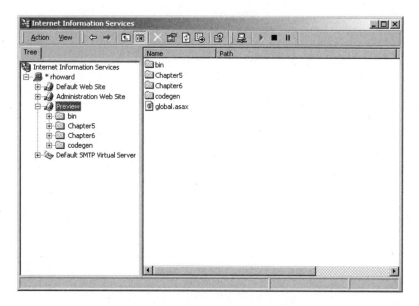

In the above screen shot, **Preview** is an IIS virtual root available on the server **rhoward**. **Preview** contains a `global.asax` file along with several sub-directories. Application files, such as ASP+ pages or Web services found within this Web site will have the settings in **Preview**\\`global.asax` applied to them.

How global.asax is Processed

When the first request comes in for an ASP+ application, `global.asax` is compiled (similar to an ASP+ page or Web service file). The application's `global.asax` instance is then used to apply application events and state for the life of each request. For example, if the Web application makes use of ASP+ sessions, the `Session_OnStart()` event would be called when the session is first initiated:

```
Sub Session_OnStart()
    ' Code goes here
End Sub
```

Using global.asax and global.asa Together

Both `global.asax` and `global.asa` are files used for application code in virtual roots or Web sites in IIS. Although both of these files may reside in the same virtual root or directory, their settings will be applied independently of one another.

> **global.asa** settings will be applied to ASP pages, while **global.asax** settings will be applied to ASP+ application files.

What this means to you as a developer, is that you cannot share application or session state between ASP and ASP+. Yes, your existing ASP applications will continue to work side-by-side with ASP+, but the two cannot share application data or events.

File Updates

ASP+ automatically detects when changes to the global.asax application file are saved on disk, and responds by completing all current requests for the application, firing the appropriate application end event, and then restarting the application. This effectively reboots the application (flushing all state) and will cause ASP+ to re-compile global.asax as well as call the appropriate application start events on the next request.

No Server Down Time

The important item to note here is that even when updates are made to global.asax, the application is constantly available for the end user. No down time is experienced when applications are 're-booted'. This is a change from ASP.

File Syntax

A global.asax file may contain several code sections:

❑ **Application Directives** – Application directives specify optional settings used by the compiler when processing files.

❑ **Events Declarations** – Event declarations define the event delegates, such as Session_OnStart().

❑ **Object Tag Declarations** – Object Tags enable developers to declare and instantiate variables using a declarative, tag-based, syntax.

❑ **Server Side Includes** – Server-Side #Includes enable developers to insert the raw contents of a specified file into global.asax.

Application Directives

If you've worked with transactions or ever specified a language for a page in ASP 3.0, you may already be familiar with application directives. For example, to enable a transaction for an ASP page, you declare a directive at the top of the page:

```
<%@ TRANSACTION=[Required, Require_New, Supported, Not_Supported]%>
```

ASP+ continues the support of application directives, but of course adding more features!

There are three directives: Application, Import, and Assembly. Each supports one or more attributes and the following semantics are used to declare directives and attribute(s):

```
<%@ directive {attribute=value}%>
```

Multiple attribute definitions per directive are supported:

```
<%@ directive {attribute=value} {attribute=value}%>
```

Let's start by looking at the Application directive:

Application

The Application directive defines attributes specific to the class instance of global.asax. This includes which classes are extended from, and a description attribute used for documentation purposes:

❑ **Inherits** - The Inherits attribute/value specifies the base class for global.asax to inherit from. You can create your own class which global.asax will inherit from:

```
<%@ Application Inherits="WroxApp.Application"%>
```

❑ **Description** - The Description attribute/value allows you to add notes or comments to the global.asax. The value of Description is ignored at compile time.

```
<%@ Application Description="My sample global.asax"%>
```

Import

The Import directive allows us to use NGWS classes within the scope of global.asax without having to declare the full **namespace** for the class.

Namespace identifies the NGWS component namespace to be available in the scope of the global.asax.

Some namespaces are imported by default:

```
System
System.Web
System.Web.UI
System.Web.UI.HtmlControl
System.Web.UI.WebControls
System.Collections
System.IO
```

Not all namespaces are imported by default. For example, the System.Net namespace provides a rich set of classes for accessing Internet resources, but it is not imported by default. If we wished to use one of its classes such as System.Net.WebRequest, we could import the System.Net namespace:

```
<%@ Import Namespace="System.Net"%>
```

Having the namespace available allows us to write (C#):

```
WebRequest webreq = WebRequestFactory.Create("http://www.microsoft.com")
```

rather than:

```
System.Net.WebRequest webreq
  = new System.Net.WebRequestFactory.Create("http://www.microsoft.com");
```

This is invaluable once you start working with longer namespaces or assemblies that you create. However, in order to use namespaces, the assembly must be available when global.asax is compiled, i.e. we need to name the file if the assembly is not imported already.

To name the resource, we use the `Assembly` application directive.

Assembly

`Assembly` allows us to specify an assembly file for a given namespace. You will use the `Assembly` directive when you wish to use assemblies, such as `System.Net`, that aren't available by default.

> **Assemblies that exist in the application's \bin directory do not need to be brought in via the `Assembly` processing directive. \bin is the application directory where compiled assemblies are deployed, and will be covered in the deployment section of this chapter.**

When the ASP+ file is compiled, the assembly file must be part of the compilation in order for the classes within the assembly to be available. Although the `Import` keyword saved us some typing, you won't even be able to access the classes – even with fully declared namespaces – without using `Assembly` to name the .dll. The `Assembly` processing directive supports one attribute: **Name**.

The **Name** attribute identifies the assembly to include in the compilation of `global.asax`. If the assembly is not named, and you attempt to import its namespace, you will get an error:

Error: BC30466: The namespace or type 'Net' for the import 'System.Net' cannot be found.

However, you can easily remedy this by using the `Assembly` processing directive:

```
<%@ Assembly Name="System.Net.dll"%>
```

After adding the above line, we re-request a resource in the application root, `global.asax` will be re-compiled, and application processing will continue as normal (since System.Net.dll is now available).

Note: we look later in the chapter at the file known as config.web that allows you to name assemblies for the entire web application, i.e. making them globally available.

Event Declarations

Events make our lives as developers easier. Rather than writing if/then blocks inline to execute code when certain behaviors occur, we can intelligently participate in the event model provided by ASP+. `Global.asax` supports more than 15 events for you to participate in. This is a big change from ASP 3.0's `global.asa`, which only had minimal `Application` and `Session OnStart/OnEnd` eventing.

For example, with ASP if we wanted code run on the beginning of every page we would more than likely add a #include file to the top of every ASP with the appropriate code in conditional blocks. Using `global.asax`'s new event model we can simply participate in the `Application_BeginRequest` event which is called at the beginning of every request for the application.

Before we look at the events, it's important to point out that events found in `global.asax` can have different event method prototypes.

Event Prototypes

Events can be coded in several different manners. It's important that we cover the various prototypes, so that when you see similar event signatures you realize they are the same.

Here are some examples in both VB and C# of how the `BeginRequest` event signature can vary:

C#

```
public void Application_OnBeginRequest()
public void Application_BeginRequest(Object sender, EventArgs e)
```

Visual Basic 7

```
Sub Application_OnBeginRequest()
End Sub
Sub Application_BeginRequest(sender As Object, e As EventArgs)
End Sub
```

The `[On]EventName` prototype is a carryover from ASP. The `EventName` prototype is the official NGWS runtime naming style. For consistency, all references to events will show the NGWS runtime style, e.g. `Application_BeginRequest`.

Event Table

The table below describes the available events we can use in `global.asax`:

Name	Description
Application_Start	The `Application_Start` event is fired once, when the application first starts. This event is useful for setting application wide settings that need to be initialized once, rather than on each request.
Session_Start	This event is fired when a user session first starts, and will be called for each user's first session.
Application_End	The `Application_End` event is fired when the application ends. It is fired only once when the application times out or is reset. This event is useful for cleaning up application code or global references created in the `Application_Start` event.
Session_End	The `Session_End` event is fired when a user session ends. It is fired only once when the session times out or is reset.
Application_Error	The `Error` event is fired when an unhandled error occurs within the application. `Error` gives you a last chance to provide any type of error handling or logging routines that you want called before presenting the error to the end user. Errors that are handled with error trapping code (such as `Try/Catch` blocks) will not cause this event to fire.
Application_BeginRequest	`Application_BeginRequest` event is fired whenever a new request is received. This event is guaranteed to always fire on each and every request.

Table continued on following page

Name	Description
Application_Authenticate Request	Used by the security module, the Application_AuthenticateRequest event signals that the request is ready to be authenticated. Use this event if you want to run any code before the user is authenticated, such as custom authentication.
Application_Authorize Request	Used by the security module, the AuthorizeRequest event signals that the request is ready to be authorized. Use this event if you want to run any code before the user is authorized for a resource, such as custom authorization to a particular URL.
Application_Resolve RequestCache	Used by the output cache module to short-circuit the processing of requests that have been cached.
Application_Aquire RequestState	Signals that per-request state (like session or user state) should be obtained.
Application_PreRequest HandlerExecute	This event signals that the request handler is about to execute. In most cases the request handler will be an ASP+ page or Web service. This is the last event that you can participate in before the handler processes the request. When we discuss the config.web file later in the chapter we'll go into more detail on what a handler is.
Application_PostRequest HandlerExecute	This event is the first event available to us after the handler, such as the ASP+ page or Web service, has completed its work.
Application_Release RequestState	This event is called when the request state should be stored, since the application is finished with it.
Application_Update RequestCache	Signals that code processing is complete and the file is ready to be added to the ASP+ cache.
Application_EndRequest	This event is the last event called when the application ends.
Application_PreRequest HeadersSent	HTTP headers are about to be sent to the client. Provides the opportunity to add, remove, or update headers and the response body.

Event Execution Order

As you may have noted, the above events have a specific execution order. Let's take a look at a diagram that shows the events that are available on each request (excluding Application and Session Start/End events):

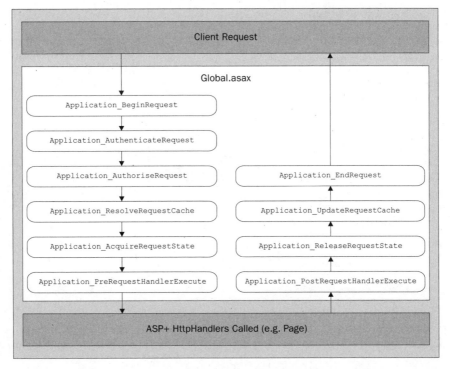

When a client request comes in, six events are available to participate in before the request is serviced by the request handler (such as an ASP+ page or Web service). For example, in the last chapter we looked at Web services. The global.asax events are called and executed before the Web service is processed for the request. After the Web service is finished with the request, global.asax events are then called before the completed request is sent to the client.

Event Participation Code Example

Our event participation example is rather simple. We have a global.asax and a default.aspx page in a virtual directory each performing a Response.Write() – this lets us know that the event has been called:

global.asax (snippet)

```
<script language="C#" runat="server">
    // Not all code shown
    ...
    public void Application_PreRequestHandlerExecute(Object sender,
                                                EventArgs e){
        Response.Write("global.asax - Application_PreRequestHandlerExecute
                    called...<br>");
    }

    public void Application_PostRequestHandlerExecute(Object sender,
                                                EventArgs e){
        Response.Write("global.asax - Application_PostRequestHandlerExecute
                    called...<br>");
    }
</script>
```

One event is shown before and after the HttpHandler is called, in this case `default.aspx`:

default.aspx (snippet)

```
<HTML>
default.aspx - Page contents written<BR>
</HTML>
```

The output of these two ASP+ application files together results in the following:

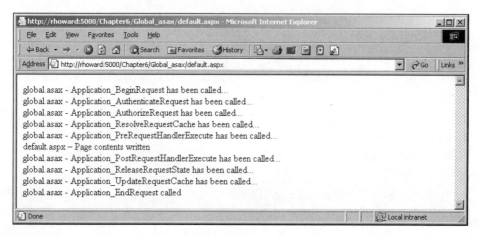

In the above screen shot we see the execution order of the `global.asax` events, along with the ASP+ page output.

Object Tag Declarations

Object tags enable us to declare and instantiate application and session objects in `global.asax` using a declarative, tag-based syntax. These tags can be used to create NGWS components, or classic COM objects specified by either ProgID or CLSID.

The type of object to create is identified using three different tag attributes: `class`, `progid`, and `classid`. These attributes are mutually exclusive, and it is an error to use more than one in our object tag declaration.

Using Object Tag Declarations

The object tag declarations are used like this:

```
<object id="id" runat="server" progid="Classic COM ProgID" scope="session"/>
```

The following table runs through the attributes that are inserted in the declaration:

Attributes	Description
ID	Unique "name" to use when declaring object on application.
runat	Must be set to `"server"` for the object to execute within ASP+.

Attributes	Description
scope	Determines where the object lives. The choices are "application" for application state, "session" for session state, and finally "appinstance" allowing each application to receive its own object instance.
[Class, ProgID, ClassID]	Determines what type of object is created; an instance of either the NGWS component, the classic COM ProgID or ClassID.

Server Side Includes

Developers often use server-side includes to insert sections of code into a file. Examples of this include sections of code that need to be run for each user when a particular file is requested, such as binding to a directory and pulling down user information to personalize a particular page instance.

The sever-side include functionaliy in ASP+ is identical to ASP, for example:

```
<!--#Include file="[path to file]" -->
```

or

```
<!--#Include virtual="[path to file]"-->
```

ASP+'s global.asax is no more complicated than ASP's global.asa. If anything, it should be simpler since there are more events to program against and there should be less case handling code that you need to write.

Now that we've looked at how we use global.asax, let's see how we set configuration settings for ASP+ applications.

Application Configuration

Developers and administrators both need ways to modify the configuration settings of a Web server without going through a user interface or requiring local access to the server. One of the goals for ASP+ is a simplified configuration system whereby updates to system settings can easily be made without the need for local system access.

ASP 3.0 Configuration Settings

Previous versions of ASP relied upon IIS settings for application configuration information. For example, settings such as session state, buffering, default languages, and script timeout settings are all configured from the Application Configuration's dialog App Options tab, found in the application's property settings (by right clicking on an IIS application):

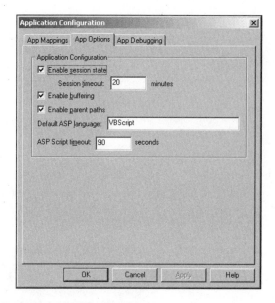

These are just some of the settings that need to be configured through the Microsoft Management Console (MMC) for application settings. All settings or modifications are then applied to the IIS metabase, which is used to compute application settings at runtime for the Web application.

The metabase is a repository for configuration information, and although it can be modified programmatically via ADSI (Active Directory Service Interfaces), it can be quite cumbersome to work with and makes application replication (especially to multiple servers) somewhat difficult.

ASP+ Configuration Settings

ASP+, on the other hand, doesn't rely upon the IIS metabase at all. Instead, it uses a declarative XML configuration file known as config.web. Having an XML configuration file gives us several benefits:

❑   You can copy your configuration with your code and content

❑   Standard text and XML editors can be used to configure settings

❑   It is easy to FTP to a Web site and modify settings

> **Although unavailable in beta 1, ASP+ will have an IIS MMC Admin tool just as ASP does. However, it will write to config.web rather than to the IIS metabase.**

In the screenshot, we saw session state settings being configured via the Application Configuration dialog and written to the metabase. Now, this is what session configuration looks like for ASP+:

```
<configuration>
  <sessionstate
        inproc="true"
        usesqlserver="false"
        cookieless="false"
```

```
            timeout="20"

            server="localhost"
            port="42424"
    />
    <configuration>
```

In the above code snippet from `config.web` it's easy to see that we're making settings to the session state behavior of the application. Let's put this code into context with a discussion of the `config.web` file and its XML syntax. We'll be coming back to what these settings mean shortly.

Config.Web

`Config.web` is an extensible configuration file that supports an open schema others can extend. This is intended so that third parties can easily extend the programming model and use `config.web` for storing their application and configuration data.

> *It is common for developers to make use of the registry or IIS metabase to store application specific data, e.g. database usernames and passwords, which could be loaded in* `global.asa` `Application_Start`. *This is no longer necessary, as config.web supports mechanisms to make storage of this type of information easy and central.*

Behavior and Location

A `config.web` file may exist in any directory, and settings declared within `config.web` are applied to all interactions with resources in that directory, and its children. For example, take the following file tree where **Preview** is a directory with `.aspx` and `.asmx` files (**wwwroot** being the default Web root).

`Config.web` setting for `<sessionstate>` in: C:\inetpub\wwwroot\Preview\\config.web:

```
<configuration>
  <sessionstate timeout="5" />
</configuration>
```

Consider, if the default `config.web` file found in \winnt\ComPlus... has the following settings:

```
<configuration>
  <sessionstate
        inproc="true"
        usesqlserver="false"
        cookieless="false"
        timeout="20"
        server="localhost"
        port="42424"
  />
</configuration>
```

We would have a cookie based session timeout setting of 20 minutes (inherited from the root `config.web`), but a setting of only 5 minutes in the \Preview Web application.

config.web or global.asax?

Don't confuse global.asax with config.web. global.asax is geared specifically for events and state, while config.web is for application settings. In addition, a config.web file does not have to be in an IIS virtual root/directory to have effect. However, config.web still has to be in the application's path, i.e., you can't put a config.web file in c:\temp and expect it to apply to c:\inetpub\wwwroot.

It's important to note that config.web files are also **optional**. When no config.web file is present in the Web application, the settings are taken from the default config.web file found at:

```
winnt\ComPlus\v2000.14.1802\config.web
```

> Note the exact directory name of **v2000.14.1802** will be different for beta 1.

File Syntax

What we have, thus far, neglected to mention in the above code snippets for <sessionstate> is the syntax for declaring these settings. Since the data is XML based, we need a top-level node to wrap it. The top-level node of our XML file is <configuration>, and any application settings will be applied within.

Within <configuration> there are two tag types we expect to find declared within this root node:

```
<configuration>
   <configsections>
     [config section handlers]
   </configsections>
   [config section settings]
</configuration>
```

In the above config.web example, [Configuration Section Handlers] identify classes that handle configuration settings. The [Configuration Section Settings] then specifies which settings to apply.

This is quite a powerful and flexible model since config.web relies upon the named (<configsections>) classes to be responsible for understanding the various settings.

Configuration Section Handlers

Configuration section handlers are classes that implement the interface: IConfigSectionHandler. These Configuration Section Handlers are declared within a config.web file using the "add" directive nested within <configsections> tags. For example, here is a subset of the configuration section handlers from the default config.web:

```
<configuration>
   <configsections>
     <add name="browsercaps"
          type="System.Web.HttpBrowserCapabilities$SectionHandler" />
     <add name="sessionstate"
          type="System.Web.SessionState.SessionStateModule$SectionHandler" />
```

```
      <add name="httphandlers"
          type="System.Web.Configuration.HttpHandlersConfigurationHandler" />
      <add name="httpmodules"
          type="System.Web.Configuration.HttpModulesConfigurationHandler" />
      <add name="compilers"
          type="System.Web.Configuration.DictionarySectionHandler" />
      <add name="iisprocessmodel"
          type="System.Web.Configuration.IgnoreSectionHandler" />
      <add name="trace"
          type="System.Web.Configuration.SingleTagSectionHandler" />
      <add name="security"
          type="System.Web.Security.SecurityConfigSettingsHandler" />
      <add name="appsettings"
          type="System.Web.Configuration.DictionarySectionHandler" />
   </configsections>
   ...
</configuration>
```

Each "add" tag identifies a configuration handler tag along with the class to handle the configuration data. Going back to our <sessionstate> example, we have the following <configsections> entry:

```
<add name="sessionstate"
    type="System.Web.SessionState.SessionStateModule$SectionHandler" />
```

The name attribute of <add> has a value of "sessionstate" which defines the tag for the configuration settings for <sessionstate>. The type attribute names the class responsible for interpreting and applying the settings found in <sessionstate>.

Declare Section Handlers Once

Configuration section handlers only need to appear once, as settings are inherited from the root. For example, if you want to take advantage of the session state features in ASP+, you don't need to re-declare <add name="sessionstate"…/> in each config.web file.

However, keep in mind that if a section handler you want applied is not specified in the default config.web, the section handler must exist in the directory or sub-directory of the application relying upon it.

Next, let's look at some of the common configuration settings that our section handlers use.

Common Configuration Settings

Configuration settings are the settings and values we apply to configuration section handlers, which in turn affect application behavior. The name="[value]" section of the configuration section handler identifies a tag (as outlined above). We'll take this section to explore some of the more common configuration settings.

<sessionstate>

The <sessionstate> configuration section handler in config.web sets the behaviors of session state throughout the application. It support five settings:

Although we haven't explored the expanded capabilities of session state in this book, we do have several new options for how to manage user sessions.

- ❑ `inproc="[true/false]"` - indicates whether or not the session state should be stored on the server, or whether it should be stored on a separate state server. The default setting is `true`; session state is stored on the server.

- ❑ `cookieless="[true/false]"` - indicates whether or not cookies should be used as the identity key. By default, the setting is `false`; cookies are used. When set to `true`, ASP+ will automatically URL munge (encode cookie data in the URL) the cookie value and pass it along with all requests.

- ❑ `timeout="[number of minutes]"` - specifies how long, in minutes, a session should be valid for. By default, it is 20 minutes.

- ❑ `server= "[server name]"` - specifies the server to use to store remote session state. It is only used when `inproc=false`.

- ❑ `port="[port number]"` - specifies the port number on the remote session state server. It is only used when `inproc=false`.

<assemblies>

Earlier we looked at the application directives in `global.asax`. The `Assembly` directive allowed us to specify assemblies that were included via its `Name` attribute:

```
<%@ Assembly Name="System.Net.dll"%>
```

The `<assemblies>` configuration settings in `config.web` also allow us to specify assemblies to include in the compilation of the resource, and settings made here will be applied to all application files. Unlike the previous settings tag, `<sessionstate>`, `<assemblies>` is a root tag and contains `<add>` tags:

```
<assemblies>
    <add assembly="mscorlib"/>
    <add assembly="System.Web"/>
    <add assembly="System.Data"/>
    <add assembly="System.Web.Services"/>
    <add assembly="System.Xml.Serialization"/>
    <add assembly="System"/>
</assemblies>
```

> **Note that assemblies such as mscorlib.dll do not have .dll appended to them.**

Each of these assemblies is now available within the scope of application files (`.aspx`, `.asmx`, etc.). But remember we would probably still want to use the `Import` processing directive in the application files to import the namespace into the scope of the page.

<appsettings>

In Chapter 3 we learned all about ADO+ and data binding. One option that was not covered was storing the Data Source Name (DSN) in a central location, rather than having it in each ASP+ application file. Earlier in this chapter we also mentioned that is possible to store configuration data such as the DSN in the `config.web` file.

Let's look at some code to show how we can do this:

```
<script language="C#" runat=server>

  public void Page_Load(Object sender, EventArgs e)
  {
    DSN.InnerHtml = (String) ((Hashtable)
                    Context.GetConfig("appsettings"))["DSN"];
  }
</script>
The DSN entry set in config.web is: <B><SPAN id=DSN runat=server/></B>
```

The above code uses the `Context` object's `GetConfig()` method to access a hashtable (similar to a dictionary object) and retrieve various values from the `config.web` file:

```
<configuration>
    <appsettings>
        <add key="DSN" value="Server=rhoward;
                        Database=advworks; UID=sa; pwd=foobar" />
    </appsettings>
</configuration>
```

This is very powerful, since we can now define all application configuration data in a central location.

<webservices>

There is one setting in the `<webservices>` section handler that we'll look at in this book: `<sdlHelpGenerator>`:

```
<configuration>
  ...
  <webservices>
    ...
    <sdlHelpGenerator href="DefaultSdlHelpGenerator.aspx" />
  </webservices>
<configuration>
```

`<sdlHelpGenerator>` is where we set the ASP+ page that is used as a template for Web services (see Chapter 5). This file can be found in winnt\ComPlus\v2000.14.1802\.

<httphandlers>

When perusing the root `config.web` file you might notice an interesting section called `<httphandlers>`. You would see the following entries:

```
<add verb="*" path="*.aspx" type="System.Web.UI.PageHandlerFactory" />
<add verb="*" path="*.asax" type="System.Web.HttpNotFoundHandler" />
<add verb="*" path="trace.axd"
              type="System.Web.InternalSamples.TraceHandler" />
<add verb="*" path="*.web" type="System.Web.HttpNotFoundHandler" />
```

An `HttpHandler` is simply an NGWS component that implements the interface `IHttpHandler` (defined in System.Web.dll), and is responsible for processing requests. `HttpHandler` is the ASP+ replacement for ISAPI.

> Notice that any requests made for the `.asax` extension (from `global.asax`) are mapped to: `type="System.Web.HttpNotFoundHandler"` which explicitly denies access to this extension type.

The entries found within `<httphandlers>` have three attributes:

- ❑ **verb** – Specifies the HTTP acceptable verb types. * indicates all, but normal HTTP verbs such as `GET`, `POST`, etc. are supported as well. The `verb` attribute simply let's you filter requests.

- ❑ **path** – The * is used as a wildcard, and as you can see from the above examples `path` is used to filter requests to different `HttpHandlers`.

- ❑ **type** – Names the NGWS component that is the handler for the request.

For example the following HttpHandler is used to map ASP+ page requests to the `PageHandlerFactory`. `PageHandlerFactory` is simply another NGWS framework component:

```
<add verb="*" path="*.aspx" type="System.Web.UI.PageHandlerFactory" />
```

> Although settings made in **<httphandlers>** are inherited, it is possible to limit the scope to apply settings only to the directory which **config.web** is located in by wrapping that **<add>** verb within a **<location>** tag.

What is really powerful about `HttpHandlers` is that you can write your own, and we'll do this at the end of the chapter.

Now that we've looked at `global.asax` and `config.web`, let's take a look at one of the ASP+ application services: **Authentication and Authorization** before we move on to deploying our application.

Authentication and Authorization Services

ASP+ supports **Microsoft Passport**, HTML forms based authentication, as well as traditional NTLM (Basic/Digest/Kerberos) authentication. A complex discussion of this topic is beyond the scope of this particular book, but what we are going to look at is the HTML Forms Authentication features of ASP+.

Those of you familiar with Microsoft's Site Server Personalization and Membership Technology should be especially intrigued by the powerful forms-based authentication model provided by ASP+.

Overview

The meanings of authentication and authorization are often confused. In this section, when we refer to **authentication**, we mean: **The process whereby the credentials used for identification are considered valid or invalid**. When authentication is complete, the server accepts the credentials input by the user for authentication and agrees upon the identity. However, no access is yet granted.

After authentication has been completed, the process of authorization may begin. When we refer to **authorization**, we mean: **The process whereby privileges are granted to a particular identity**. When authorization is complete, the server grants privileges to allow the user to access resources.

> **Simply put, authentication is about identifying the user by validating a username and password, while authorization is about granting or denying an authenticated user access to a resource.**

Writing authentication and authorization code is no simple task with ASP today. ASP+, however, provides several mechanisms for authentication and authorization, one of which is HTML Forms Authentication.

HTML Forms Authentication

For those of you familiar with Site Server 3.0 Personalization and Membership, you may recall the HTML Forms based authentication feature. This authentication mechanism was cookie based, and used a redirection system whereby un-authenticated requests for system resources are redirected to an HTML forms login page. ASP+ provides similar functionality, but with a more flexible design. Before we look at the code that makes ASP+ HTML Forms Authentication work, let's look at a high level overview of request/response exchanges between client and server:

Overview

When a user makes a request for a resource that is using ASP+ HTML Forms Authentication, ASP+ will attempt to authenticate the user by employing the following logic:

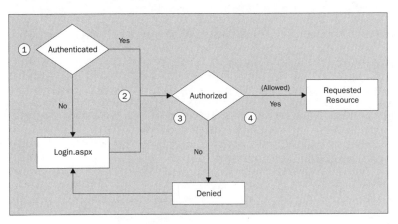

Authentication and Authorization Flow Chart

ASP+ will authenticate (**1**) any requests for a resource marked to require security. Clients such as Internet Explorer, will either (**2**) provide a valid cookie used for identification, or if no valid cookie is found will be redirected to a login page.

In our flowchart above, this login page is `login.aspx`. Within our login page, we present the user with an HTML form whereby they provide a username and password used for authentication:

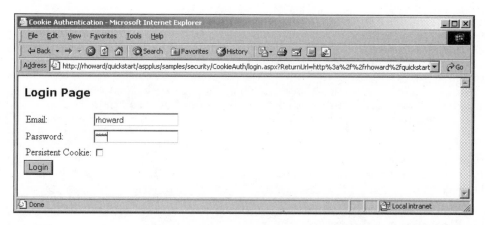

Once the HTML form is submitted, code will run that determines whether or not the user is valid. If the user *is* valid, the system issues a cookie that contains the credentials (in an encrypted key) for re-acquiring the user's identity. Once a valid cookie is obtained, subsequent resource requests will skip the HTML Forms Authentication login page and move straight to authorization.

> *Cookieless authentication will possibly be supported in the final version. Cookieless authentication would embed the cookie id within the querystring for each request.*

Next, we determine if the user is (3) authorized to access the given resource. Authorization to the resource is controlled by <allow> and <deny> settings in config.web (which we'll look at briefly in a moment). If the user is denied access, the browser is redirected to an 'Access Denied' page or back to the login page. However, if the user is allowed access, the browser is redirected to the resource originally requested.

This authentication and authorization process is repeated for each secured resource.

Why HTML Forms Authentication?

HTML Forms based login pages are great because they provide us with the greatest amount of flexibility. We can customize the "look-and-feel" of the HTML form to match that of our site. But if we were using basic authentication, we would have to use the clunky HTTP Basic Authentication pop-up (which can tend to confuse some novice end users):

HTTP Basic Authentication Dialog

HTTP Basic Authentication dialogs are confusing, and can interrupt the flow of a site:

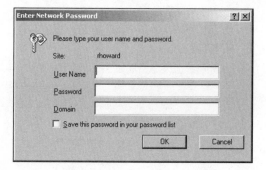

HTML Forms Authentication

Unlike HTTP Basic Authentication dialog boxes, we can heavily customize ASP+ HTML Forms Authentication login screens:

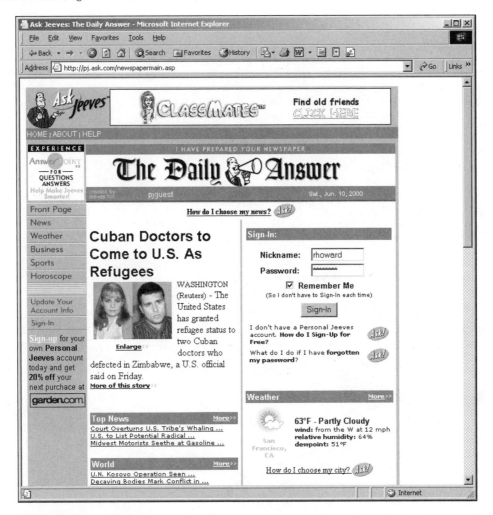

Custom Credential Verification

We can have greater control about the rules used for authentication. Additionally, we have more control over what type of security to apply to the request. For example, you could choose to use no encryption and pass the data in clear-text (only if the contents within the site are not sensitive of course), or you could use SSL or certificates for a more secure way of identifying the user.

Next, let's look at a sample HTML Forms Authentication implementation.

Sample Implementation

First, let's create a `config.web` file, set the authentication and authorization settings, and name the users that we want to authenticate. We'll rip these files apart and explain them afterwards:

Config.web

```
<configuration>
  <security>
    <authentication mode="Cookie">
      <cookie cookie=".ASPXAUTH" loginurl="login.aspx"
              decryptionkey="autogenerate">
        <credentials passwordformat="Clear">
          <user name="jonnic" password="password"/>
        </credentials>
      </cookie>
    </authentication>
    <authorization>
      <deny users="?" />
    </authorization>
  </security>
</configuration>
```

Next, let's create the `default.aspx` page that we want to ensure is authenticated and the `login.aspx` page that we want to authenticate users from:

Default.aspx

```
<script language="c#" runat=server>
  public void Page_Load(Object sender, EventArgs e) {
      user.InnerHtml = User.Identity.Name;
  }
</script>
Hello, <SPAN id=user runat=server/>, you have been authenticated by ASP+!
```

`Default.aspx` has some simple logic (that we'll explore later) that helps us determine which user has been authenticated.

Login.aspx

```
<script language="C#" runat=server>
public void Login_Click(Object sender, EventArgs E){
  if (CookieAuthentication.Authenticate(txtUser.Value, txtPwd.Value)) {
    // We always persist the cookie
    CookieAuthentication.RedirectFromLoginPage(txtUser.Value, true);
  } else {
    lblStatus.InnerHtml = "Invalid login";
  }
}
</script>
<form method=post runat=server>
  Username: <INPUT type=text name=txtUser id=txtUser runat=server/><BR>
  Password: <INPUT type=password name=txtPwd id=txtPwd runat=server/><BR>
<INPUT type=submit OnServerClick="Login_Click" runat=server/>
</form>
<SPAN id="lblStatus" runat=server/>
```

`Login.aspx` contains the code to authenticate the user.

Configuring Authentication

Finally, we add these files into our Web application. Since we want our secure section separate from our main application, we must mark it as a Web application:

> **Config.web <authentication> sections must be defined within an IIS application root or directory.**

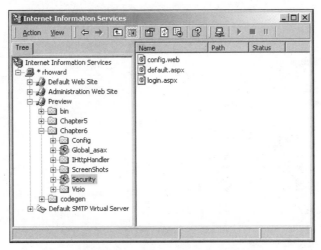

Now we can request our `default.aspx` page from our Web server and we will be redirected to `login.aspx` where we must enter our credentials. If the credentials aren't accepted we are redirected back to `login.aspx` and informed that it was an "Invalid login".

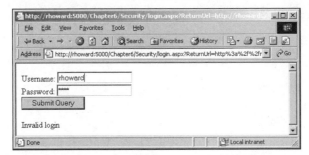

However, if we enter a valid username and password, as defined in our `config.web` file, we are granted access to `default.aspx`:

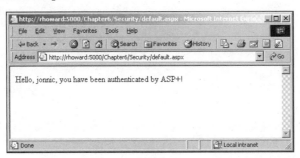

Now that we've coved both an overview and a sample implementation, let's take a look at the code and suggested strategies for HTML Forms Authentication. We'll start by looking at `config.web`.

Config.web

Like all ASP+ settings, HTML Forms Authentication is configured in `config.web`:

```
<configuration>
  <security>
    <authentication mode="Cookie">
      <cookie cookie=".ASPXAUTH" loginurl="login.aspx"
              decryptionkey="autogenerate">
        <credentials passwordformat="Clear">
          <user name="jonnic" password="password"/>
        </credentials>
      </cookie>
    </authentication>
    <authorization>
      <deny users="?" />
    </authorization>
  </security>
</configuration>
```

The HTML Forms configuration settings are wrapped first in <security>, then in <authentication> and <authorization> tags. Let's review both of these, as well as some of the other tags found in `config.web`.

<authentication>

As mentioned in the introduction to this section, several different types of authentication are supported. ASP+ is configured to use a particular authentication mode by specifying the mode value in the <authentication> tag.

```
<authentication mode="Cookie">
```

The following options are supported:

Mode Value	Description
None	No ASP+ authentication will be used for the requested resources. However, the Windows NT/2000 Access Control Lists (ACLs) on a file or directory may still deny access to the requestor.
Windows	ASP+ will use Windows NT/2000 based authentication to validate credentials provided via NTLM or another supported Security Support Provider (Basic/Digest/Kerberos/NTLM). Once authenticated a Windows NT SID will be used on the thread to allow/deny access based on Windows NT security permissions.
Cookie	ASP+ will attempt to authenticate users based on a cookie that uniquely identifies a user.
Passport	ASP+ will attempt to authenticate users based on Microsoft's Passport Web Service.

Again, we are only looking at `Cookie` (HTML Forms) authentication mode in this book.

<cookie>

Allows us to configure settings of the cookie such as name and decryption key, as well as the page which un-authenticated requests are directed to:

```
<cookie cookie=".ASPXAUTH" loginurl="login.aspx"
        decryptionkey="autogenerate">
```

Attribute	Description
`cookie="[string]"`	This setting simply specifics the name of the cookie. Due to the vagaries of casing, Path='/' is set on authentication cookies as, otherwise, URLs like /path and /Path would be treated differently by the browser when returning cookies. So, if you have multiple apps on a single server using cookie authentication, you probably want to make this unique per application.
`decryptionkey="[string]"`	The current setting is set to `"autogenerate"`, which tells the system to auto generate a random key. In a single server environment this works great, but for server farms each `decryptionkey` needs to be set to the same value as the client won't always land on the same server. The `decryptionkey` should be in hex format – and make sure that the size of the key (number of hex characters), matches the encryption package installed on your machine, e.g. with 128 bit encryption support installed on Windows 2000, provide any 32 char hex string (such as 1122334455AABBCCCCBBAA5544332211), or 14 or 16 characters for 56 or 64 bit encryption.
`loginurl="[string]"`	The ASP+ resource to which un-authenticated requests are going to be directed. In our example above, un-authenticated requests will be sent to `login.aspx`, which you can customize to your heart's desire.

> The login URL does not have to be on the same server in order to validate a user. However, a common **decryptionkey** must be used across all machines.

<credentials>

Within the `<credentials>` we specify usernames and passwords used when accessing our system; support for encrypted passwords is managed in this tag.

```
<credentials passwordformat="Clear">
```

> **Storing usernames and passwords in `config.web` is not required; as we'll see when we look at `login.aspx`, we can use any credential store, e.g. database, directory, etc.**

We have three different options for storing the password data in `config.web`:

Attribute	Description
`passwordformat="[Clear,SHA1,MD5]"`	❑ **clear** - Passwords are stored in clear text. The user password is compared directly against this value without further transformation.
	❑ **SHA1** - Passwords are stored using the SHA1 hash digest. When credentials are validated, the user password will be hashed using the SHA1 algorithm and compared for equality with this value. The clear text password is never stored or compared.
	❑ **MD5** - Passwords are stored using an MD5 hash digest. When credentials are validated, the user password will be hashed using the MD5 algorithm and compared for equality with this value. The clear text password is never stored or compared.

Although we've covered all three of the encryption types supported, we need to use a special API to perform the encryption if we wish to use SHA1 or MD5. We won't be using it in the chapter, but I will list the API in case you wish to explore:

```
CookieAuthentication.HashPasswordForStoringInConfigFile([password],
                                                        [SHA1 | MD5])
```

The result of `HashPasswordForStoringInConfigFile` should then be entered into `config.web`, and the appropriate `passwordformat` type must be specified.

Since we are not covering how we get the SHA1 and MD5 encrypted passwords, all examples will be done using cleartext.

Once we specify the credentials password format, we must still list the users.

<user>

The user tag lets us specify the name of the user as well as the password that the user will use for authentication.

```
<user name="jonnic" password="password"/>
```

Attribute	Description
`name="username"`	Name of the user.
`password="password"`	Password of the user.

\<authorization>

Now that we have specified how to authenticate users, we still need a way to authorize user's access to a resource. This is done through the \<authorization> section.

Within this section we can specify \<allow> and \<deny> sections for both users and roles.

The use of roles is really beyond the scope of this book, so we won't be covering it in detail.

We can either specify whether to allow or deny all users with `<[allow|deny] users="*"/>`, or deny all anonymous users with `<deny users="?"/>`. We can also list the users or roles by name, separated by commas, to allow or deny access:

```
<deny users="brian, hans, brad"/>
<allow users="*"/>
```

Authorization is applied in order of the rule. So in our code example above, brian, hans, and brad, would all be denied access, and all others would be allowed.

Now that we've looked at `config.web`, let's look at some of the specific files and APIs that make HTML Forms Authentication work. We'll start with the login page.

Login Page

When we use HTML Forms Authentication we redirect the user to a page that processes and checks the provided credentials. The sample that we used above redirected the user to an ASP+ page, `login.aspx`:

```
<script language="C#" runat=server>
public void Login_Click(Object sender, EventArgs E) {
  if (CookieAuthentication.Authenticate(txtUser.Value, txtPwd.Value)){
    // We always persist the cookie
    CookieAuthentication.RedirectFromLoginPage(txtUser.Value, true);
  } else {
    lblStatus.InnerHtml = "Invalid login";
  }
}
</script>
<form method=post runat=server>
  Username: <INPUT type=text name=txtUser id=txtUser runat=server/><BR>
  Password: <INPUT type=password name=txtPwd id=txtPwd runat=server/><BR>
<INPUT type=submit OnServerClick="Login_Click" runat=server/>
</form>
<SPAN id="lblStatus" runat=server/>
```

Login.aspx is simply a generic HTML form with a Login_Click server-side event handler that is called when the form is submitted. Within our event handler we perform the authentication of the user using the CookieAuthentication class. We have two options here:

❑   Authenticate from config.web

❑   Authenticate from another data store

Let's look at both of these options.

Authenticate Users From Config.web

We've already seen the `<user>` settings in `config.web`:

```
<user name="jonnic" password="password"/>
```

If we wish to authenticate users from config.web, we use the `CookieAuthentication` class's `Authenticate` method in our login page:

```
if (CookieAuthentication.Authenticate(txtUser.Value, txtPwd.Value)){
  ...
}
```

In our `login.aspx` example, we simply pass the name and password from our form. This method then examines the users and their passwords in `config.web`. If a match is found, the method returns `true` and we execute the code to issue the cookie and redirect the user to the resource originally requested. If a match is not found, the `Authenticate()` method returns `false`.

We can also choose to use our own user/password store such as a directory or a database.

Authenticate Users From Custom User/Password Store

This simply consists of us writing our own logic to determine whether or not the credentials supplied by the user are considered valid. For example, if we possessed an XML file that listed our users (users.xml):

```
...
<Users>
    <UserEmail>jdoe@somewhere.com</UserEmail>
    <UserPassword>password</UserPassword>
</Users>
...
```

We could easily re-code our `login.aspx` to use this XML file:

```
...
String cmd = "UserEmail='" + UserEmail.Value + "'";
DataSet ds = new DataSet();

FileStream fs = new
FileStream(Server.MapPath("users.xml"),FileMode.Open,FileAccess.Read);
StreamReader reader = new StreamReader(fs);
ds.ReadXml(reader);
fs.Close();

DataTable users = ds.Tables[0];
DataRow[] matches = users.Select(cmd);

// Did we find a match?
if( matches != null  && matches.Length > 0 ) {
  DataRow row = users.Rows[0];
  String pass = (String)row["UserPassword"];
  if( 0 != String.Compare(pass, UserPass.Value, false) ) {
    ...
```

```
      } else {
        CookieAuthentication.RedirectFromLoginPage(UserEmail.Value,
                                        PersistCookie.Checked);
      }
    }
    ...
```

Again, if we find a match for the username:

```
    if( matches != null  && matches.Length > 0 ) {
```

and the password:

```
    if( 0 != String.Compare(pass, UserPass.Value, false) ) {
```

we execute the code to issue the cookie and redirect the user to the resource originally requested.

This is very flexible, since any username/password store can work with ASP+ HTML Forms Authentication. We just need to write the code to wire the two systems together. Either way, all we're actually doing is determining if we have a valid username and password. We have another method on the CookieAuthentication class to issue the cookie and redirect the user to the requested resource.

Issuing the Cookie

Once we have authenticated the user's credentials we use the CookieAuthentication class to issue the cookie:

```
    CookieAuthentication.RedirectFromLoginPage(txtUser.Value, true);
```

We have a several options here. Each of the following methods supports the same parameters (String username, bool createPersistenCookie):

❑   String username – The username of the authenticated user

❑   bool CreatePersistentCookie – Whether or not the cookie should be kept around after the browser is closed

Here are the three methods we can use to issue the cookie and/or redirect the user to the originally requested resource:

Method	Description
RedirectFromLoginPage()	Issues the cookie and then redirects the user to the originally requested resource. For example, when we requested default.aspx we were redirected to login.aspx. Once successfully authenticated we were redirected to default.aspx.
GetAuthCookie()	Returns an instance of a cookie class: HttpCookie. This method does not set the cookie for us, but rather allows us to control when the cookie is to be issued.
SetAuthCookie()	Sets the cookie (in the Response.Cookies collection) for the user without performing a server redirect.

Now that we've issued the cookie (in our `login.aspx` we used `RedirectFromLoginPage`) and authenticated the user, the authorization section of `config.web` will still be checked to see if the user is allowed access to the resource. Assuming the user is authorized; let's look at how we can access the authenticated user from our `default.aspx` page.

Programmatically Accessing User Identity

After we have successfully authenticated a user, by any of the supported means, we can use the `User` class to access the user name and authentication type used. The `User` class is available to us intrinsically from an ASP+ page and it supports several properties:

User.Identity Properties

Property	Description
IsAuthenticated	We can use this method to determine whether or not the user that is currently accessing a resource has been authenticated or not.
Name	Returns the name of the authenticated user. If, for example, we authenticated as rhoward, rhoward would be the return value of Name.
Type	Returns the authentication type used to authenticate the user.

Here's the example from our `default.aspx` page that tells the user they've been authenticated:

```
<script language="c#" runat=server>
  public void Page_Load(Object sender, EventArgs e) {
     user.InnerHtml = User.Identity.Name;
  }
</script>
Hello, <SPAN id=user runat=server/>, you have been authenticated by ASP+!
```

It is very easy to see that with the simplified programmatic access to a user's identity we can easily build a personalization system on ASP+ that uses the user's name as a key into a database table or directory resource. In fact, personalization is one of the features we expect to see in the final product.

Signing Off the User

Although not always necessary, users often wish to log-off the system and have the cookie removed from their computer. ASP+ HTML Forms Authentication has a method that allows us to sign-out the user:

```
CookieAuthentication.SignOut()
```

This will invalidate the cookie (even if the cookie is marked not to persist past the current browser session).

Unfortunately, there is much that we have left out of the security discussion. At a high level, some of these items include:

❑ Role based authorization (similar to what is in Microsoft Transaction Server or COM+ 1.0)

❑ User impersonation

However, you easily have enough information and context to start using ASP+'s powerful HTML Forms Authentication system.

Now that we've looked at `global.asax`, `config.web`, and how we can take advantage of one of the ASP+ application services, let's look at how we deploy our application.

Deploying the Application

Deployment of Web applications today can be somewhat difficult. Especially in large Web server farms when local machine access is required to make changes. For example, here are some tasks most developers will perform when deploying an application:

❑ **IIS Metabase Changes** – Changes to the number of ScriptEngineCaches, modification of session state, or changes to the way pages are authenticated, e.g. NTLM or Basic.

❑ **Security** – Changing the authorization aspect of a page requires server access to modify the Access Control List on file resources. This can be especially painful on large server farms.

❑ **COM and COM+ Component Registration/Updates** – Objects require registration in the registry to provide mechanisms for discovery. The command line tool `regsvr32.exe` is used to register new components, but it must be used on the local machine. In addition, when a particular object must be updated, the potential exists for both COM and IIS to 'pin' or 'lock' the associated .dll to a process. This translates to system administrators having to stop the IIS service, un-register the component, register the new component, and restart the service.

With ASP+, these types of headaches have gone away.

It Just Works

One of the goals of ASP+ was to make deployment of Web applications a simple matter of copying a file tree to a new location and 'it just works'. This is true of all ASP+ application details: Web pages, Web services, `config.web`, `global.asax`, NGWS components, etc.

Configuration Settings

We already know that `config.web` is an XML configuration file for configuring Web server settings. ASP+ uses `config.web` for all its settings and has no dependencies upon IIS beyond creating the application virtual or Web root and the associated \bin directory for compiled assemblies.

Assembly Deployment (\bin)

There are no administration or registration tools (such as regsvr32) to register objects. Assemblies contain their own metadata (object description information), and simply dropping them in the \bin directory of the application suffices for the assembly to be available to the application.

Since the \bin directory is relied upon as part of an application, it follows the same rules as `global.asax`. It must be located within an IIS Web application. This includes both IIS Web roots and virtual directories:

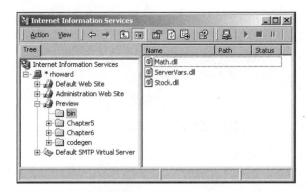

In the above screen shot the \bin directory exists within the Preview IIS Web root. Any assemblies found within, such as Math.dll, ServerVars.dll, and Stock.dll are available to the entire Preview Web application.

Application Isolation

Each Web application assembly, such as Math.dll from our screenshot above, is isolated from other Web applications. For example, our Web service Math.dll is available only within the scope of the Preview Web application. Other Web roots such as Default Web Site and Administration Web Site do not have access to Math.dll.

Thus, assemblies can be private to the application (since each contains its own \bin directory). Other applications cannot load the private assemblies or classes of a different application. So, separate applications can use different versions of the same objects without collisions on the system. For example, if we created another Math Web service that supported a Subtract() method, we could publish this version in another Web application and it would not conflict with the version that only supported Add().

Removing the Application

In addition to no regsvr32 registration, there is no regsrv32 for 'un-registration'. No entries are made into the Windows registry, thus when you delete an assembly it is completely removed from the system. In fact the entire application supports this 'delete' to uninstall philosophy, making the task of administering a Web server very easy.

Always Running

ASP+ allows us to copy an assembly (.dll files) over an existing assembly (.dll files) in a running application, even when the assembly is being used. Assemblies, which all live in the \bin directory of the application, are shadow copied by the ASP+ system. The shadowed copied is locked, but the original file in \bin is not. When an update is made to the \bin directory, ASP+ will begin handling all new requests on the new assembly, but will simultaneously compete all existing requests on the existing assembly. The application never needs to be stopped and started, and is always available to the end user.

Process Based

ASP+ is also now process based rather than thread based. The benefit is that multiple processes can be used and recycled on the system without any downtime being experienced by the end users. Settings in config.web (not discussed in this chapter) allow us to configure how many processes to use and when those processes should be 're-booted'. This process-based model is similar to Apache in that processes can die (or be killed) and restarted as other processes continue to fulfill user requests.

For beta 1, the areas of deployment that you need to be familiar with have more to do with building and using assemblies than deployment. When you write custom assemblies, or use those provided by the ASP+ quickstart samples, you will have to run batch files to compile the files.

Let's take a look at some of the common command line switches we should be familiar with when working with the command line compilers.

Command Line Compilers

In Chapter 5 we discussed a Math assembly that we used for Web services (generated by our `WebServiceUtil.exe` tool). A batch file is provided with the sample, and we deferred the discussion of command line compilers to Chapter 6. Let's look at how we would compile our Math assembly without the benefit of the batch file:

```
csc /t:library /r:system.web.services.dll /r:system.dll
    /r:system.xml.serialization.dll /out:math.dll math.cs
```

The Visual Basic 7 command line compiler is `vbc.exe` and the C# command line compiler is `csc.exe`.

Here's the before and after of running the C# compiler with the line from above:

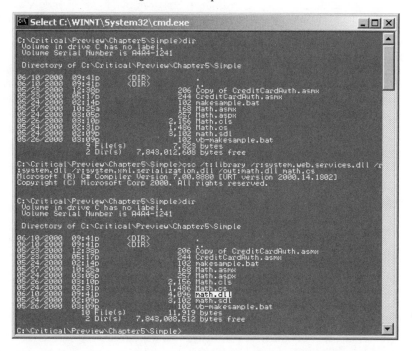

We are using the C# compiler to build an assembly from the C# source file Math.cs with an output file of Math.dll (highlighted). Once the file(.dll) is compiled we still need to register it in our application's \bin directory for it to be available to our application.

You can find the command line compilers in the \winnt\ComPlus\v2000.14.1802\ directory tree after installing the NGWS SDK bits.

Let's examine the compiler switches used above in more detail.

Frequently Used Compiler Switches

Here are the compiler switches you should be familiar with when using the command line compiler for VB7 and C#:

Switch	Description
/t[arget]: [module|library|exe|winexe]	The target switch specifies the target output type of the compiled resource. library is used to create a standalone file that contains code plus metadata for a given class or classes. We use /t:library whenever we want to build an assembly that we use in an ASP+ resource (page, global.asax, Web Service, etc.).
/r[eference]:<file>	When you use the processing directive Assembly in either global.asax or on a page, you are specifying an assembly that contains metadata and classes that you need within your class instance. The /r switch is used to perform a similar function within a compiled resource. For example, if you created a new namespace and used the using keyword to bring System.Web namespace into the scope of the class, you would need to specify [path]\System.Web.dll with an /r: switch, otherwise you would get a compiler error.
/out:<file>	The out switch simply specifies the output of the compiler. For libraries we specify [filename].dll and for exe's we specify [filename].exe – simple!

Now that we've seen the compiler switches to create assemblies, let's talk about how we view the resources in a assembly.

Viewing Assemblies

Now that we've learned how to create assemblies with the command line compilers, how do we view them? If you to open up an assembly with Visual Studio 6 OLE-VIEW you're going to be disappointed, as OLE-VIEW can't be used to view assemblies.

However, as you would expect, we do have an alternative solution!

Class Browser

Once you've created an assembly or when you wish to familiarize yourself with some of the NGWS components, the Class Browser is an invaluable tool:

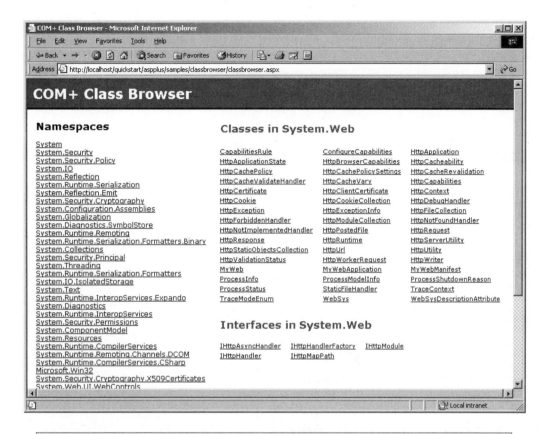

The class browser is accessible from
/quickstart/aspplus/samples/classbrowser/classbrowser.aspx.

We're not going to drill into the details of the Class Browser, as it is fairly self-explanatory. However, we do need to know how we can add additional assemblies to the Namespace view.

Viewing other assemblies

We can modify the assemblies available in the Class Browser by editing the `config.web` in the /classbrowser/ directory:

```
<configuration>
    <configsections>
        <add name="ClassBrowser"
             type="System.Web.Configuration.DictionarySectionHandler"/>
    </configsections>

    <ClassBrowser>
        <set key="ASP+ Class Library" value="System.Web.dll" />
        <set key="Base Class Library" value="mscorlib.dll" />
    </ClassBrowser>
</configuration>
```

To add assemblies, we simply add the appropriate entry for the `<ClassBrowser>` configuration section settings. For example, if we wanted to view classes in `System.Net`, we would make the following addition:

```
<set key="Net Class Library" value="System.Net.dll" />
```

The same is true for custom assemblies that you have written or purchased.

Writing a Custom HttpHandler

Microsoft Internet Information Server exposes its raw API via ISAPI (Internet Service Application Programming Interface). ASP 3.0 is, in fact, an ISAPI extension (`ASP.dll`). ISAPI, however, requires the developer to code the implementation in a language that supports multi-threading, most usually C++, and to the exclusion of most ASP script and VB COM developers.

ASP+ builds upon something known as the HTTP runtime framework. We'll save the complete discussion of the HTTP Runtime Framework for another book. However, there are a few things you should know.

HTTP Runtime

Similar to ISAPI, the HTTP Runtime Framework provides a solution for developers who want to get to the low-level request/response semantics of the Web server. However, unlike ISAPI, programming this low-level request/response framework can be done in any NGWS runtime language, so enabling a broader developer audience to leverage this technology.

Creating our Own HttpHandler

As we read earlier, requests (`.aspx`, `.asmx`) are serviced through HttpHandlers named in `config.web` by `<httphandlers>` tags. Let's take a look at how we could write a custom HttpHandler that simply returns the server variables of the Web server using the HTTP Runtime.

> *Before we walk through the code, I think it is worthwhile noting that I wrote the same code in C++ using ISAPI, and the HttpHandler sample took 1/3 as much code, and is infinitely easier to understand.*

To create our own HttpHandler, we need to implement the `IHttpHandler` interface.

IHttpHandler Interface

`IHttpHandler` is an interface defined in the `System.Web.dll` assembly, and defines two abstract methods:

```
void ProcessRequest(class System.Web.HttpContext)
bool IsReusable()
```

All HttpHandlers implement these two methods. In fact, the entire ASP+ programming framework is simply an implementation on top of the HTTP Runtime Framework, and `System.Web.UI.Page` class (which all ASP+ pages derive from) implements IHttpHandler.

Let's take a look at a sample `IHttpHandler` written in C# that dumps the server variables:

C# IHttpHandler Implementation

```
using System.Web;
using System.Collections;
```

We first bring in the namespaces of both `System.Web` and `System.Collections`. We'll be using the `IHttpHandler` interface defined in `System.Web` and we'll be using the `NameValueCollection` defined in `System.Collections`.

Next, we implement the two methods from `IHttpHandler`: `ProcessRequest()` and `IsReusable()`:

```
namespace Simple
{
  // Returns the Server Variables
  public class ReturnServerVariables : IHttpHandler
  {
    public void ProcessRequest(HttpContext context)
    {
      // Initialize method variables
      NameValueCollection ServerVars;

      // Grab the headers and Server Variables
      ServerVars = context.Request.ServerVariables;

      // Enumerate ove items
      for (int i = 0; i < ServerVars.Count; i++)
      {
        context.Response.Write( (string) ServerVars.GetKey(i) + ": ");
        context.Response.Write( (string) ServerVars.Get(i));
        context.Response.Write("<BR>");
      }
    }

    public bool IsReusable()
    {
      return true;
    }
  }
}
```

`IsReuable()` returns `true` or `false` and is used to specify whether this class can be reused. The interesting method is `ProcessRequest()`; this is where we do the work of the `HttpHandler`.

Inside of `ProcessRequest()` we create a method variable named `ServerVars` of type `NameValueCollection`. We then assign this variable the ServerVariables collection, which is available to us as a property of the Request object.

Next, we simply iterate over the available number of keys in the `NameValueCollection` of `ServerVars` and write out the key and the value:

```
for (int i = 0; i < ServerVars.Count; i++)
{
  context.Response.Write( (string) ServerVars.GetKey(i) + ": ");
  context.Response.Write( (string) ServerVars.Get(i));
  context.Response.Write("<BR>");
}
```

We then must compile `ServerVars.dll` by running a batch file that uses the command line C# compiler and move the resulting `.dll` to our application's \bin directory. Next, we create a `config.web` file that has an entry for our custom HttpHandler.

Config.Web <httphandler> entry

```
<configuration>
    <httphandlers>
        <add verb="*" path="sv.aspx"
            type="ServerVars#Simple.ReturnServerVariables" />
    </httphandlers>
</configuration>
```

In our `config.web` file we allow all HTTP verbs and match only with the path `sv.aspx`. When a match to this path comes in, we call our HttpHandler: `ServerVars#Simple.ReturnServerVariables`, and we can then make a request for `sv.aspx`:

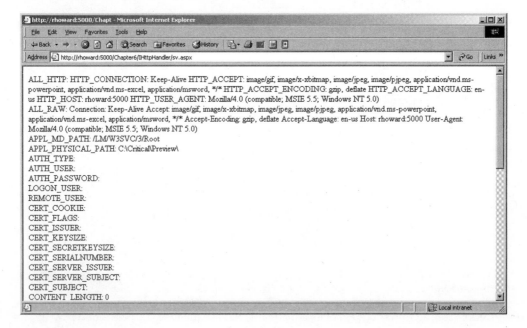

Summary

In this chapter we covered `global.asax` where we learned that there are new events available that we can participate in, and that, just like ASP+ pages, `global.asax` is compiled. In addition we learned that we no longer need to start and stop the Web server in order to make changes to `global.asax`.

Next, we looked at the XML based `config.web` file used to configure various features, and we saw how we no longer have a dependency upon the IIS metabase. We also looked at the various sections of `config.web` and learned that we can easily extend it for our own purposes.

After looking at `config.web` we explored one of (the many) great features of ASP+: HTML Forms Authentication. We looked at several of the classes and methods and then built a small sample.

Next, we looked at what is involved with deploying the application. In this discussion, we covered the command line compiler switches, and looked at the Class Browser.

Finally, we wrote our own HttpHandler implementation to dump the server variables.

Overall, the topics we covered were:

- ❑ Using the global application file: `global.asax`
- ❑ Application Configuration
- ❑ Authentication and Authorization Services
- ❑ Deploying the Application
- ❑ Writing a Custom HttpHandler

In the next chapter we'll delve deeper into building custom controls that we can reuse or sell.

Building Custom ASP+ Controls

7

Since the early days of OLE and COM, developers around the world have been building reusable visual controls. In the early 90s building such controls required significant time and investment to understand the myriad of COM interfaces that a control had to implement. And this didn't include the numerous interfaces a control had to use to talk to a container application such as Microsoft Word, where it had to correctly negotiate screen real estate for its UI, merging menus etc.

In the mid/late 90s, C/C++ frameworks like the Microsoft Foundation Classes (MFC) and the Active Template Library (ATL) made control development a little easier. They provided ready-reusable classes and templates that hid a lot of complexity, but the true breakthrough in popular control development was in 1996 with the release of the Visual Basic Control Creation edition. It was then that control creation became truly simple and very popular.

The upside of control development, and the reason why people still write so many controls today, is reusability. Once you have conquered visual control development, the reward of being able to write a control once (the grid control being the canonical example) and then reuse it in numerous **control containers** (such as Word, Excel, etc.) makes it worth all the pain. You can, of course, reuse the control in your own suite of products, not to mention that fact you could also make a good living selling the control to other developers. These same advantages apply in the world of ASP+ controls, but there is one big difference: **ASP+ controls are easy to write from day one**.

ASP+ allows you to build reusable visual controls that render themselves as HTML or other text based formats such as WML. Many parallels can be drawn between COM controls and ASP+ controls, as they both enable reuse within UIs. But in reality, they are very different in the way they are implemented. ASP+ provides a clean and easy-to-use class hierarchy for implementing controls, and there are no esoteric interfaces or threading models that are difficult to understand (i.e. what they are there for, when they are called, and by what containers). ASP+ still uses some interfaces, but there really aren't more than three or four that you'll use on a regular basis.

In this chapter we're going to look at ASP+ control development covering:

❑ When, why, and how you can build ASP+ controls in VB and C#

❑ How controls form the basis of **all** page rendering in ASP+

❑ How controls persist state across page invocation

❑ Building controls that themselves use other controls to render their UI

❑ Building controls with a user interface that can be customized using templates

Writing a Simple Control

To demonstrate the basic principles of control development and to show how easy ASP+ control development is, we'll kick off the chapter by writing a simple Label control that can render a text message. We'll initially develop the control in C#, review the code, and then rewrite it using VB. This example will hopefully prove to you that control development really isn't that difficult, and it is, at the very least, worth understanding how controls are written so you can better understand how ASP+ renders pages.

Creating a C# Control

Like the rest of this book, everything in this chapter is created using Windows NotePad and the command line compilers.

Fire up your text editor of choice and enter the following C# code:

```
using System;
using System.Web;
using System.Web.UI;

namespace WroxControls
{
    public class MyFirstControl : Control
    {
        protected override void Render(HtmlTextWriter writer)
        {
            writer.Write("<h1>ASP+ Control Development in C#</h1>");
        }
    }
};
```

Save the file and call it QuickStart.cs. Let's briefly examine the code. The first few lines of the code import three **code namespaces** that controls typically use:

❑ System – contains core system classes like String. The code will compile without this, but as 99.99% of controls make use of the core classes it is always good practise to include it.

❑ System.Web – the parent namespace for all ASP+ classes. This contains classes like HttpRequest (the ASP+ Request object) and HttpResponse (the ASP+ Response object). Again, the code will compile without this, but as with the System namespace, most control classes will use the ASP+ intrinsic objects so it is good practice to add it

❏ System.Web.UI – contains the ASP+ control classes, many of which are divided up into child code namespaces based upon their family (System.Web.UI.WebControls , System.Web.UI.HtmlControls, etc.). This reference is needed as we are using the Control and HtmlTextWriter classes in the control.

> **Namespaces are used to group related classes and interfaces logically in COM+ and help reduce name clashes.**

The next line of the code marks the beginning scope of a new namespace we have chosen for our control, called WroxControls:

```
namespace WroxControls
{
```

Anything declared within the next section of the code, until the closing namespace statement seven lines later, is a member of the WroxControls namespace. This means that the full namespace-qualified reference to our control is WroxControls.MyFirstControl. Any code using our class must use this full name unless the Using directive is included to import all definitions within our namespace into its default scope.

The next five lines of code declare the class for our control:

```
public class MyFirstControl : Control
{
    protected override void Render(HtmlTextWriter writer)
    {
        writer.Write("<h1>ASP+ Control Development in C#</h1>");
    }
}
```

The class is called MyFirstControl. It is derived from the class Control, is declared as public, and has one protected function called Render.

The name of the class is arbitrary and you can call your controls whatever you like, as they are defined in your own namespace. Where possible you should avoid using names that are already used by ASP+ (or any other part of the runtime), as name conflicts will occur if two namespaces are imported using the @Import directive by a page or the using directive inside a source file. If you decided to create your own label control, do not call it Label; call it YourLabel or some other meaningful name such as WroxLabel.

By marking our class as public we are stating that **anybody** can create an instance of our class and use it. If we specify that it is private (by omitting the public attribute), the class will only be usable by other classes within the same namespace. If an ASP+ page attempts to access a private class, the runtime will raise an error saying the class/type is not defined. This is somewhat confusing when trying to track down an error, so it is always worth checking the access control of a class as it is easy to forget to add the public keyword when developing.

If you mark a class using the internal attribute, it can only be used by other classes within the same assembly.

The Render function is declared using the override attribute. This attribute tells the compiler that the base class Control implements the Render function, but our class wants to override the function so that it can control the output created at runtime itself. The implementation of this method calls the Write method of the HtmlTextWriter object, which results in the HTML "<h1>ASP+ Control Development in C#</h1>" being written to the page output stream.

> **We don't cover the HtmlTextWriter class in any more detail in this chapter. Make sure you check out the class in ILDASM if you are developing controls that output lots of HTML. The class can automatically generate element tags, attributes, and styles for you.**

The position of the HTML that a control creates in the final page depends upon where that control is declared inside the ASP+ page code. The Render method is called by the ASP+ page framework when it encounters one or more elements in an ASP+ page that have been associated with our ASP+ control using the @Register page directive:

```
<%@ Register TagPrefix="Wrox" Namespace="WroxControls" %>
<html>
<body>

<Wrox:MyFirstControl runat="server" />

</body>
</html>
```

This directive tells the ASP+ runtime that when it hits any element in the 'Wrox:' namespace it should search the namespace WroxControls for a class whose name matches the element name (i.e. MyFirstControl). If the control exists, create an instance of it, and call its Render function to allow it to write data to the output stream being created (the page).

In this example, once our control has inserted its HTML into the output stream, the final page will look like this:

```
<html>
<body>

<h1>ASP+ Control Development in C#</h1>

</body>
</html>
```

The actual rendering of which is shown here:

To test the ASP+ page yourself and view the output, you need to compile the C# source code to create an assembly. This is placed into the bin directory of the application on your Web server, causing the ASP+ runtime to scan the assembly and make an internal note of the namespaces and classes/controls within it.

Compiling the C# Control and Creating an Assembly

To compile the class, bring up your text editor, enter the following batch commands, and save the file as make.bat:

```
set outdir = \aspplus\bin\MyFirstControl.dll
set assemblies = System.dll, System.Web.dll

csc /t:library /out:%outdir% /r:%assemblies% MyFirstControl.cs
```

> For the class to compile correctly, you'll need to change the **aspplus** directory to match a directory on your machine that is configured as a virtual directory.

The first two lines of the make.bat file declare a couple of variables. These make the line that actually does the compilation more readable. The compiler options are discussed in Chapter 6. The important points to note about this file are:

❑   A reference to the System.dll and System.Web.dll assemblies is added using the /r parameter. We have to do this so that the compiler knows where to search for the namespaces/classes we import into our control with the using directive. If you do not add a reference to the assembly containing referenced classes you'll get a compile error.

❑   The output of the compiler (MyFirstControl.dll) is placed directly into our Web application's bin directory. When the ASP+ detects that a file assembly is placed into the bin directoy it will examine metadata it contains and know where to locate the WroxControls namespace we specify in the page's @Register directive. By doing it as part of the compilation, we are less likely to forget to copy the assembly.

Save the file, then run it from a command prompt. The output you see should look something like this:

If all goes well, check that the `bin` directory contains the compiled assembly. If it exists, you should be able to open the test page we described earlier and see the output of the control.

Control Complete

Although the C# control we have just developed is about as simple as it gets, you have just seen the full development cycle required for a simple ASP+ control. Hopefully you now believe that: (a) control development is nothing like it was in the COM days, and (b) maybe control development is worth checking out in more detail. Things will get more advanced from here on in, but all of the code is clean and fairly easy to understand once you've grasped the basic concepts that we've been discussing.

To show that control development in Visual Basic is just as painless, we'll create an almost identical control called `MyFirstControlInVB`.

Control Development in Visual Basic

One of the great things about version 7.0 of Visual Basic is that the language has been dragged into the 21st Century with a bang (see Appendix B). It now has all the object-oriented (OO) features that make it a first class programming language (and, coming from a seasoned C/C++ programmer, that's not an easy thing to admit!). However, as you'd expect, the VB team and C# teams at Microsoft are competing with each other for adopters, and as a result they have used different names for certain attributes and directives that they feel are more suitable for their audience of programmers. This is fair enough, but it does means that switching between the languages can be a little confusing at first.

Here are a few notes on the language differences that should help you convert any of the samples in this chapter between C# and VB:

C# Example	VB Example
`Using System;`	`Imports System`

`Namespace WroxControls {`
    `...`
`};`
	`Namespace WroxControls`
	    `...`
	`End Namespace`

`Public class A : B {`
    `...`
`}`
	`Public Class A`
	    `Inherits B`
	    `...`
	`End Class`

Creating the VB Label Control

Create a new file for the VB control called `MyFirstControlInVB.cls` and enter this code:

```
Imports System
Imports System.Web.UI

Namespace WroxControls

    Public Class MyFirstControlInVB

    Inherits Control
```

```
        Overrides Sub Render(writer as HtmlTextWriter)
          writer.Write("<h1>ASP+ Control Development in VB</h1>")
        End Sub

    End Class

End Namespace
```

Using the table above, you should be able to see how the code has been translated from C#. The main changes are:

- All references to `Using` have been replaced with `Imports`.

- All the trailing C-style syntax semicolons have been removed.

- All opening curly brackets have been removed, and the closing curly brackets replaced with the more verbose VB syntax of `End Class`, `End Namespace`, etc.

- The `Class` declaration has had the trailing `': Control'` text removed, and a separate line, `Inherits Control`, has been added to replace it.

- The method declaration order has been switched around as VB declares the name of a variable first and then the type, whereas C# does the opposite.

The other change to note is that we have changed the HTML output to say **VB** rather than C#, so the browser output is now rendered like this:

To build the assembly containing this new class, create a file called `makevb.bat` and enter the following commands:

```
set outdir = \aspplus\bin\MyFirstControlInVB.DLL
set assemblies = c:\winnt\complus\v2000.14.1715\System.Web.dll
vbc /t:library /out:%outdir% /r:%assemblies% MyFirstControlInVB.cls
```

This is similar to the C# `make` file except that the compiler name is now `vbc` rather than `csc`, the output file is now `MyFirstControlInVB.DLL`, and the `assemblies` parameter has been changed to a full path. This last point is a requirement of the current VB compiler, but it will probably change and behave like C# in the final release.

Run the make file to compile the control, then bring up your text editor and enter following ASP+ page code. Save it as `testpagevb.aspx`:

```
<%@ Register TagPrefix="Wrox" Namespace="WroxControls" %>
<html>
<body>

<Wrox:MyFirstControlInVB runat="server" />

</body>
</html>
```

The page is pretty much identical to the ASP+ page that used the C# version of the control, but we have changed the line in the `<body>` element to specify the class `MyFirstControlInVB` instead of `MyFirstControl`. The ASP+ runtime knows where this class lives (it will have scanned the `MyFirstControlInVB.DLL` assembly), so it can exist side by side with the C# control, and the namespace logically spans the two assemblies.

After you have viewed the page to prove your VB control is working, add an additional line to the page to render both the C# and VB controls on the same page:

```
<%@ Register TagPrefix="Wrox" Namespace="WroxControls" %>
<html>
<body>
<Wrox:MyFirstControlInVB runat="server" />
<Wrox:MyFirstControl runat="server" />
</body>
</html>
```

View this in the browser and you should see the output from the two label controls:

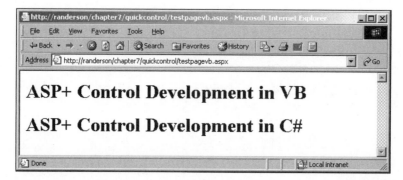

As expected, both controls have rendered themselves in the output stream depending upon their location in the ASP+ page. The ASP+ page framework doesn't care what language the controls are written in, as long as they are derived from the `Control` class.

Now we have run though the basics of control building in C# and VB, let's look a little closer at why you might want to write your own control. We'll look at alternative ways of rendering output, and the additional features like event handlers that you can add to your controls to make them more functional and sophisticated.

Why Create Your Own Controls?

All ASP+ dynamic pages are created by the ASP+ runtime using ASP+ controls. Although you may not have realised it, we have already built several ASP+ controls in the earlier chapters of this book just by creating ASP+ pages and pagelets. The ASP+ page framework (NGWS framework) automatically compiles the files you create into ASP+ controls behind the scenes, and somewhere in their class hierarchy, these classes eventually derive from the `Control` class we have just been using:

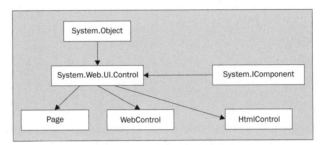

If you open up the `.dll` assembly that ASP+ created for our `testpage.aspx` page earlier (it will be one of the files located in the `codegen` directory), you can see that ASP+ has created a class called `testpage_aspx`, which extends (i.e. derives from) the class `System.Web.UI.Page`:

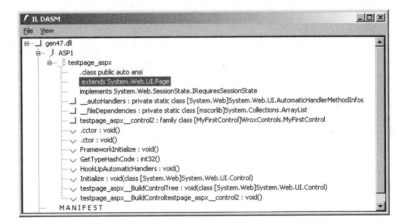

The page object (located in the assembly `System.Web.dll`) in turn derives from the `Control` class:

The actual code generated by ASP+ for the `testpage.aspx` page is not that different to the code we have just written for our `Label` controls. It is more advanced, because it uses **control composition** to actually generate the page, but the basic principles of creation and rendering are similar. So 'Why Create Your Own Controls?' isn't really the right question to ask.

Instead, the decision you actually have to make as an ASP+ developer is whether you let ASP+ build the controls automatically (by just building your sites using ASP+ pages and/or pagelets), or whether you take over some of the control creation yourself. In the latter case, you can build your site using a mixture of ASP+ pages, pagelets, and custom server controls. So there is no single answer to the original question, but here are a few pointers that should help you choose:

❑ ASP+ controls enable a fine-grained level of black box reuse. ASP+ pagelets and pages can also provide this reuse, but since they are far more course-grained and have fixed UI traits, they are likely to provide far less reuse.

❑ ASP+ controls ultimately provide the most flexibility, but take longer to write and require more coding skill.

❑ If you think you want a custom control, but are not 100% sure, start with a pagelet as you can always change it to be a custom control later. All the code you write will work as a control, but you will need to convert any HTML section of your pagelet into code using control composition.

❑ Only custom controls can be 'lookless', and therefore support templates. If you want people to be able to extend and manage the UI of your control, create it as a custom ASP+ control.

❑ Pagelets and custom controls can be written in different languages, and then used within the same hosting page. At present only one language can be used directly within any single ASP+ page.

Now we've established that everything you do is based around controls, lets go back to the simple control we created earlier and rewrite it using **control composition**.

> From this point on, we will only be showing the code samples in C#, but using the table shown earlier you should be able to understand and convert the code. And although we are using C#, we could just as easliy have used VB. However, you might be interested to know that ASP+ is written in C#, which is an indication that the language has a strong following inside of Microsoft.

Composite Controls

The `Render` method for the control we wrote earlier places its output directly into the HTML output steam using the `Write` method of the `HtmlTextWriter` object. An alternative is to use other controls to output the HTML you require. The `Control` class has a `Controls` property of the type `ControlsCollection` to which child controls can be added as shown in this code:

```
using System;
using System.Web.UI;

namespace WroxControls
{
    public class MyFirstControl : Control
    {
        protected override void CreateChildControls()
        {
            LiteralControl text;
```

```
            text = new LiteralControl(
                    "<h1>ASP+ Control Development in C#</h1>" );
        Controls.Add(text);
    }
  }
};
```

In this code we have removed the Render function and replaced it with this CreateChildControls function. The ASP+ framework calls this function before a control is rendered, allowing it to populate its child control collection (Controls), and prepare its UI by creating one or more controls to represent it. By removing the Render method from our class, the default implementation of the Render function defined in the Control class is called some time after CreateChildControls.

The default Render function enumerates the Controls collection and invokes the RenderControl method of each child control in sequence. This effectively causes our control's UI to be drawn, by allowing each child control to output HTML by either using the HtmlTextWriter object, or by also using child controls.

Using control composition for our simple control really doesn't buy us any advantage over rendering the HTML directly using HtmlTextWriter. To see when there is actually a greater advantage in using it, however, let's increase the complexity of our control's UI by creating an HTML table below our <h1> element. The table will contain 10 rows, each with 5 cells. We could render this using the HtmlTextWriter or by creating lots of LiteralControl objects, but it makes a lot more sense to use the high level ASP+ Web controls we have seen in earlier chapters of this book. Although we have typically only made references to these controls in early parts of the book, creating these controls is straightforward:

```
using System;
using System.Web;
using System.Web.UI;
using System.Web.UI.WebControls;

namespace WroxControls
{
    public class MyFirstControl : Control
    {
        Table _table;  // Make table a member so we can access it at any point

        protected override void CreateChildControls()
        {
            LiteralControl text;

            text = new LiteralControl(
                    "<h1>ASP+ Control Development in C#</h1>");
            Controls.Add(text);

            TableRow row;
            TableCell cell;

            // Create a table and set a 2 pixel border

            _table = new Table();
            _table.BorderWidth = 2;
```

```
            Controls.Add(_table);

            // Add 10 row each with 5 cells

            for(int x = 0; x < 10; x++) {
                // Create a row and add it to the table

                row = new TableRow();
                _table.Rows.Add(row);

                // Create a cell that contains the text

                for(int y = 0; y < 5; y++) {

                    text = new LiteralControl("Row: " + x + " Cell: " + y);

                    cell = new TableCell();
                    cell.Controls.Add(text);

                    row.Cells.Add(cell);
                }
            }
        }
    }
};
```

This code may look at bit complex at first, but what it's doing is very simple. Firstly, it adds the
LiteralControl containing the <h1> element as a child control. Next, it creates a Table object
(System.Web.UI.WebControls.Table), sets the border width to two pixels, and adds that as a
child control:

```
_table = new Table();
_table.BorderWidth = 2;

Controls.Add( _table );
```

The table is then populated with rows by running a for loop for ten iterations, creating and adding a
TableRow object using the Rows collection property:

```
row = new TableRow();
table.Rows.Add( row );
```

Finally, for each row that is added, an inner loop is executed for five iterations adding a TableCell
object that has a LiteralControl as its child. The Text of the LiteralControl is set to indicate the
current row and cell. Compiling and executing this code produces the following:

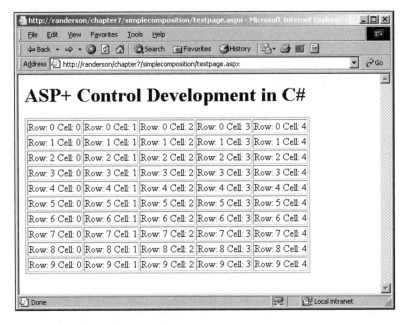

All of the controls we have used (`Table`, `TableRow`, `TableCell` etc.) derive from the `Control` class somewhere in their hierarchy, and it's therefore logical to assume that they all use control composition. We can picture this control hierarchy as follows:

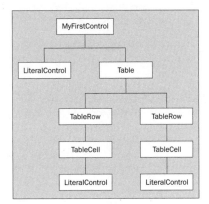

If you view the source for this page you'll see around **130** lines of HTML. We didn't directly create any of the HTML, and we have gained a number of key advantages by using control composition over direct rendering:

- ❑ We have saved ourselves a great deal of error-prone coding.

- ❑ We have programmatically created objects, called methods, and set properties. The code we've written is therefore simple to read, clean, and easily extendable at a later date.

- ❑ We have not been exposed to the underlying HTML generated by the various controls we have used.

❑ The fact that they actually render `table`, `tr` and `td` HTML elements to the page is an implementation detail we do not have to concern ourselves with. In theory, the output can be WML or any other markup language – and our control will still work just fine.

❑ The control we are writing can focus on its objective, rather than being bogged down by lots of HTML generation code.

The argument for using composite controls gets stronger as the child controls we use, such as the `Table` control, provide more and more functionality – and hence save us more time and effort. For example, let's modify our table so that the user can edit each of the cells within it by using a `TextBox` control within our `TableCell` control, rather than a `LiteralControl`:

```
for( int y=0; y < 5; y++ ) {

    TextBox textbox;

    textbox = new TextBox();
    textbox.Text = "Row: " + x + " Cell: " + y;

    cell = new TableCell();
    ...
```

By changing three lines of code we now have an editable table – we've changed the values in a few cells to show that it really is editable:

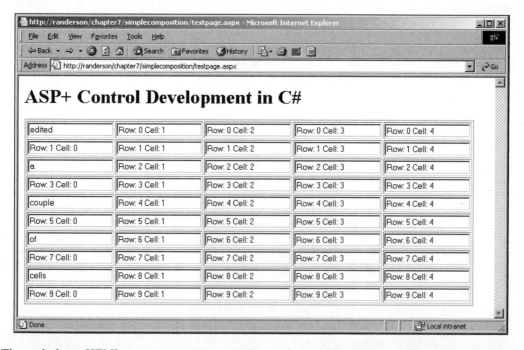

The underlying HTML is now even more complex, with the ASP+ Web controls creating all the `input` elements needed within the `td` elements. It has also automatically assigned each input box a unique name:

```
...
<tr>
  <td>
    <input name="ctrl23" type="text" value="Row: 1 Cell: 0">
  </td><td>
    <input name="ctrl26" type="text" value="Row: 1 Cell: 1">
  </td><td>
    <input name="ctrl29" type="text" value="Row: 1 Cell: 2">
  </td><td>
    <input name="ctrl32" type="text" value="Row: 1 Cell: 3">
  </td><td>
    <input name="ctrl35" type="text" value="Row: 1 Cell: 4">
  </td>
</tr>
...
```

The control `ids` are assigned sequentially by ASP+ as the child controls are created and added to our control. When a post-back occurs, ASP+ uses these `ids` to push the data that the user entered in the textboxes into the server side objects that are created by our `CreateChildControls` function.

Control Properties

To make our table a little more flexible, we'll add three properties that make our control dimensions and header text configurable:

Name	Type	Description
Rows	Integer	The number of rows to draw
Columns	Integer	The numbers of cells to draw
Title	String	The title to display at the top of the table

These properties will be set in our test page as attributes of the `Wrox:MyFirstControl` element:

```
<%@ Register TagPrefix="Wrox" Namespace="WroxControls" %>
<html>
<body>
<Wrox:MyFirstControl id="table" rows="3" columns="5"
       title="My Table Control" runat="server" />
</body>
</html>
```

When ASP+ sees these attributes it will treat the attribute names as property names, and expect our control to implement the appropriate property `Set` handlers. If we don't implement these properties on our control, or the user mistypes the name, an error will be displayed.

Attribute Value Conversion

When ASP+ matches an attribute to a property it will perform intelligent conversion of the value if needed. If our class property is a string, then ASP+ will just do a simple mapping. If the property is an integer or long, the attribute value will be converted to a number, then set. If a value is an enumeration, ASP+ will match the string value against an enumeration name, and then pass in the associated integer value for that enumeration value. The same type of logical conversion occurs for others types such as `Boolean`.

229

> **Never use integer values like 0, 1 or 2 to represent options such as Day, Month and Year in your controls. Always try use an enumeration, as the ASP+ runtime can then help you and your users catch errors earlier. Of course, this means that you should try not to change your enumeration values once a control goes into production.**

Adding Properties

To implement the property get/set code for the `Title`, `Rows` and `Columns` properties, we add the following code to our class:

```
public class MyFirstControl : Control
{
    int _rows;
    int _columns;
    string _title;

    public int Rows {
        get {
            return _rows;
        }
        set {
            _rows = value;
        }
    }

    public int Columns {
        get {
            return _columns; .
        }
        set {
            _columns= value;
        }
    }

    public string Title {
        get {
            return _title;
        }
        set {
            _title = value;
        }
    }
    ...
```

These property handlers just map the various properties to some local variables that we have defined within the class. With the property handlers in place, we just need to change our `CreateChildControl` function to use these handlers to create the correct number of rows and columns (or cells):

```
    ...
    protected override void CreateChildControls()
    {
        LiteralControl text;
```

```
        text = new LiteralControl("<h1>" + Title + "</h1>");
        Controls.Add(table);
        ...

    // Add rows

    for(int x = 0; x < Rows; x++) {
        ...

        // Create a cell that contains the text

        for(int y = 0; y < Columns; y++) {
        ...
```

Compile the changes, and view the page with our new attributes, and you'll see that the table has used the attributes and rendered itself accordingly:

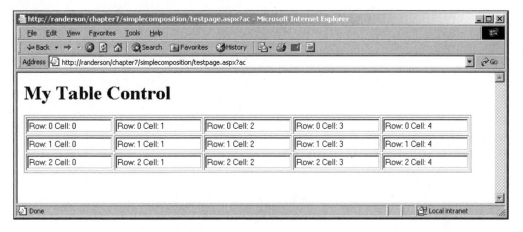

Now our control is starting to take shape, let's spend a little time looking at state management.

State Management and Naming Containers

If our control allows a user to edit the values, we obviously want to process the new values and do something with them when a post-back occurs. Given that the CreateChildControls code always initializes the cell Text property, you might think that any changes made by the user will be lost. To see if this is the case, we'll modify the page, wrapping our control in a server-side <form> element (containing the runat="server" attribute), and adding an ASP:Button element that we can click to cause a post-back:

```
<%@ Register TagPrefix="Wrox" Namespace="WroxControls" %>
<html>
<body>
<form runat="server">
<Wrox:MyFirstControl id="table" rows="3" columns="5"
        title="My Table Control" runat="server" />
<p>
<asp:Button Text="Post Back" runat="server" />
</form>
</body>
</html>
```

View this page in the browser, edit some values then click the Post Back button. The values you entered seem to have been lost. The TextBox control is capable of retaining state during post-back, but the problem is that our control has not signalled to the ASP+ runtime that it is an **ID naming container**. In other words, it contains child controls that want to manage state. To signal to the ASP+ runtime that our child controls should be given the opportunity to be invoked when the serialization process of our control occurs, we must implement the INamingContainer interface.

INamingContainer

The INamingContainer interface is a **marker interface,** and therefore has no methods that our class has to implement. The ASP+ runtime just checks for its presence in our control's class hierarchy to decide whether serialization of our child control's state should occur.

To support this interface, we change our class statement to derive from the INamingContainer interface:

```
public class MyFirstControl : Control, INamingContainer
```

At runtime, ASP+ now knows to enumerate our control's child controls and persist their values. If we go back to our page now, edit some values, and click the button to cause a post-back, we'll see that our values have been retained. To understand why this now magically works, we have to look at some of the HTML for our control:

```
<tr>
  <td>
    <input name="table:ctrl4" type="text" value="Row: 0 Cell: 0">
  </td><td>
    <input name="table:ctrl7" type="text" value="Row: 0 Cell: 1">
  </td><td>
    <input name="table:ctrl10" type="text" value="Row: 0 Cell: 2">
  </td><td>
    <input name="table:ctrl13" type="text" value="Row: 0 Cell: 3">
  </td><td>
    <input name="table:ctrl16" type="text" value="Row: 0 Cell: 4">
  </td>
</tr>
```

Each of the input elements generated by our textboxes now has a **hierarchical name** where the "table" section of the name represents the name of our control (Wrox:MyFirstControl) and ctrl*nn* represents the various textboxes that are created as **children** of that parent control. During a post-back, ASP+ uses these hierarchal names to walk the control tree of the ASP+ page to track down individual controls, seeding them with the state that was originally rendered as part of the page or entered by the user. The control creation code in CreateChildControls occurs before this, so any initial default values we create just get overwritten.

A Control's StateBag

Before ASP+ renders the final output of a page, each child control on the page is given an opportunity to persist its state. This serialization process is carried out by calling the SaveState function (defined in the Control class) of each control. The default implementation of the SaveState function (it can be overridden) returns the State object property. This is declared as a StateBag class in the Control class, and is essentially a simple wrapper around the Hashtable class.

The `object` reference returned from `SaveState` is converted into a special encoded string by the ASP+ runtime, and saved as part of the viewstate for a page. When a post-back occurs and controls on a page are recreated, and the `LoadState` method of each control that had state is called, the call to this function is passed in an `object` reference created from the viewstate. The object instance is different to that returned by `SaveState`, but all of the properties are the same.

The default implementations of `SaveState` and `LoadState` mean that controls like the `TextBox` typically manage their state using the `State` object property. Any values placed into this 'state bag' are seemingly magically persisted across roundtrips to the server. To introduce state management into our controls and understand why/when it is needed, we'll add four buttons to our test ASP+ page that manipulate the state of our control. These buttons will increase and decrease the `Rows` and `Columns` properties for our control:

```
<%@ Page Trace="True" %>
<%@ Register TagPrefix="Wrox" Namespace="WroxControls" %>
<html>
<body>
```

```csharp
<SCRIPT language="C#" runat="server">

    protected void AddRow(object sender, EventArgs e) {
        table.Rows++;
    }

    protected void RemoveRow(object sender, EventArgs e) {
        table.Rows--;
    }

    protected void AddColumn(object sender, EventArgs e) {
        table.Columns++;
    }

    protected void RemoveColumn(object sender, EventArgs e) {
        table.Columns--;
    }

</SCRIPT>
```

```
<form runat="server" >
<Wrox:MyFirstControl id="table" rows="3" columns="5"
     Title="My Table Control" runat="server" />
<p />
```

```
<asp:button Text="Add Row" OnClick="AddRow" runat="server" />
<asp:button Text="Remove Row" OnClick="RemoveRow" runat="server" />
<asp:button Text="Add Column" OnClick="AddColumn" runat="server" />
<asp:button Text="Remove Colum" OnClick="RemoveColumn" runat="server" />
```

```
</form>
</body>
</html>
```

View this page in the browser and you'll see that nothing happens if you press the buttons. The post-back occurs, but the table doesn't render any differently. The problem is that the Rows and Columns properties are actually set after our CreateChildControl method has been called, so the number of rows and columns that are created is not affected. To compound this problem, the values are lost from the control shortly after the page is rendered, because the control has not had its values persisted.

To retain the values, we need to modify the Rows and Columns property handlers to store their values in the control's StateBag, via the State property:

```
public int Rows {
    get {
        return (int) State["_rows"];
    }
    set {
        State["_rows"] = value;
    }
}

public int Columns {
    get {
        return (int) State["_columns"];
    }
    set {
        State["_columns"] = value;
    }
}
```

By using the control's state bag, the ASP+ framework will save the state of our control when it is destroyed, and restore it when it's created. If we compile the control with this small change and look at the HTML that is created, we can just about make out these properties in the hidden form field named __VIEWSTATE:

```
<FORM name="ctrl1" method="post" action="testpage.aspx?freddysatar" id="ctrl1">
<INPUT type="hidden" name="__VIEWSTATE" value="a0z-
2006470177_a0z_hz5z1x_a0z_hz5z1x_a0zhz\_columns_5z4x_\_rows_5z4xx_xxxxx_azrestrictSi
\zexx">
```

If you view the page and click the **Add Rows** button, you'll see nothing happens for the first click. Click it again and the table will grow. As we saw earlier, the properties are set by the ASP+ runtime after our child controls have been created. The changes therefore come too late, and have no effect until next time the control is rendered. To address this we have to override the PreRender method, and check that the number of child controls created (rows and cells) matches our control's properties.

The PreRender Method

All controls have a PreRender method that can be overridden to carry out last minute changes before a control's state is saved and its UI is rendered. By adding code to this method to ensure that the number of rows and columns in our table matches our control's properties, we can make certain that any changes to these properties are correctly reflected in the UI. So, if there are too many rows based upon the current control properties, we remove them. If there are too few, we add them. The same logic applies for columns. The following code shows this resizing logic in action:

```
protected override void PreRender() {

    // Increase the number of rows if needed

    while ( _table.Rows.Count > Rows ) {
        _table.Rows.RemoveAt( _table.Rows.Count -1 );
    }

    // Decrease the number of rows if needed

    while ( _table.Rows.Count < Rows ) {
        createNewRow( _table.Rows.Count );
    }

    // Check each row has the correct number of columns

    for(int i = 0; i < _table.Rows.Count; i++) {

        while( _table.Rows[i].Cells.Count < Columns )
            appendCell( _table.Rows[i], i, _table.Rows[i].Cells.Count );

        while( _table.Rows[i].Cells.Count  > Columns )
            _table.Rows[i].Cells.RemoveAt(  _table.Rows[i].Cells.Count -1 );

    }

}
```

As we now need code to create the table rows and columns in more than one place within our control (in CreateChildControls and PreRender), we've created a couple of utility functions for building the table:

❑   createNewRow – creates a new row with the correct number of cells

❑   appendCell – creates a new cell and appends it to the specified row

> *These functions are just a repackaging of the table/row/cell creation code we saw earlier. We've not shown it here, but the CreateChildControls method also uses these functions in the sample code we provide.*

If you compile the new code and view the ASP+ page, you'll see that button clicks now cause the table to render itself as expected. However, as you add and remove rows and columns, you might notice that the values you entered into the various cells start jumping about, and sometimes even disappear. This problem arises because, as we increase the number of rows and columns into our table, the automatic id control assignment performed by ASP+ is getting out of sync.

Advanced ID Naming Managment

If we look at the ids generated for a table with two rows and two columns, we see the following HTML in the browser:

```
<table rules="all" style="border-width:2px;border-style:solid;">
  <tr>
    <td>
```

```
      <input name="table:ctrl4" type="text" value="Row: 0 Cell: 0">
    </td><td>
      <input name="table:ctrl7" type="text" value="Row: 0 Cell: 1">
    </td>
  </tr><tr>
    <td>
      <input name="table:ctrl11" type="text" value="Row: 1 Cell: 0">
    </td><td>
      <input name="table:ctrl14" type="text" value="Row: 1 Cell: 1">
    </td>
  </tr>
</table>
```

If we then add an additional column, we'll see the id assignment changing, as you would expect:

```
<table rules="all" style="border-width:2px;border-style:solid;">
  <tr>
    <td>
      <input name="table:ctrl4" type="text" value="Row: 0 Cell: 0">
    </td><td>
      <input name="table:ctrl7" type="text" value="Row: 0 Cell: 1">
    </td><td>
      <input name="table:ctrl10" type="text" value="Row: 0 Cell: 2">
    </td>
  </tr><tr>
    <td>
      <input name="table:ctrl14" type="text" value="Row: 1 Cell: 1">
    </td><td>
      <input name="table:ctrl17" type="text" value="Row: 1 Cell: 1">
    </td><td>
      <input name="table:ctrl20" type="text" value="Row: 1 Cell: 2">
    </td>
  </tr>
</table>
```

The runtime does its best to match the state to the control based upon thesis ids, but we cannot rely on this behavior if our child controls are going to change dynamically. The solution is to generate our own ids for each cell. That's actually quite easy for a table, because the row/column number will always uniquely identify the same cell, no matter how many rows and/or cells we delete.

To implement the id assignment, we add an additional line just after we create each TextBox to set the id property:

```
            textbox = new TextBox();
            textbox.ID = "r" + rowNumber + "c" + cellNumber ;
```

> Note that you cannot use the colon character in your id properties, as that is the value used by the ASP+ framework (NGWS) to delimit its hierarchal control path.

If we then view the HTML generated for a two by two table, we see our assigned id being used:

```
<table rules="all" style="border-width:2px;border-style:solid;">
  <tr>
    <td>
      <input name="table:r0c0" type="text" value="Row: 0 Cell: 0" id="table_R0C0">
    </td><td>
      <input name="table:r0c1" type="text" value="Row: 0 Cell: 1" id="table_R0C1">
    </td>
  </tr><tr>
    <td>
      <input name="table:r1c0" type="text" value="Row: 1 Cell: 0" id="table_R1C0">
    </td><td>
      <input name="table:r1c1" type="text" value="Row: 1 Cell: 1" id="table_R1C1">
    </td>
  </tr>
</table>
```

No matter how many rows or columns we add, these ids will not change and therefore our data will not jump and around and get lost.

> **If the ASP+ runtime cannot match an id to a control during a post-back, an error is *not* raised, but the redundant state is silently disposed of.**

Supporting Events Using Delegates

ASP+ provides a fairly unique server-side event model. As a page is being constructed, controls can fire events that are caused either by aspects of a client-side post-back, or by controls responding to page code that is calling their methods or changing properties. To demonstrate events in action, our control will generate an event whenever the control size changes (somebody sets the Rows or Columns properties). We'll handle this event with some example code that checks the new control dimensions, and constrains the size of the control if it goes beyond acceptable limits.

Supporting events in an ASP+ page requires two public methods to be implemented for each event: Add*xxxx* and Remove*xxxx* where *xxxx* represents the event name. These methods are called by the ASP+ runtime when it detects an attribute name in a control declaration like this:

```
<Wrox:MyFirstControl id="table" rows="3" cColumns="5" Title="My Table Control"
    OnSizeChanged="SizeChanged" runat="server" />
```

The event names should match two method names, when Add or Remove is prefixed to the attribute name (in this case OnSizeChanged). In our example the event is called OnSizeChanged, and our control will have the methods AddOnSizeChanged and RemoveOnSizeChanged. ASP+ will detect the OnSizeChanged attribute and use it as a trigger to wire up the event handling when the page is being created, and to unwire it when the page is being destroyed.

The two methods that we implement to handle the wiring/unwiring of the event are implemented as follows:

```
private EventHandler _onSizeChanged;

  // Add onSizeChanged Handler

  public void AddOnSizeChanged(EventHandler handler)
  {
     if (handler != null)
        _onSizeChanged =
           (EventHandler)Delegate.Combine(_onSizeChanged,handler);
  }

  // Remove onSizeChanged Handler

  public virtual void RemoveOnSizeChanged(EventHandler handler)
  {
     if (handler != null)
        _onSizeChanged =
           (EventHandler)Delegate.Remove(_OnSizeChanged ,handler);
  }
```

Both methods delegate their event handling 'wiring-up' code to the COM+ delegate class EventHandler. This is declared as part of the mscorlib.dll assembly, and is used throughout COM+. The Combine method of the delegate class takes the event handler passed in by ASP+ and adds it to an internal list. EventHandler is derived from the class MultiCastDelegate. This means that more than one section of code (for example multiple parts of our page code) can sink (receive) the event. The Remove method just removes the specified event handler from the internal list.

In order actually to generate the event, we add a fireEventSizeChanged method to our control:

```
protected void fireEventSizeChanged() {
    if ( _onSizeChanged != null )
       _onSizeChanged.Invoke(this, EventArgs.Empty);
}
```

Before firing the event, this code checks to see if anybody has actually registered an interest in the event. If nobody has registered an event handler the _onSizeChanged variable will be null. We can then call this method in our property handlers for Rows and Columns to generate events when their values are changed:

```
public int Rows {
      get {
          return (int) State["_rows"];
      }
      set {
          State["_rows"] = value;
          fireEventSizeChanged();
      }
  }
```

```
public int Columns {
    get {
        return (int) State["_columns"];
    }
    set {
        State["_columns"] = value;
        fireEventSizeChanged();
    }
}
```

With all the event hook-up and generation code in place, we can add some page code to sink the event, which ensures that the dimensions of the control never go below 2 rows x 2 columns, or exceed 5 rows by 5 columns:

```
protected void SizeChanged( object sender, EventArgs e ) {

    if ( table.Rows < 2 )
        table.Rows = 2;

    if ( table.Rows > 5 )
        table.Rows = 5;

    if ( table.Columns < 2 )
        table.Columns = 2;

    if ( table.Columns > 5 )
        table.Columns = 5;

}
```

If you view this page in the browser, you'll see the control cannot exceed the dimensions specified in the code.

Initialising Controls with Data

When our control is used within a page, it is very likely that users will want to fill the cells within the control with initial data. To do this we have a number of choices:

❑ **Expando attributes** – We let the user set any attribute on our control (eg. R2C4 = "aaa") and we map those attribute values to the cells as we build the table.

❑ **Child Controls** – We let the user declare controls within our control and initialize their values.

Expando Attributes – IAttributeAccessor

When the ASP+ runtime sees a custom control tag, it will by default raise an error if any attributes on that element are not exposed as properties by that control. This makes sense, as it helps to reduce the number of errors caused by typing mistakes. However, there will be times when you want your attributes to be dynamic. For example, our table control has a variable number of rows and columns. It would be nice if these values could be pre-initialised using attributes, for example:

```
...
<Wrox:MyFirstControl R0C0="Hello" R0C1="From"
    R1C0="Sunny" R1C1="Peterborough"
    id="table" rows="2" columns="2"
    Title="My Table Control" runat="server" />
...
```

For this to work, and not raise a runtime error because we have not exposed R0C0, R0C1, R1C0 and R1C1 as attributes, we have to derive our class from the IAttributeAccessor interface and implement the methods SetAttribute and GetAttribute. These methods are called when attributes do not match a property exposed by a control, enabling a control to decide what to do with them. For our table control, the implementation of this interface will store the attributes in a hashtable and use them later when creating cells.

The first step is to derive our control from the interface:

```
public class MyFirstControl : Control, INamingContainer,
                                          IAttributeAccessor
```

Following which we declare the two functions for IAttributeAccessor along with their implementation:

```
Hashtable _attributes = new Hashtable();

public virtual string GetAttribute(string name)
{
    return (string) _attributes[name];
}

public virtual void SetAttribute(string name, string value)
{
    _attributes[name] = value;
    Context.Trace.Write("IAttributeAccessor", name );
}
```

The code behind these two functions uses the Hashtable class to store and retrieve the values. Each time an attribute is not exposed as a property, the SetAttribute method will be called and the name/value pair will be stored in the Hashtable. This table is then used in the CreateChildControls function when we build each cell to see if an initial value has been specified:

```
textbox = new TextBox();
textbox.ID = "r" + x + "c" + y;

// See if an attribute was set

if ( _attributes[ textbox.ID ] != null )
    textbox.Text = (string) _attributes[ textbox.ID ];
else
    textbox.Text = "Row: " + x + " Cell: " + y;
    cell = new TableCell();
```

The code checks the hashtable to see if an attribute was specified for the cell, and uses it if present. If no value is specified, the default-generated text is used instead. As our earlier control declaration example had two columns and two rows, and we specified a value for all four cells using attributes, the browser will render a fully populated table:

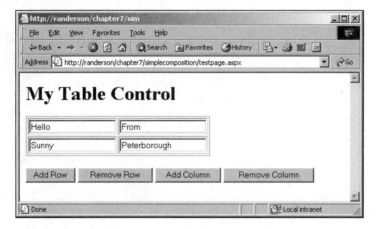

This expando attribute support is pretty neat, but it isn't suitable if we want to specify more than one attribute for each cell. For example, consider this control declaration:

```
<Wrox:MyFirstControl
        R0C0="Hello" R0C1BackColor="Yellow" R0C1="From" R0C1BackColor="Green"
        R1C0="Sunny" R1C1="Peterborough"
        id="table" rows="2" columns="2"
        title="My Table Control" runat="server" />
```

Here we have indicated that we want all the cells populated with text, but we also want some nice background colors for two of the cells. There are some fairly obvious problems with this approach:

- ❑   It's getting messy – there are just too many attributes now.

- ❑   It is going to be inefficient – our code would have to check to see if multiple attributes existed for each cell. As we add more attributes the number of checks goes up exponentially.

A much better approach for our control declaration syntax would be to have a sub-element for each cell, for example:

```
<Wrox:MyFirstControl id="table" rows="2" columns="2"
        title="My Table Control" runat="server" >

  <Wrox:MyCell id="R0C0"  BackColor="Red"    Text="Hello" />
  <Wrox:MyCell id="R0C1"  BackColor="Yellow"  Text="From" />
  <Wrox:MyCell id="R1C0"  BackColor="Green"  Text="Colorful" />
  <Wrox:MyCell id="R1C1"  BackColor="Blue"   Text="Peterborough" />

</Wrox:MyFirstControl>
```

The declaration is much cleaner than using attributes – and the relationships between the various elements and attributes are now more explicit. ASP+ supports this approach of sub-elements (sub-objects) using **Control Builders**.

Control Builders

A control builder is responsible for processing the element declarations within a control declaration. At runtime a control builder is given the opportunity to examine the declarations that are defined. It can specify a COM+ class that is created for each element declaration, and which is then responsible for processing it.

By default, all custom ASP+ controls are associated with the default ASP+ control builder. This control builder simply maps the contents within a control declaration to literal controls, unless they are marked with a `runat="server"` attribute, in which case it will actually create the specified class and add it as a child control to the parent control. For example, if we added the `<Wrox:MyCell>` declarations into our test page we'd actually see these declarations appearing in the HTML of the client:

```
<html>
<body>

<form name="ctrl1" method="post" action="testpage.aspx" id="ctrl1">
<input type="hidden" name="__VIEWSTATE" value="a0z1552392154__x">
    <Wrox:MyCell id="R0C0" BackColor="Red"    Text="Hello" />
    <Wrox:MyCell id="R0C1" BackColor="Yellow"  Text="From" />
    <Wrox:MyCell id="R0C2" BackColor="Green"   Text="Colorful" />
    <Wrox:MyCell id="R0C3" BackColor="Blue"    Text="Peterborough" />
<h1>My Table Control</h1>
<table rules="all" style="border-width:2px;border-style:solid;">
...
```

If we also changed the inner declarations to contain an `asp:button` declaration:

```
<Wrox:MyFirstControl
        R0C0="Hello" R0C1="From" R1C0="Sunny" R1C1="Peterborough"
        id="table" rows="2" columns="2"
        title="My Table Control" runat="server">
    <asp:button Text="An unwanted button" runat="server" />
    <Wrox:MyCell id="R0C0" BackColor="Red"    Text="Hello" />
    <Wrox:MyCell id="R0C1" BackColor="Yellow"  Text="From" />
    <Wrox:MyCell id="R1C0" BackColor="Green"   Text="Colorful" />
    <Wrox:MyCell id="R1C1" BackColor="Blue"    Text="Peterborough" />
</Wrox:MyFirstControl>
```

the button would actually appear as part of our custom control UI:

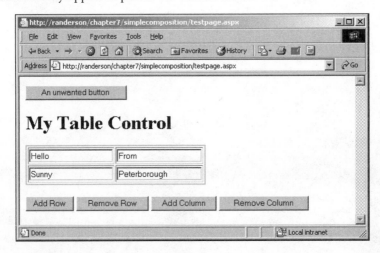

This is certainly not the behavior we want the control to exhibit, so either we have to implement a custom control builder to handle the inner content, or if your control just doesn't want any inner content to effect its UI there is a way of preventing it. The easiest way to stop users from adding strange UI elements to your control is by adding one line to your `CreateChildControls` methods that removes any controls added by the ASP+ runtime due to users misusing the control:

```
protected override void CreateChildControls()
{
    Controls.Clear();
```

Implementing a Custom Control Builder

Implementing a custom control builder requires four main steps:

1. Implement a COM+ class for each sub-control you want to support.

2. Implement the custom control builder that associates element names with your custom control classes.

3. Tell ASP+ that your control wants to use a custom control builder.

4. Make your control do something with the sub-controls when ASP+ passes them to it.

Step 1 – Create the Sub-Controls

A sub-control is simply a COM+ class (control) that is created by the ASP+ runtime to deal with the declarations within your controls. It is no different to a standard ASP+ custom control, except that it doesn't have to derive from `Control` unless you are going to use it to render any UI. Here is the COM+ class used to handle our `Wrox:MyCell` declarations:

```
public class MyCell {

    string _id;
    string _value;
    string _color;

    public string ID {
        get {
            return _id;
        }
        set {
            _id = value;
        }
    }

    public string Value {
        get {
            return _value;
        }
        set {
            _value = value;
        }
    }
```

```
        public string Color{
            get {
                return _color;
            }
            set {
                _color = Value;
            }
        }
    };
```

In many ways, the sub-control will behave and be treated the same as a normal control at runtime. When the ASP+ runtime encounters an attribute on the element that causes the sub-controls to be created, it will try and set a property just like it does with controls.

Step 2 – Implement the Custom Control Builder

Once our COM+ `MyCell` class is in place to deal with the sub-controls, we need to implement a custom control builder to associate the element names used within our control with the COM+ class we have just created. To do this, we create a COM+ class that derives from the `ControlBuilder` class:

```
    internal class MyControlBuilder    : ControlBuilder {

        public override Type GetChildControlType(string tagName, IDictionary
    attribs) {
            // override to allow TableRow without runat=server to be added

            if (tagName.ToLower().EndsWith("mycell"))
                return typeof(MyCell);

            return null;
        }

        public override void AppendLiteralString(string s) {
            // override to ignore literals between rows
        }
    }
```

In this code we implement two methods:

❑ `GetChildControlType` – indicates to the ASP+ runtime that any element named `mycell` should result in the COM+ class `MyCell` being created.

❑ `AppendLiteralString` – tells the ASP+ runtime to ignore any text between elements. If we did not implement the default implementation it would create one or more `LiteralControl` controls for text in between the control definitions.

The `GetChildControlType` implementation shown above is designed to be very flexible. Element names can use upper or lower case, and they can have any namespace prefix (e.g. `Wrox:MyCell`). If the method returns a COM+ class, that class will be created, otherwise a return value of `null` will result in no class being created.

Now the custom control builder is in place, we need to tell ASP+ to use it for our control. We do this using a class level attribute.

Step 3 – Tell ASP+ to use a Custom Control Builder

To define a control builder for our ASP+ custom control, we add an attribute section to the class definition, and specify the `ControlBuilderAttribute` attribute:

```
[
    ControlBuilderAttribute(typeof(MyControlBuilder))
]
public class MyFirstControl : Control, INamingContainer,
                                       IAttributeAccessor
...
```

The attribute section starts with the left square bracket and ends with the right square bracket. The attribute we have specified accepts one parameter – the COM+ class type that should be created for building the controls inner content. The attribute and class type are stored as metadata within our assembly, and ASP+ interrogates this at runtime to detect that we want to use a custom control builder. ASP+ then knows that is has to create our custom control builder, which in turn will create our `MyCell` COM+ class.

Step 4 – Make the Control Do Something with the Sub-Controls

Whenever a sub-control is created, the method `AddParsedSubObject` is invoked. This is defined within the `Control` class, and should be overridden to decide how to handle sub-controls. The default implementation simply appends object references to the `Controls` collection that are passed in, so we need to override this and store the `MyCell` objects that are passed to it in another `Hashtable`. In the example code we have called this `_cellObjects` Hashtable:

```
Hashtable _cells2;

public override void AddParsedSubObject(object obj) {
     if (obj is MyCell) {
         MyCell cell;
         cell = (MyCell) obj;
         _cells2.Add( cell.ID, cell );
     }
 }
```

With this new hashtable in place, we modify the code that creates the text boxes to check this – in the same way as we did earlier with the hashtable used for expando attributes:

```
textbox = new TextBox();
textbox.ID = "r" + x + "c" + y;

// See if an attribute was set
if ( _attributes[textbox.ID] != null )
    textbox.Text = (string) _attributes[textbox.ID];

// Check for MyCell sub-object
else if ( _cellObjects[textbox.ID] != null ) {

    MyCell cellLookup;
    cellLookup = (MyCell) _cellObjects[textbox.ID];
    textbox.Text = cellLookup.Text;
```

```
                        textbox.BackColor = cellLookup.BackColor;
                     }
                 else
                     textbox.Text = "Row: " + x + " Cell: " + y;

             cell = new TableCell();
             cell.Controls.Add(textbox);
             row.Cells.Add(cell);
             }
```

If you compile this code and view the page that uses it in the browser, you'll see that the colors are now rendered:

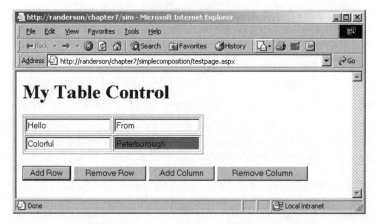

Control builders allow you to provide a very flexible configuration mechanism for your controls. You'll have noticed that we didn't have to specify the `runat="server"` attribute on every sub-element, which can often be a very tedious exercise for users. The same approach is implemented by many of the built-in ASP+ controls.

Other Controls Topics

So far in this chapter, we've covered the most common aspects of ASP+ control development. To round off, we'll briefly cover some of the more advanced aspects of ASP+ control development.

Class Properties

Class properties allow a control declaration to set the attributes of a sub-object exposed from a control as a property. Given the following COM+ class that allows two string values to be set via the properties A and B:

```
public class SampleClassProperty {

    string _valueA;
    string _valueB;

    public string A {
        get {
            return _valueA;
        }
```

```
        set {
            _valueA = value;
        }
    }

    public string B {
        get {
            return _valueB;
        }
        set {
            _valueB = value;
        }
    }

};
```

we can expose it as a property from our control:

```
    ...
    SampleClassProperty _exampleObjectProperty = new SampleClassProperty();

    public SampleClassProperty MyObject {
        get {
            return _exampleObjectProperty;
        }
    }
```

We can then directly set the properties of the object (A and B) by using the **Object Walker** syntax in our control declaration where a hyphen (-) separates each object/property:

```
<Wrox:MyFirstControl MyObject-A="hello" MyObject-B="World"
    rows="3" columns="5" title="My Table Control" runat="server" />
```

The syntax can walk any number of objects. Its major benefits are that it allows a control to group related attributes (consider the style object used by most ASP+ controls), and the syntax also saves controls having to expose manually public properties of contained objects – which means simple control interfaces and less code to write.

Lookless UI

Most of the built-in ASP+ controls in System.Web.UI allow their UI to be customized by using templates, and some even mandate templates (such as the asp:repeater control). Templates work by allowing users of a control to define sections of the UI using standard HTML and ASP+ elements. At runtime these elements are compiled into a COM+ class that, given a reference to a control, can add one or more controls to it (recursively – depending upon the complexity of the template) to represent the template UI. The created COM+ object exposes the ITemplate interface, which has a single Initialize method:

```
    void Initialize(Control control);
```

To support templates, a control exposes one or more properties of type ITemplate. The name assigned to the properties can then be used in conjunction with the template element. For example, the following HTML shows how we might make our control's title section of the UI definable using a template:

```
<Wrox:MyFirstControl OnSizeChanged="SizeChanged" id="table"
      rows="3" columns="5" title="My Table Control" runat="server">

  <template name="HeaderTemplate">
    <h1>Templates Rock!</h1>
    <h4>and they Roll too...</h4>
  </template>

  <Wrox:MyCell CellID="r0c0" BackColor="Red" Text="Hello" />
  <Wrox:MyCell CellID="r0c1" BackColor="Cyan" Text="From" />
  <Wrox:MyCell CellID="r1c0" BackColor="Yellow" Text="Colorful" />
  <Wrox:MyCell CellID="r1c1" BackColor="Gray" Text="Peterborough" />

</Wrox:MyFirstControl>
```

To support this, we have to implement the HeaderTemplate property, which ASP+ will call when it hits the above template element:

```
private ITemplate _headerTemplate = null;


[
Template(typeof(MyFirstControl))
]
public ITemplate HeaderTemplate {

    get {
        return _headerTemplate;
    }
    set {
        _headerTemplate = value;
    }
}
```

The Template attribute specified for the method tells the ASP+ runtime that any usage of the Container syntax should result in code being generated that is early bound, i.e. Container is of the type MyFirstControl.

To use the ITemplate instance we modify our CreateChildControls method to optionally create the control's header UI:

```
protected override void CreateChildControls()
{
    LiteralControl text;
    Controls.Clear();

    // no header template ?

    if (HeaderTemplate == null) {
        text = new LiteralControl("<h1>" + _title + "</h1>");
```

```
                Controls.Add(text);
                }
        else {
            _headerTemplate.Initialize(this);
        }
```

This code checks to see if the header template has been supplied. If it hasn't, it adds the default child control. Otherwise it calls the _headerTemplate Initialize method to add the child controls defined by the template to our control as children. Viewing this page in the browser shows the customized header created by our template:

Using the same technique, we can make cells capable of being template-aware, although there are two key implications that we need to understand:

❑   Currently we assign our unique IDs (r0c0, r1c1 etc) to the TextBox object. As we cannot rely on this being present any more when using templates, we have to set that id on the TableCell object instead.

❑   The TableCell class does not derive from the INamingContainer interface, so we'll experience non-persistence of any child state unless we define our own TableCell class that derives from TableCell and the INamingContainer interface:

```
public class MyTableCell : TableCell, INamingContainer {};
```

With these points taken into consideration, lets look at the implementation for cell templates.

Adding Support for Cell Templates

Firstly, we define the CellTemplate property as we did before with the HeaderTemplate:

```
        private ITemplate _cellTemplate = null;

        [
        Template(typeof(MyTableCell))
        ]
```

```
    public ITemplate CellTemplate {

    get {
        return _cellTemplate;
    }
    set {
        _cellTemplate = value;
    }
}
```

The main difference here is that the Template attribute states that the Container type will not be the MyTableCell class. As discussed earlier, this allows the ASP+ page compiler to generate early bound code whenever the Container syntax is used.

Next, we modify the appendCell function to use the CellTemplate property to initialize the child controls of the MyTableCell object if it has been specified. If the CellTemplate property has not been set, the original code we saw earlier in this chapter is called:

```
protected void appendCell( TableRow row, int rowNumber, int cellNumber ) {
    TableCell cell;
    TextBox textbox;

    if  (CellTemplate != null) {
        cell = new MyTableCell();
        cell.ID = "r" + rowNumber + "c" + cellNumber;
        CellTemplate.Initialize(cell);
        row.Cells.Add(cell);
        return;
    }

    cell = new TableCell();
    textbox = new TextBox();
    cell.Controls.Add( textbox );
    textbox.ID = "r" + rowNumber + "c" + cellNumber;

    // See if an attribute was set
    if ( _attributes[ textbox.ID ] != null)
        textbox.Text = (string) _attributes[textbox.ID];

    // Check for MyCell sub-object

    else if ( _cellObjects[textbox.ID] != null) {
        MyCell cellLookup;
        cellLookup = (MyCell) _cellObjects[textbox.ID];
        textbox.Text = cellLookup.Text;
        textbox.BackColor = cellLookup.BackColor;
    }
    else
        textbox.Text = "Row: " + rowNumber  + " Cell: " + cellNumber;

    row.Cells.Add(cell);
}
```

This is the first time we have seen the appendCell method in this chapter. It's simply the original code repackaged to make it easier to update.

Finally, we can update our control declaration to specify a template for each cell. In this example we create a checkbox to enter your sex, and a textbox for entering your name:

```
<Wrox:MyFirstControl OnSizeChanged="SizeChanged" id="table" rows="2" columns="5"
    title="My Table Control" runat="server">

  <template name="HeaderTemplate" runat="server">
    <h1>Templates Rock!</h1>
    <h4>and they Roll too...</h4>
  </template>

  <template name="CellTemplate" runat="server">
    <asp:checkbox id="sex" Text="Male" runat="server" /><br />
    <font size="2">Enter your name: <asp:TextBox id="name" runat="server" />
  </template>

  <Wrox:MyCell CellID="r0c0" BackColor="Red" Text="Hello" />
  <Wrox:MyCell CellID="r0c1" BackColor="Cyan" Text="From" />
  <Wrox:MyCell CellID="r1c0" BackColor="Yellow" Text="Colorful" />
  <Wrox:MyCell CellID="r1c1" BackColor="Gray" Text="Peterborough" />

</Wrox:MyFirstControl>
```

Viewing this in the browser, and entering some data, shows that we can quite easily create a sophisticated data entry form using the control:

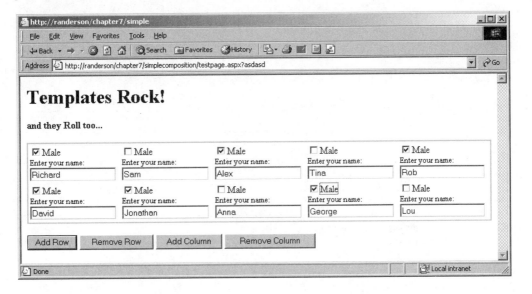

As an exercise, you might like to try exposing the `Table` *object within the control as a property and processing data contained within it in a post-back.*

Error Handling – Throwing Exceptions

If an ASP+ control reaches a point where it just cannot continue, or it wants to raise an error, it can throw an exception to halt execution. For example, here is an updated `Rows` property handler that throws an exception if the `Row` property exceeds 10:

```
public int Rows {
    get {
        return (int) State["_rows"];
    }
    set {
        if  (Rows > 10)
            throw new Exception("You cannot have more than 10 rows");
        State["_rows"] = value;
        fireEventSizeChanged();
    }
}
```

If the limit is exceeded the ASP+ runtime will display the error:

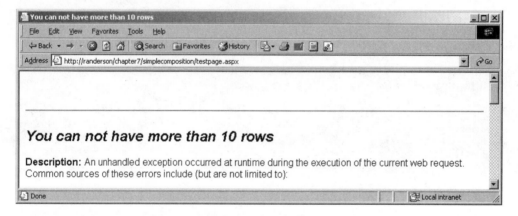

As a small exercise, try deriving your own class from `Exception` and throwing that in your code. This enables you to throw custom exceptions that can contain customized error information.

Threading and Threading Models

As an ASP+ developer, you really don't have to concern yourself with threading models any more. Threading models have always been a hack at the best of times to fit in with the way that COM was originally implemented on Windows Queues, and they are a thing of the past as far as ASP+ is concerned. ASP+ will automatically create controls that are **both threaded**.

The ASP+ runtime will ensure that a control is never accessed by more than one thread at a time when a page is being rendered. This means you typically do not need any code to deal with multiple thread concurrency, unless your class accesses shared state or object references located in the ASP+ application object or cache object.

Control Navigation

The `parent` property of a control can always be used to walk up the control hierarchy. The `controls` property is used to walk down the control hierarchy.

Summary

In this chapter we have briefly covered ASP+ control development in VB and C#. We started the chapter by developing a simple control in C# and VB, showing key language differences and how to convert between them.

The main section of the chapter focused on incrementally developing an ASP+ grid control, showing a number of ASP+ control techniques including properties, control composition, state management, pre-render changes, expando attributes, custom control builders, class properties, and templates.

We have not had time to cover all aspects of ASP+ control development in this chapter, but do keep an eye on http://www.wrox.com/beta for more examples showing data binding and validation controls.

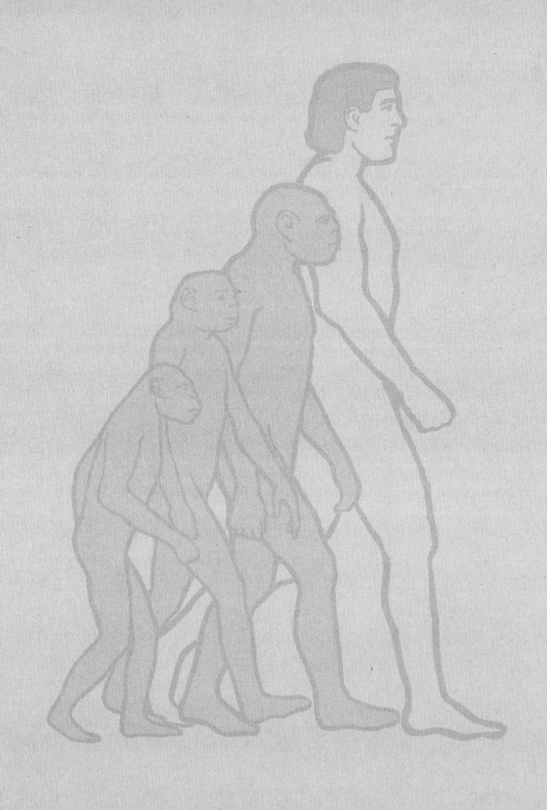

8

A Simple E-Commerce Application

Adventure Works 2000

In the previous chapters of this book you have learned about the individual features of ASP+, such as Web controls, data binding, configuration and security. On their own, each of these features is pretty cool and powerful, but individually they are like a number of jigsaw pieces: the final objective is to figure out how to put them all together correctly to create a picture. Like jigsaw pieces, the individual features of ASP+ are ultimately there for composition into an ASP+ application.

In this chapter we are going to show you how we've used ASP+ to create a simple n-tier e-commerce application that is scalable yet still relatively simple to code and understand. Along the way we'll discuss and review:

- ❑   How to design and write an n-tier e-commerce application using ASP+
- ❑   Using cookie based authentication to secure an e-commerce application
- ❑   Scalability considerations when creating an e-commerce site that must scale in a Web farm
- ❑   Using business objects to encapsulate business logic and data access
- ❑   Using 'code behind' to share common page logic

Overview of the Application

For those who can remember back to ASP 2.0, you may recall that it shipped with a sample application called **Adventure Works**. This application allowed you to shop for climbing equipment suitable for extreme conditions. Adventure Works featured all the basic features of a typical e-commerce application, including product viewing and selection, user registration and a shopping cart. In this chapter we are going to use ASP+ to create a simple variant of the Adventure Works application called **Adventure Works 2000**, or **AW2000** for short. Throughout the rest of this chapter we are going to review the code and functionality of this application, and discuss some of the design decisions we made while creating it.

> All the files for the Adventure Works 2000 application are available for download from the Wrox website, www.wrox.com, and will include set up and installation instructions.

Adventure Works 2000 (AW2000)

If you haven't seen or used the old ASP Adventure Works application before, don't worry. We'll be covering the ASP+ AW2000 application from the ground up, and we will only be porting a small subset of features from the original application. This approach allows us to demonstrate using ASP+ to create real-word e-commerce applications, without getting distracted by too many application specific features that would simply dilute the goals of this chapter.

> *If you do have access to the original Adventure Works application we do recommend that you spend some time comparing the original ASP code and ASP+ code in this chapter. Sections of the code, such as the shopping basket and page layout code, really show the power and simplicity of ASP+.*

The Target Audience

The Adventure Works 2000 application is aimed at allowing climbing enthusiasts to check out and buy the latest climbing equipment over the Internet from the comfort of their home or tent. The application will let customers view different products grouped by category (boots, pants, tents etc.), and enable them to add items to their shopping cart at any time. The application uses just-in-time registration, so customers can fill their shopping carts with products and not have to register or login until they actually proceed to the checkout. This approach is pretty common on most major sites like Amazon.com, and really is a must-have feature in any e-commerce application today.

Scalability – Windows DNA 2000 Architecture

The Adventure Works application needs to be scalable and capable of supporting hundreds, if not thousands of concurrent users. To achieve this goal the application has been designed according to the guidelines set out by Windows DNA 2000 (http://www.microsoft.com/dna). The application therefore adopts an *n*-tier architecture as described by Windows DNA, where the application is split into a number of tiers for presentation, business logic and data:

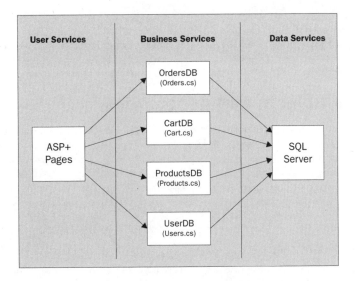

By adopting an *n*-tier architecture the Adventure Works application can easily be deployed on a single machine or multiple machines (one or more physical tiers). In theory it should be possible, using this architecture, to deploy the ASP+ pages, COM+ components, and SQL server on their own dedicated servers. All the ASP+ pages in Adventure Works access the backend database using a set of COM+ components that enforce business logic and encapsulate the underlying database. These components are fairly thin, and for the most part simply wrap a series of ADO+ routines similar to those that were covered in Chapter 3, returning a `DataSet` from the methods that are called to retrieve data.

Designing for Enterprise Scalability

To cater for enterprise level scalability (the use of Web farms) the application uses **no session level state**. All state is either stored client-side within hidden fields, or within the backend SQL server database. When a user first visits the site, the ASP+ session ID is used to track the user and any shopping items they add to their cart (and therefore the database). After registering or logging in, any references to the session ID stored in the database are updated with the customer name.

By taking this approach, the application can easily be deployed in a Web farm without the need to use sticky sessions. Each Web server that receives a request can simply use the session ID or user name (provided by the cookie based authentication) to lookup user details and cart items from a central database.

> **Sticky Sessions is a term used to describe ASP/ASP+ user sessions that must always be redirected to the same front-end Web server in a Web farm. Generally sticky sessions are required in applications that depend upon state stored in the session object. This is typically a bad design decision because if the machine hosting the sticky session falls over, all session state is lost and the user effectively has to start again.**

Using a database to store session state (such as the shopping cart) does add a degree of overhead to our application, but it makes it more resilient in the case of failures. If a Web server fails during a user's request, another server can handle it and no information will be lost. If we'd used a session-based shopping cart, our customers would lose everything created during their session if the machine hosting that session failed.

> ASP+ was designed around the principle that servers do fail and applications/ components do leak memory and crash from time to time. By designing the Adventure Works application to use no session state we work well with the ASP+ philology.

The Business Objects and Assemblies

Four business objects written in C# provide the various ASP+ pages with all the business logic and data access code they require. As all of the COM+ classes are fairly similar in terms of structure and the ADO+ code they use to access the SQL server database, we won't review every single method of every single object. Instead we'll look at one of the components in detail (ProductsDB) to see the basic structure of our components, and then use the ILDASM utility to show the methods and properties of each of the remaining business objects for reference purposes. As we encounter pages that use these functions we'll expand on their purposes.

ProductsDB Business Object

The ProductsDB class provides functions for retrieving product information. The complete C# code for the class is shown here:

```
using System;
using System.Data;
using System.Data.SQL;

namespace AdvWorks
{
  public class ProductsDB
  {
    string m_dsn;

    public ProductsDB( string dsn ) {
      m_dsn = dsn;
    }

    public DataSet GetProduct(string productCode) {

        SQLConnection sqlConn = new SQLConnection(m_dsn);
        SQLDataSetCommand sqlAdapter1 =
            new SQLDataSetCommand(
    "SELECT * FROM Products WHERE ProductCode='"+productCode+"'",
    sqlConn);

    DataSet products = new DataSet();
    sqlAdapter1.FillDataSet(products, "products");

    return products;
    }

    public DataSet GetProducts(string category) {
```

```
            SQLConnection sqlConn = new SQLConnection(m_dsn);
            SQLDataSetCommand sqlAdapter1 =
                new SQLDataSetCommand(
                    "SELECT * FROM Products WHERE ProductType='"+category+"'",
                    sqlConn);

            DataSet products = new DataSet();
            sqlAdapter1.FillDataSet(products, "products");

            return products;
        }

        public DataSet GetProductCategories() {

            SQLConnection sqlConn = new SQLConnection(m_dsn);
            SQLDataSetCommand sqlAdapter1 =
                new SQLDataSetCommand(
                    "SELECT Distinct ProductType FROM Products", sqlConn);

            DataSet products = new DataSet();
            sqlAdapter1.FillDataSet(products, "products");

            return products;
        }
    }
}
```

This class has four methods including the constructor:

❑   ProductsDB – Initializes the class with a data source string.

❑   GetProduct – Returns a dataset containing details for a single product.

❑   GetProducts – Returns a dataset containing the details for all products in a specified category.

❑   GetProductCategories – Returns a dataset containing the list of product categories.

The first three lines of the component declare the namespaces we are using:

```
using System;
using System.Data;
using System.Data.SQL;
```

All of our class files have these lines and they indicate that we are using the standard system namespace and the namespaces for ADO+ and the SQL Server specific parts of ADO+ (System.Data.SQL). We use the SQL specific elements of ADO+ because they provide high performance SQL Server access using TDS (Tabular Data Stream) via the classes SQLConnection and SQLDataSetCommand. If we needed to support a different backend database we could recode our classes to use the ADOConnection and ADODataSetCommand classes, which perform database access through OLEDB. These classes were discussed in Chapter 3.

One important point to note about all of the ADO+ code in the business object is that it does not contain any exception handlers. It is therefore up to the code that uses these classes to catch exceptions like SQLException, which can be thrown if any error occurs when performing the data access (e.g. the existence of duplicate rows etc.).

We haven't included any exception handling in our ASP+ pages to keep them terse, but the basic format is shown here:

```
try
{
  someObject.SomeMethodUsingADOplus()
}
catch (SQLException e)
{
  if (e.Number == 2627)
    Message.InnerHtml = "Record exists with the same primary key";
  else
    Message.InnerHtml = e.Message;
}
```

In this code, we are checking for a known SQL server error code using the SQLException Number property. If the error code we are checking for is matched, we display a custom error message. If the known error code is not encountered we display the exception's Message property. The Message property of an exception object typically contains very descriptive and helpful text that can help resolve a problem quickly. In your applications you're unlikely to check for specific error codes unless you want to perform some type of action. For example, you may check for the error code above if you want to delete a row that may already exist.

> **You should always proactively add exception-handling code to commercial applications. The ADO+ classes (including SQLException) are located in the assembly System.Data.DLL. Use the ILDASM tool for the class browser example from the quick start to explore the classes in more detail.**

The Connection String Constructor

The ProductsDB class has a constructor that accepts the connection string used to establish a connection to the backend database. By passing the string in like this we prevent people from forgetting to specify it, and hopefully we prevent business objects from containing hard-coded strings, which is always bad practice.

The string passed in is stored in the member m_dsn in the constructor code:

```
...
string m_dsn;

public ProductsDB( string dsn ) {
   m_dsn = dsn;
}
...
```

The m_dsn member is then used when constructing the SQLConnection object:

```
    public DataSet GetProduct(string productCode) {

        SQLConnection sqlConnection = new SQLConnection(m_dsn);
        SQLDataSetCommand sqlAdapter1 = new SQLDataSetCommand("SELECT * FROM
Products WHERE ProductCode='"+productCode+"'", sqlConnection);

        DataSet products = new DataSet();
        sqlAdapter1.FillDataSet(products, "products");
```

```
        return products;
    }
```

Anybody using the `ProductsDB` business object (and any of the other business objects) must therefore pass the connection string when creating an instance of the class:

```
AdvWorks.ProductsDB inventory = new AdvWorks.ProductsDB(getDSN());
```

The `getDSN` function in this example retrieves the connection string from the `config.web` file:

```
<configuration>
  <advworksdb>
    <add key="connstring"
         value="server=localhost;uid=sa;pwd=;database=advworks" />
    <add key="specialOffer" value="AW042-03" />
  </advworksdb>
</configuration>
```

By using the `config.web` file to store the connection string for our components we do not have connection strings duplicated throughout business objects and ASP+ pages. This makes it much easier to manage the connection string should we decide to rename the database or change any of the connection string properties.

> The **getDSN** function is implemented using a 'code behind' class that we'll review later in this chapter. You could alternatively use an include file to define such functions in your application, but the 'code behind' technique is my preferred approach.

Now we have reviewed the `ProductsDB` class let's take a brief look at a couple of ILDASM screen shots showing the methods for our other business objects.

The ILDASM output for AdvWorks.DLL

The follow screen shows the ILDASM output for the `AdvWorks.dll` assembly:

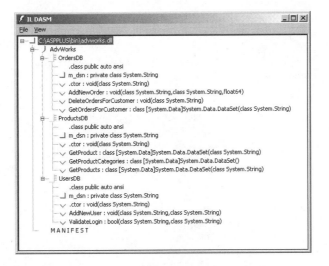

The IDLASM Output for AdvWorksCart.dll

The following screen shows the ILDASM output for the AdvWorksCart.dll assembly:

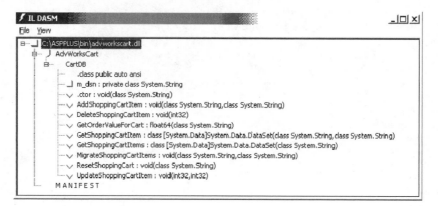

Assemblies

As we discussed in Chapter 6, assemblies are the key deployment mechanism in ASP+ applications. The business objects for Adventure Works are divided into two assemblies, which are both dependant upon the System.Data.dll assembly as they use ADO+:

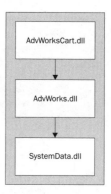

The AdvWorksCart.dll contains the CartDB business object, which is used for manipulating the shopping cart. This is dependant upon the ProductsDB class that is contained within the AdvWorks.DLL assembly.

> Although assemblies have a **DLL** extension, they are, for the most part, not DLLs. The extension was kept only to aid interoperability between COM+ managed code and classic COM unmanaged code.

The AdvWorksCart.dll assembly isn't strictly necessary, but it does show that partitioning classes into different assemblies in an ASP+ application isn't a difficult task. The decision as to when to create assemblies will typically be influenced by a number of more real-life factors:

❑   The functionality of the classes within the assembly. Assemblies should ideally contain functionally related classes.

❑   The number of developers working on an application. Assemblies are a key unit of deployment in ASP+ applications so it makes sense for different development teams to create their own assemblies to ease co-development.

Compiling the Assemblies

All of the business object source code for the Adventure Works application is located in the **components** directory. This directory contains the file `make.bat` that uses the C# command line compiler (`csc.exe`) to create the two assemblies:

```
csc /out:..\..\bin\advworks.dll /t:library ProductsDB.cs OrdersDB.cs UsersDB.cs
/r:System.Web.dll /r:System.Data.dll

csc /out:..\..\bin\advworkscart.dll /t:library CartDB.cs /r:System.Web.dll
/r:System.Data.dll /r:..\..\bin\advworks.dll
```

> *The compiler options for C# are discussed in more details in Chapter 6.*

The first line compiles the business objects `ProductsDB`, `OrdersDB`, and `UsersDB`, which are respectively located within the files `ProductDB.cs`, `OrdersDB.cs`, and `UsersDB.cs`. The output from this line is the `AdvWorks.DLL` assembly. The second line compiles the business object `CartDB`, which is located in the file `CartDB.cs`. The output from this is the `AdvWorksCart.DLL` assembly. Both assemblies are compiled into our ASP+ application `bin` directory so that they are available to our ASP+ pages.

Naming Conventions

The Adventure Works business objects `ProductsDB`, `OrdersDB`, and `UsersDB` are declared within the namespace **AdvWorks**. This reflects the name of the assembly they are contained in, so making it easy to locate and determine what files to ship when it comes to deploying an application that contains pages that are dependant upon those classes. The same naming convention applies to the `CartDB` business object, which is declared within the namespace `AdvWorksCart`, and contained within the assembly `AdvWorksCart.DLL`. Microsoft also uses this naming convention for most of its assemblies. The exceptions to the rule are core classes such as strings that tend to live in assemblies called `mscor[*].dll`.

The AW2000 Database

Adventure Works is driven by a SQL Server database with four tables (`Accounts`, `Products`, `ShoppingCarts`, and `Orders`) as shown in the next diagram:

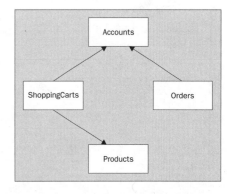

The business objects encapsulate each of these tables, so pages never perform direct database access.

The Accounts Table

The `Accounts` table is used to store the login information for registered customers and has the following structure:

Column Name	Type	Length	Description
CustomerName	Char	50	The name or e-mail address of the registered user. This field is used as the key against all of the tables, and should therefore be unique.
Password	Char	25	The password specified by the user during their registration.

The Orders Table

The `Orders` table is used to store a summary of all orders made by customers and has the following structure:

Column Name	Type	Length	Description
CustomerName	Char	50	The name or e-mail address of the registered user. This field is used as the key against all of the tables, and should therefore be unique.
Ordered	DateTime	8	The date the order was placed.
TotalValue	Float	8	The total value of the order.

When a user hits the **Confirm Order** button and moves to the checkout page to process an order, an entry is added to this table. The individual items within the shopping cart are not actually saved to the database when an order is confirmed, although this would obviously be a requirement for a commercial application.

The Products Table

The `Products` table contains a list of all products that a customer can purchase from Adventure Works. The table has the following structure:

Column Name	Type	Length	Description
ProductID	Int	4	A unique ID for the product.
ProductCode	Char	10	The unique code for the product.
Description	Char	255	A description of the product.
UnitPrice	Float	8	The price for this product.
ProductType	Char	20	The category for the product.
Product Introduction Date	DateTime	4	The date when the product was first added to the catalogue.

Column Name	Type	Length	Description
ProductName	Char	50	The name of the product shown in the catalogue.
ProductImage URL	Char	255	The URL of the image to display for the product.
OnSale	Int	4	A flag to indicate whether or not the unit price is a sale price. 1 = sale, 0 = not sale.
Rating	Float	8	A rating out of five for this product in terms of overall quality.

Adventure Works has just less than 50 products grouped into 12 categories.

The ShoppingCarts Table

The ShoppingCarts table holds all of the current product details for each user's shopping cart. The table has the following structure:

Column Name	Type	Length	Description
CustomerName	Char	50	The name or e-mail address of the registered user that currently has the specified product in their basket. **If the user is not currently registered or logged in, this contains the session ID of their ASP+ session.**
ProductCode	Char	10	The unique code for the product.
Description	Char	255	A description of the product.
UnitPrice	Float	8	The price for this product.
Quantity	Int	4	The number of units wanted.
Shopping CartId	Int	4	An auto-generated ID (identity) for the entry.

Every time an item is added to a user's shopping cart, an entry is added to this table.

> The Adventure Works sample application does not clean up the database and remove rows that are associated with sessions that have expired. This would need to be done in a commercial application.

The Application User Interface

When a user first visits the Adventure Works site they are presented with an ASP+ page that gives them a brief introduction to the site contents and provides all the standard promotion material, special offers, and navigation buttons you'd expect from an e-commerce application:

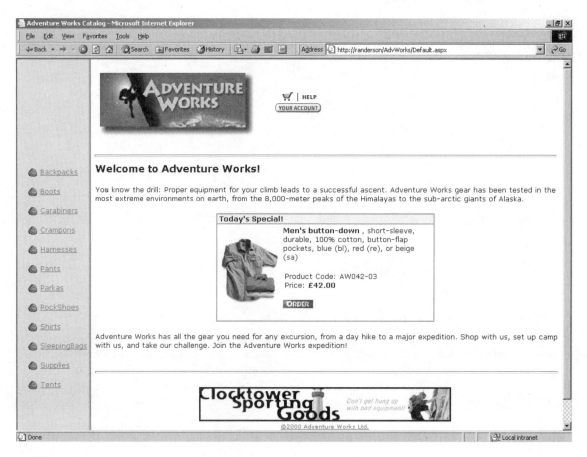

The welcome page provides a fairly intuitive user interface that should enable customers to browse, register, and buy goods. The top of the page contains the Adventure Works logo and navigation buttons that let the user register, login, and view their current/previous orders. The left hand side of the screen details all of the product categories that are defined in the Adventure Works database. The bottom of the screen contains the product-advertising banner and the rest of the screen's middle section contains the special offer.

All pages on the site have the same basic structure as the front page, so each page uses at least three pagelets:

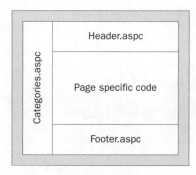

Using Pagelets in AW2000

The pagelets are defined at the top of each page using the @Register directive. This allows you to associate a pagelet with an ASP+ tag prefix (i.e. an element **namespace**). When the ASP+ runtime finds these special tags it knows to create the appropriate pagelet and render the necessary output thanks to these associations.

The @Register directives common to each page are shown here:

```
<%@ Register TagPrefix="Ecommerce" TagName="Header"
          Src="Pagelets\Header.aspc" %>
<%@ Register TagPrefix="Ecommerce" TagName="Categories"
          Src="Pagelets\Categories.aspc" %>
<%@ Register TagPrefix="Ecommerce" TagName="Footer"
          Src="Pagelets\Footer.aspc" %>
```

The pagelets that we've registered are then inserted into a page in the same way as we've seen in previous chapters:

```
<Ecommerce:Header id="Header" runat="server" />
```

Most of the pages in the Adventure Works application have the same basic format containing an HTML table. We'll therefore review the complete page code for Default.aspx that shows all of the pagelets being declared, the language and 'code behind' page directive, the default output cache directive, and the basic HTML page structure:

```
<%@ Page Language="C#" Inherits="AdvWorks.PageBase"
       Src="components/stdpage.cs" %>
<%@ Register TagPrefix="Ecommerce" TagName="Header"
       Src="Pagelets\Header.aspc" %>
<%@ Register TagPrefix="Ecommerce" TagName="Categories"
       Src="Pagelets\Categories.aspc" %>
<%@ Register TagPrefix="Ecommerce" TagName="Special"
       Src="Pagelets\Special.aspc" %>
<%@ Register TagPrefix="Ecommerce" TagName="Footer"
       Src="Pagelets\Footer.aspc" %>
<%@ OutputCache Duration="600" %>

<html>
  <head><title>Adventure Works Catalog</title></head>

  <body background="images/back_sub.gif">
    <form runat="server">
    <font face="Verdana,Arial,Helvetica" size="2">
      <table border="0" cellpadding="0" cellspacing="0">
        <tr>
          <td colspan="5">
             <Ecommerce:Header id="Header" runat="server" />
          </td>
        </tr>
        <tr>
          <td colspan="3" align="left" valign="top">
            <Ecommerce:Categories id="Categories" runat="server" />
          </td>
```

```
            <td>  </td>
            <td align="left" valign="top">
                <h3>Welcome to Adventure Works!</h3>
                <p>
                <font face="Verdana,Arial,Helvetica" size="2">
                  You know the drill: Proper equipment for your climb
                  leads to a successful ascent. Adventure Works gear
                  has been tested in the most extreme environments on
                  earth, from the 8,000-meter peaks of the Himalayas
                  to the sub-arctic giants of Alaska.
                </p>
                <Ecommerce:Special runat="server" />
                <p />
                Adventure Works has all the gear you need for any
                excursion, from a day hike to a major expedition.
                Shop with us, set up camp with us, and take our
                challenge. Join the Adventure  Works expedition!
                <br />
                <Ecommerce:footer runat="server" />
                </font>
            </td>
        </tr>
      </table>
    </font>
    </form>
  </body>
</html>
```

Although the appearance of the front page is fairly rich, the amount of code within the page is actually quite small because much of the HTML and code is encapsulated within the three pagelets. Default.aspx, like most pages, uses the @OutputCache directive to specify that pages are cached for 600 seconds. This reduces database overhead, but you should consider a couple of issues:

❏   Cached information is stored in memory so the working set of your application will be larger.

❏   The same page will be cached multiple times if it has different query parameters, and you have to allow for that increase in the working set.

❏   If a page is cached, then all the output for that page is also cached. This might sound obvious, but it does mean that, for example, the **AdRotator** control for the Adventure Work application doesn't rotate as often as a normal site (i.e. the advert changes once every 600 seconds on the pages that use caching). In the release version of ASP+, you should be able to do page fragment caching and so this shouldn't be an issue.   Fragment caching allows a **portion** 'of the page to be rendered from the cache, while other parts of the page are computed dynamically.

> **At present, ASP+ only performs page caching for HTTP GET requests, and not for HTTP POST requests; so pages will be regenerated when post-backs occur within a page.**

Only One Server-Side <form> Element

One important point to note about the default.aspx page is that it contains a single <form> element with the runat="server" attribute. This form contains the majority of the page's HTML, including all of the pagelets. None of the pagelets has a server-side <form> element. This is important because <form> elements **cannot** be nested, so the single form must include **ALL** pagelet code. If you attempt to define a <form> element with the runat="server" attribute anywhere within the outer <form> element, you will be get an error.

Using C# for the Pagelets and Code

The first line of all our pages in Adventure Works contains the @Page directive:

```
<%@ Page Language="C#" Inherits="AdvWorks.PageBase"
         Src="components/stdpage.cs" %>
```

We saw this directive earlier in the book. Our particular directive informs the ASP+ compiler of two key points about our pages:

❑ All of the page code is written using C# (pagelets and controls could of course be written in other languages).

❑ Each page uses 'code behind', and derives from the COM+ class PageBase that provides common functionality.

The main motivation for using C# to write the Adventure Works application was to show that it really isn't so different to JScript and VB, and it is easy read and understand. ASP+ itself is written in C# which indicates as a language that it has a solid future.

The 'code behind' class specified using the Inherits and Src attributes causes the ASP+ compiler to create a page that derives from the class PageBase rather than Page. The implementation of PageBase is very simple:

```
using System;
using System.Collections;
using System.Web.UI;

namespace AdvWorks
{

  public class PageBase : Page
  {
    public string getDSN() {
      return (String) ((Hashtable)
              Context.GetConfig("advworksdb"))["connstring"];
    }
  }
}
```

By deriving each page from this class we make the getDSN function available within each of our ASP+ pages. This function retrieves the DSN string from the config.web file, and is called in our pages when constructing business objects that connect to the back end data source. The config.web file is cached, so accessing it frequently in our pages should not have any detrimental effect on performance. Should you want to cache just the DSN string you could use the data cache to hold it, just accessing the config.web initially to retrieve the value when creating the cache entry:

```
    // An alternative way of accessing the DSN via the data cache

public String getDSNCached() {

    string connectionString;

    // Check the Cache for the ConnectionString
    connectionString = (string) Context.Cache["DSN"];

    // If the ConnectionString is not in the cache, fetch from Config.web

    if (connectionString == null) {
        connectionString =
        (String) ((Hashtable)
                    Context.GetConfig("advworksdb"))["connstring"];

        //store to cache
        Cache["DSN"] = connectionString;
    }

    // Return the Connection String

    return connectionString;
    }
```

One point to consider when using the data cache is that the values held within it **will** be updated if somebody changes the config.web file. ASP+ automatically creates a new application domain and essentially restarts the Web application to handle all new Web requests when the config.web file is changed. As this results in a new data cache being created, the new DSN string will be cached after the first call to getDSNCached.

> As discussed in Chapter 6, applications settings should always be stored in the
> **appsettings** section of **config.web**. Values within the section are cached
> automatically.

If you decided to store application configuration in another location (maybe your own XML file on a central server) you can still invalidate the cache when your files change, by creating file dependency. This allows a cache item to be automatically flushed from the cache when a specific file changes:

```
//store to cache
Cache.Insert("DSN", connectionString,
        new CacheDependency(Server.MapPath("\\someserver\myconfig.xml")));
```

File dependencies are just one of the cache dependency types ASP+ supports. The other types supported include:

❑ **Scavenging** – flushing cache items based upon their usage, memory consumption and rating

❑ **Expiration** – flushing cache items at a specific time or after a period of inactivity/access

❑ **File and key dependencies** – flushing cache items when either a file changes or another cache entry changes

The Specials Pagelet – Special.aspc

As you might have noticed, the `default.aspx` page we saw earlier, which implements the welcome page, actually uses one additional pagelet (`Pagelets\Special.aspc`) to display today's special product, so the page structure is slightly more complex:

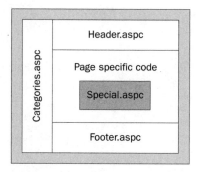

The product on offer is stored in the `config.web` file, making it easy for the site administrator to change the product displayed:

```
<configuration>
    ..
    <advworksdb>
      <add key="connstring"
           value="server=localhost;uid=sa;pwd=;database=advworks" />
      <add key="specialOffer" value="AW042-03" />
    </advworksdb>
    ...
</configuration>
```

The specials pagelet reads this value in its `Page_Load` event handler, retrieving the product information using the `ProductsDB` component, and then updates the page using server-side controls:

```
...
<script language="C#" runat="server">

  void Page_Load(Object sender, EventArgs e) {

    // Obtain today's special product.

    AdvWorks.ProductsDB inventory = new AdvWorks.ProductsDB(getDSN());
    string specialOffer;

    specialOffer = (String) ((Hashtable)
                Context.GetConfig("advworksdb"))["specialOffer"];

    // Read Product form DB
    DataSet specialDetails = inventory.GetProduct(specialOffer);

    // Update UI with product details
```

```
      ProductImageURL.Src =
        (String) specialDetails.Tables[0].Rows[0]["ProductImageURL"];
      ProductName.Text = (String)
                specialDetails.Tables[0].Rows[0]["ProductName"];
      ProductDescription.Text = (String)
                specialDetails.Tables[0].Rows[0]["ProductDescription"];
      ProductCode.Text = (String)
                specialDetails.Tables[0].Rows[0]["ProductCode"];
      UnitPrice.Text =
          String.Format("{0:C}",
                specialDetails.Tables[0].Rows[0]["UnitPrice"]);
      OrderAnchor.HRef =
          "ShoppingCart.aspx?ProductCode=" +
          (String) specialDetails.Tables[0].Rows[0]["ProductCode"];
      ...
  }
</script>

<table width="400" align="center" border="1"
        cellpadding="0" cellspacing="0">
  <tr bgcolor="#f7efDe">
    <td>
      <font face="Verdana" size="2"><b>Today's Special!</b></font>
    </td>
  </tr>
  <tr>
    <td>
      <table>
        <tr>
          <td align="left" valign="top" width="110">
             <img id="ProductImageURL" runat="server" />
          </td>
          <td align="left" valign="top"><font size="2">
            <b><asp:label id="ProductName" runat="server" /></b>,
            <asp:label id="ProductDescription" runat="server" /><br />
            <table>
              <tr>
                <td><font size="2">
                  Product Code:
                  <asp:label id="ProductCode" runat="server" />
                  <br />Price: <b>
                  <asp:label id="UnitPrice" runat="server" />
                  </b></font>
                </td>
                <td>
                    
                  <img src="images/saleTag1.gif" id="sale" runat="server" >
                </td>
              </tr>
            </table>
            <br>
            <a id="OrderAnchor" runat="server"
              href="ShoppingCart.aspx?ProductCode=AW109-15" />
              <img src="images/order.gif" width="55" height="15"
                   alt="Order" border="0">
            </a><br /><br /></font>
          </td>
```

```
        </tr>
      </table>
    </td>
  </tr>
</table>
```

The pagelet code is very simple, and just updates the server controls with values from the DataSet returned by the function call to GetProduct. The String.Format function is called using a format string of {0:C} to show the UnitPrice as a numerical value that represents a locale-specific currency amount.

The Categories Pagelets – Categories.aspc

This product category list (categories.aspc), shown on the left-hand side of most pages (it is not shown on checkout or account pages), is dynamically built using the asp:DataList control and the ProductsDB business object. The DataSource property for the control is set in the Page_Load event:

```
<script language="C#" runat="server">

  void Page_Load( Object sender, EventArgs e ) {
    AdvWorks.ProductsDB inventory = new AdvWorks.ProductsDB(getDSN());
    CategoryList.DataSource =
          inventory.GetProductCategories().Tables[0].DefaultView;
    CategoryList.DataBind();
  }

</script>
```

The ItemTemplate for this data list control is specified in the pagelet, and specifies the layout of the data:

```
<asp:DataList id="CategoryList" border="0" runat="server">

  <template name="ItemTemplate">
    <tr>
      <td valign="top">
        <asp:image ImageURL="/AdvWorks/images/bullet.gif"
                AlternateText="bullet" runat="server" />
      </td>
      <td valign="top">
        <font face="Verdana,Arial,Helvetica" size="2">
          <asp:hyperlink
               NavigateURL='<%#DataBinder.Eval(Container.DataItem,
                                  "ProductType",
                                  "/AdvWorks/Catalogue.aspx?ProductType={0}")%>'
               Text='<%#DataBinder.Eval(Container.DataItem, "ProductType")%>'
               runat=server />

        </font>
    </td>
  </tr>
  </template>

</asp:DataList>
```

The `asp:DataList` control was seen in Chapter 3. It is bound to a data source of items in a collection, and it renders the `ItemTemplate` for each of these items.

The `asp:DataList` control outputs an HTML table; so the `ItemTemplate` we've written outputs a `<tr>` element containing two columns (`<td>` elements), which ensure the table and page are correctly rendered. The first column contains an `asp:image` control that renders the small 'rock' bullet bitmap, the second column contains an `asp:hyperlink` control that has two fields (`NavigateURL` and `Text`). These fields are bound to the current row of the `DataSet` returned by the `ProductDB` business object.

The hyperlink rendered in the `ItemTemplate` allows the user to view the product details for a specific category. The `NavigateURL` attribute is a calculated field consisting of a fixed URL (`/AdvWorks/catalogue.aspx`) and a dynamic query parameter, `ProductType`, whose value is set to equal the `ProductType` field in the current dataset row. To build the URL we have specified a replacement value of `{0}` in the third parameter to `DataBinder.Eval`. At runtime ASP+ replaces this marker value with the contents of the `ProductType` value specified by the second parameter. This method of constructing strings is much cleaner than the traditional ASP way of concatenating strings. Finally, the `Text` is also set to equal the `ProductType` field in the current dataset row.

The `DataBinder` class is used to retrieve the values stored in these properties. In case you're wondering, the `DataBinder` class is just a 'helper' class provided by ASP+ to keep our code simpler (fewer casts) and more readable, especially if we also need to format a property. We could also have directly accessed the current `DataSet` row ourselves and retrieved the `ProductType` value using this code:

```
((DataRowView)Container.DataItem)["ProductType"].ToString()
```

This format is slightly more complex, but may be preferable if you're happy using casts and prefer the style. One advantage of this code is that it is early bound, so it will execute faster than the late bound `DataBinder` syntax.

When one of the product category hyperlinks is clicked, the ASP+ page `Catalogue.aspx` is displayed:

This page shows the products for the selected category by using the `ProductType` query string parameter in the Page_Load event to filter the results returned from the ProductDB component:

```
void Page_Load(Object sender, EventArgs e) {

    // Determine what product category has been specified and update section image

    String productType = Request.Params["ProductType"];
    CatalogueSectionImage.Src = "images/hd_" + productType + ".gif";

    // Use business object to fetch category products and databind
    // it to the <asp:datalist> control

    AdvWorks.ProductsDB inventory = new AdvWorks.ProductsDB(getDSN());
    MyList.DataSource =
        inventory.GetProducts(productType).Tables[0].DefaultView;
    MyList.DataBind();
}
```

A subtle design issue here is that we have used a hyperlink and not a post-back to change the products shown. This hyperlink produces an HTTP GET action to send the values to the Web server, which – as mentioned earlier – means that page output caching will be employed.

Each of the products shown for the selected category has a number of details:

- ❑ **Product Name** – the name of the product (Everglades, Rockies, etc.).

- ❑ **Product Info** – facts about the product that will be of interest to customers and help them make purchasing decisions (whether the item is water-proof, its color, etc.).

- ❑ **Product Code** – the unique ID for the product across the site.

- ❑ **Price** – The price of the product.

- ❑ **On Sale** – If the price is reduced in price, the 'SALE PRICE' image is displayed.

- ❑ **Order Button** – to add the product to the shopping basket the user clicks the 'Order' image.

The main body of this page is also generated using an `asp:DataList` control, by setting the data source in the Page_Load event and using an `ItemTemplate` to control the rendering of each product. Unlike the categories pagelet, the `asp:datalist` on this page takes advantage of the `RepeatDirection` and `RepeatColumns` attributes:

```
<asp:datalist id="MyList" BorderWidth="0"
    RepeatDirection="horizontal" RepeatColumns=2 runat="server">
```

These attributes automatically perform the page layout for us, and make the application look professional. All we do in our `ItemTemplate` is define a two-column table that contains the image in the first column and the details in the second column. The `asp:DataList` control then works out how to flow the rows, so changing the page to use vertical flowing is simply a matter of changing one attribute value:

```
<asp:datalist id="MyList" BorderWidth="0"
    RepeatDirection="vertical" RepeatColumns=2 runat="server">
```

Now, we get a different layout of the items:

Without the `asp:DataList` control providing this functionality, we'd have to write a reasonable amount of code ourselves. If you review the original ASP Adventure Works application, you'll see this requires 100-200 lines of code in total.

When an item is in a sale the bitmap is shown:

To determine whether or not this image is displayed, we use inline code to hide the image. We do this by setting the `Visible` property of the `saleItem` server control (our `img` element) to `false` if the `OnSale` property is equal to zero:

```
...
<%
DataRowView myRowView;
myRowView = (DataRowView) Container.DataItem;

if  ((int) myRowView["OnSale"] == 0) {
    Container.FindControl("saleItem").Visible = false;
}
%>
...
<img src="images/saleTag1.gif" id="saleItem" runat="server" />
...
```

This code is an extract taken from within the ItemTemplate.

By setting the `Visible` property to `false`, the ASP+ runtime does not render the control or any child controls – as it would if we'd used something like a `<span>` element to contain the image and text. This is a very powerful approach for preventing partial page generation, and is much cleaner than the inline `if...then` statements that ASP required us to write.

> **When using inline code like this, the code must occur before the elements in the page it references, otherwise the code is executed too late and the page contents for the referenced elements have already been rendered.**

An alternative to using inline code to hide and show elements, is to wire up a function to the `OnItemCreated` event that the `asp:datalist` fires each time an item is created. The function prototype required for the event is shown here:

```
void ItemCreated(Object sender, DataListItemCreatedEventArgs e);
```

The `DataListItemCreatedEventArgs` argument contains an `Item` property that effectively returns the same object as calling `Container.DataItem`. By accessing this in your event handler, it's possible to locate any controls within your `Item` template using the `FindControl` method, and then manipulate them.

The following code shows this approach:

```
void DataList_ItemCreated(object sender, DataListItemCreatedEventArgs e) {
    // Only if this is an Item
    if ((e.Item.ItemType != ListItemType.Header) &&
        (e.Item.ItemType != ListItemType.Footer) &&
        (e.Item.ItemType != ListItemType.Separator))
    {
        int onsale = (int) ((DataRowView)e.Item.DataItem)["OnSale"];
            if (onsale == 0) {
            Container.FindControl("saleItem").Visible = false;
        }
    }
};
```

The advantage of this approach is that the code is somewhat clean and easier to maintain, but more importantly, any changes made by the code to controls that persist their state survive post-backs. As inline code is executed during the render phase of an ASP+ page, view state (state saved by the page and/or any child controls) has **already** been saved, so any changes made in inline code will not be round-tripped during a post back. The reason for using inline code in this chapter is to show that ASP+ applications can still make use of inline code, but better (and sometimes mandatory) alternative approaches exist that allow you to maintain a much stronger separation of code from content.

Product Details

For each product shown in the `catalogue.aspx` page, the product name is rendered as a hyperlink. If a customer finds the product overview interesting, they can click the link to see more details about the product (admittedly there is not a great deal of extra detail in our sample application):

This page is called `details.aspx` in the samples accompanying this book.

Everglades Details

Information:

medium-weight, waterproof leather boots, good traction, brown (br)

AW098-04

Product first introduced 20/05/1996

SALE PRICE £98.00

ORDER

Adventure Works Rating 4.5 out of a possible 5

The additional information on this screen includes the date when the product was first introduced and a product rating assigned by the reviewer team at Adventure Works. The team always tests out the gear it sells first hand and assigns a rating. The Rating field in the Products table predetermines the rating bar shown for each product. The bar itself is generated using a custom server control written for Adventure Works. The source code for this rating meter control is located in the Controls directory, and it should be easily understood if you have read Chapter 7. Like the Components directory, the Controls directory contains a make.bat file for building the control.

The control is registered and assigned an element name (tag prefix) at the top of the details page:

```
<%@ Register TagPrefix="Wrox" Namespace="WroxControls" %>
```

Although it only shows a single product, the details.aspx page still uses an asp:DataList control. The motivation for this was that future versions of Adventure Works could potentially allow multiple products to have their details viewed at once. The rating control is therefore declared within the ItemTemplate for the asp:DataList control as the Score property, using the field named Rating in the database table:

```
<Wrox:RatingMeter runat="server"
      Score=<%#(double)DataBinder.Eval(Container.DataItem, "Rating")%>
      Votes="1"
      MaxRating="5"
      CellWidth="51" CellHeight="10" />
```

While the properties of the rating control may seem a little confusing at first, you should understand that it is a generic control that is suitable for many tasks. If you have seen the MSDN article rating system it probably makes sense, but if not, consider the case where 200 people have rated a product, so you have 200 votes. For each vote a score between 0 and MaxRating can be assigned, and the Score attribute reflects the total sum for all votes.

The rating control actually supports more functionality than is needed by the Adventure Works application, so we set the Votes property to 1, since only a single staff member rates the products. The idea is that future versions of the application will support customer ratings and reviews.

We won't be covering the functionality of the rating control any further in this chapter, so to help you out, here is a run down of the properties which should set you in the right direction:

Property	Description
CellWidth	The size of each cell within the bar.
MaxRating	The maximum rating that can be assigned by a single vote. This value determines the number of cells that the bar has.
CellHeight	The height of each cell.
Votes	The number of votes that have been cast.
Score	The current score or rating.

The Shopping Cart

When surfing through the site, a customer can add items to their shopping basket at any time by hitting the Order image hyperlink:

This image is inserted into the catalogue.aspx page as it is created, and clicking it results in the browser navigating to the ShoppingCart.aspx page:

```
<a href='<%#DataBinder.Eval(Container.DataItem,
                            "ProductCode",
          "ShoppingCart.aspx?ProductCode={0}")%>'>
  <img src="images/order.gif" WIDTH="55" HEIGHT="15" ALT="Order" BORDER=0>
</a>
```

Which looks like this:

SHOPPING CART

You have selected 1 items so far:

Remove	Product Code	Product Name	Description	Quantity	Unit Price	Unit Total
☐	AW098-04	Everglades	medium-weight, waterproof leather boots, good traction, brown (br)	1	£98.00	£98.00

Total is £98.00

Recalculate   Go To Checkout

When the ShoppingCart.aspx page is being generated, the Page_Load event checks to see if a new product is being added to the cart by looking for a Request parameter called ProductCode. This is added to the URL as a query string by the code in the Catalogue.aspx page (as shown earlier). The AddShoppingCartItem function of the CartDB object is then invoked to add it to the shopping cart for the current user.

The `Page_Load` event handler for the `ShoppingCart.aspx` page is shown here:

```
void Page_Load(Object sender, EventArgs e) {

    AdvWorks.CartDB cart = new AdvWorks.CartDB(getDSN());

    // If new product is specified, add it to the shopping cart

    if (Request.Params["ProductCode"] != null) {
        cart.AddShoppingCartItem( GetCustomerID(),
                                Request.Params["ProductCode"]);
    }

    // If page is not being loaded in response to postback

    if (Page.IsPostBack == false) {
        PopulateShoppingCartList();
        UpdateSelectedItemStatus();
    }
}
```

The `ProductCode` parameter is optional because the shopping cart can also be displayed by clicking on the shopping cart symbol shown in the navigation bar. If this is clicked, the user has not selected a product so we do not want to add anything. The `GetCustomerID` function used here returns the unique ID for the current customer, which is then passed as a parameter to the `AddShoppingCartItem` function. If the customer has not registered and logged in, the ID returned by the `GetCustomerID` function is the current ASP+ session ID, otherwise it is the current user name:

```
String GetCustomerID() {

    if (User.Identity.Name != "") {
        return User.Identity.Name;
    }
    else {
        return Session.SessionID;
    }
}
```

The implementation of the `AddShoppingCartItem` method of the `CartDB` business object is worth reviewing at this point, because it contains two interesting sections of code:

```
public void AddShoppingCartItem(string customerName,
                                string productCode) {

    DataSet previousItem = GetShoppingCartItem(customerName, productCode);

    if (previousItem.Tables[0].Rows.Count > 0) {
        UpdateShoppingCartItem(
            (int)previousItem.Tables[0].Rows[0]["ShoppingCartID"],
            ((int)previousItem.Tables[0].Rows[0]["Quantity"]) + 1);
    }
    else {
```

```
        AdvWorks.ProductsDB products;
        products = new AdvWorks.ProductsDB(m_dsn);

        DataSet productDetails = products.GetProduct(productCode);

        String description =
          (String) productDetails.Tables[0].Rows[0]["ProductDescription"];
        String productName =
          (String) productDetails.Tables[0].Rows[0]["ProductName"];
        Double unitPrice =
          (double) productDetails.Tables[0].Rows[0]["UnitPrice"];
        String insertStatement = "INSERT INTO ShoppingCarts (ProductCode, "
            + "ProductName, Description, UnitPrice, CustomerName, Quantity) "
            + "VALUES ('" + productCode + "', @productName, @description, "
            + unitPrice + ", '" + customerName + "' , 1)";

        SQLConnection sqlConnection = new SQLConnection(m_dsn);
        SQLCommand myCommand = new SQLCommand(insertStatement,
                                              sqlConnection);
        myCommand.Parameters.Add(new SQLParameter("@ProductName",
                        SQLDataType.VarChar, 50));
        myCommand.Parameters["@ProductName"].Value = productName ;
        myCommand.Parameters.Add(new SQLParameter("@description",
                        SQLDataType.VarChar, 255));
        myCommand.Parameters["@description"].Value = description;
        myCommand.ActiveConnection.Open();
        myCommand.Execute();
        myCommand.ActiveConnection.Close();
    }
  }
```

The first interesting point about the code is that it checks if the item is already in the shopping cart by calling GetShoppingCartItem, and if it does already exist it simply increases the quantity for that item and updates it in the database using the UpdateShoppingCartItem function.

The second interesting point comes about because the ADO+ code that adds a new cart item uses the SQLCommand class. Since the Adventure Works product descriptions can contain single quotes, we need to ensure that any quotes within the description do not conflict with the quotes used to delimit the field. To do this we use the SQLCommand object to execute our query, making use of parameters in our SQL such as @description to avoid any conflict. The values for the parameters are then specified using the Parameters collections of the SQLCommand object:

```
myCommand.Parameters.Add(new SQLParameter("@description",
                    SQLDataType.VarChar, 255));
```

Once the SQL statement is built, the command object can be connected, the statement executed, and then disconnected:

```
myCommand.ActiveConnection.Open();
myCommand.Execute();
myCommand.ActiveConnection.Close();
```

Displaying the Shopping Cart and Changing an Order

The shopping cart allows customers to specify a quantity for each product in the cart, and displays the price per item and total price for the quantity ordered. At any time, a customer can change the order quantity or remove one or more items from the cart by checking the Remove box and clicking Recalculate. An item will also be removed if the customer enters a quantity of zero.

To implement this functionality we have used the asp:Repeater control. Implementing this functionality today in ASP isn't an easy task, and requires significant code. In ASP+ it's fairly simple.

The asp:Repeater control was used as the base for building the shopping cart as it doesn't need to use any of the built-in selection and editing functionality provided by the other list controls such as the asp:DataList and asp:DataGrid. All of the items are always checked and processed during a post-back, and the cart contents (i.e. the data set bound to the asp:Repeater control) is always generated during each post-back.

The asp:Repeater control is also 'lookless' (i.e. it only generates the HTML element that we specify using templates), which fits in well with the design for our shopping cart page. We don't need a complete table to be generated by the control (the table start and header row are part of the static HTML).

Data Source/HTML/ASPX for the Shopping Cart

The shopping cart data source is provided by the CartDB component, which is bound to the myList asp:repeater control:

```
void PopulateShoppingCartList() {

    // Populate list with updated shopping cart data

    AdvWorksCart.CartDB cart = new AdvWorksCart.CartDB(getDSN());

    DataSet ds = cart.GetShoppingCartItems(GetCustomerID());

    MyList.DataSource = ds.Tables[0].DefaultView;
    MyList.DataBind();
    ...
```

The HTML used to render shopping cart, including the ItemTemplate rendered for each item in the MyList.DataSource is shown next, although some parts of the HTML page formatting (e.g. the font settings) have been removed to keep it short and more readable:

```
<table colspan="8" cellpadding="5" border="0" valign="top">
<tr valign="top">
  <td align="center" bgcolor="#800000">Remove</td>
  <td align="center" bgcolor="#800000">Product Code</td>
  <td align="center" bgcolor="#800000">Product Name</td>
  <td align="center" bgcolor="#800000" width="250">Description</td>
  <td align="center" bgcolor="#800000">Quantity</td>
  <td align="center" bgcolor="#800000">Unit Price</td>
  <td align="center" bgcolor="#800000">Unit Total</td>
</tr>
```

```
<asp:Repeater id="MyList" runat="server">

  <template name="ItemTemplate">
    <tr>
    <td align="center" bgcolor="#f7efde">
      <asp:checkbox id="Remove" runat="server" />
    </td>
    <td align="center" bgcolor="#f7efde">
      <input id="ShoppingCartID" type="hidden" value=
'<%#DataBinder.Eval(Container.DataItem,"ShoppingCartID")%>'
        runat="server" />
      <%#DataBinder.Eval(Container.DataItem, "ProductCode")%>
    </td>
    <td align="center" bgcolor="#f7efde">
      <%#DataBinder.Eval(Container.DataItem, "ProductName")%>
    </td>
    <td align="center" bgcolor="#f7efde">
      <%#DataBinder.Eval(Container.DataItem, "Description")%>
    </td>
    <td align="center" bgcolor="#f7efde">
      <asp:textbox id="Quantity" text=
'<%#DataBinder.Eval(Container.DataItem, "Quantity")%>'
        width="30" runat="server" />
    </td>
    <td align="center" bgcolor="#f7efde">
      <asp:label id="UnitPrice"
        runat="server">
        <%#DataBinder.Eval(Container.DataItem, "UnitPrice", "{0:C}")%>
      </asp:label>
    </td>
    <td align="center" bgcolor="#f7efde">
      <%# String.Format("{0:C}",
 (((int)DataBinder.Eval(Container.DataItem, "Quantity"))
 * ((double) DataBinder.Eval(Container.DataItem, "UnitPrice")) )) %>
      </td>
    </tr>
  </template>

</asp:Repeater>

<tr>
  <td colspan="6"></td>
  <td colspan="2" align="right">
  Total is <%=String.Format(fTotal.ToString(), "{0:C}") %>
  </td>
</tr>
<tr>
  <td colspan="8" align="right">
  <asp:button text="Recalculate" OnClick="Recalculate_Click"
            runat="server" />
  <asp:button text="Go To Checkout" OnClick="Checkout_Click"
            runat="server" />
  </td>
</tr>

</table>
```

The code shown above is similar to that which we've seen earlier, so it should be easy to follow. The important point to note, is that all the fields that need to be available when a post-back occurs are marked with the id and runat="server" attributes. When the customer causes a post-back to occur by pressing the Recalculate button, the ASP+ page can access the Remove checkbox control, the database cart ID hidden field control, and the Quantity field control for each list item – and update the database accordingly.

For each row in the ShoppingCarts table for this customer, the asp:Repeater control will contain a list item with these three controls – which can be programmatically accessed:

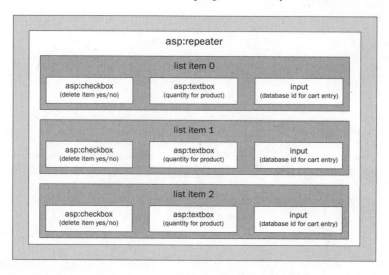

To associate each list item within the asp:Repeater control with a specific database cart item, a hidden field is used to store the unique ID for the entry:

```
<input id="ShoppingCartID" type="hidden" value=
'<%#DataBinder.Eval(Container.DataItem,"ShoppingCartID")%>'
runat="server">
```

As discussed earlier, the contents of the shopping cart are always stored in the SQL server table named ShoppingCarts, and manipulated using the business object named CartDB. To populate the shopping cart with items, the ASP+ page invoked the PopulateShoppingCartList function. This occurs when the page is loaded for the first time (i.e. Page.PostBack==false), and after each post-back that leads to the database being modified – items added, deleted or the quantities changed. To retrieve the cart items and data bind the asp:Repeater control, this function uses the GetShoppingCartItems method of the CartDB object:

```
void PopulateShoppingCartList() {

    // Populate list with updated shopping cart data

    AdvWorks.CartDB cart = new AdvWorks.CartDB(getDSN());
    DataSet ds = cart.GetShoppingCartItems(GetCustomerID());
    MyList.DataSource = ds.Tables[0].DefaultView;
    MyList.DataBind();
    ...
```

Once the list is bound, the data set is then enumerated to calculate the total value of the items within the cart:

```
DataTable dt;
dt = ds.Tables[0];

int lIndex;
double UnitPrice;
int Quantity;

for ( lIndex =0; lIndex < dt.Rows.Count; lIndex++ ) {
   UnitPrice = (double) dt.Rows[lIndex]["UnitPrice"];
   Quantity = (int) dt.Rows[lIndex]["Quantity"];
   if ( Quantity > 0 ) {
      fTotal += UnitPrice * Quantity;
   }
 }
}
```

The total stored in the `fTotal` parameter is defined as a `Double` earlier in the page definition:

```
// Total for shopping basket
double fTotal = 0;
```

and then referenced by inline code that executes just after the `asp:Repeater` control:

```
...
</asp:repeater>
<tr>
  <td colspan="6"></td><td colspan="2" align="right">
    Total is <% = Double.Format(fTotal, "C") %>
  </td>
</tr>
    ...
```

When a customer changes the order quantity for products in their cart, or marks items to be removed, they click the **Recalculate** button. This button was created using the `asp:button` control with its `OnClick` event wired up to the `Recalculate_Click` function:

```
<asp:button text="Recalculate" OnClick="Recalculate_Click"
            runat="server" />
```

The `Recalculate_Click` function updates the database based upon the changes the user has made to the quantities and the items they've added or deleted. It then retrieves the updated cart items from the database, rebinds the repeater control to the updated data set, and finally creates a status method informing the user how many items (if any) are currently in the cart. These functions are delegated within the event handler to three different functions:

```
void Recalculate_Click(Object sender, EventArgs e) {

  // Update Shopping Cart
  UpdateShoppingCartDatabase();
```

```
  // Repopulate ShoppingCart List
  PopulateShoppingCartList();

  // Change status message
  UpdateSelectedItemStatus();
  }
```

The `UpdateShoppingCartDatabase` method is called first in the event handler, when the post-back data for the `asp:Repeater` control describing the cart and any changes made will be available. The function can therefore access this post-back data before any database updates and deletions that may be required. Next, calling `PopulateShoppingCartList` causes the shopping cart to be re-read from the database and bound to the `asp:Repeater` control. This will cause the page to render an updated view of the cart to the user.

To perform the required database updates, the `UpdateShoppingCartDatabase` function iterates through each of the list items (i.e. the rows) within the `asRepeater` control and checks each item to see if it should be deleted or modified:

```
void UpdateShoppingCartDatabase() {

AdvWorks.ProductsDB inventory = new AdvWorks.ProductsDB(getDSN());
AdvWorksCart.CartDB cart = new AdvWorksCart.CartDB(getDSN());


// Iterate through all rows within shopping cart list

for (int i=0; i<MyList.Items.Count; i++) {

  // Obtain references to row's controls

  TextBox quantityTxt = (TextBox) MyList.Items[i].FindControl("Quantity");
  CheckBox remove = (CheckBox) MyList.Items[i].FindControl("Remove");
  HtmlInputHidden shoppingCartIDTxt = (HtmlInputHidden)
  MyList.Items[i].FindControl("ShoppingCartID");

  // If Remove checkbox selected then delete the item
  // Otherwise update the quantity for this item

  // Convert quantity to a number
  int Quantity = Int32.Parse(quantityTxt.Text);

  if (remove.Checked == true || Quantity  == 0) {
    cart.DeleteShoppingCartItem(Int32.Parse(shoppingCartIDTxt.Value));
    }
  else
    cart.UpdateShoppingCartItem(Int32.Parse(shoppingCartIDTxt.Value),
                                Quantity);
  }
}
```

This code takes a brute force approach by updating every item in the shopping cart that isn't marked for deletion. In a commercial application, you should consider having a hidden field that stores the original quantity and only updates items when the two quantity fields differ. This could potentially reduce database IO considerably if you have users who keep changing their order quantities and deleting items.

Another alternative would be to hook the OnChange event fired by the TextBox controls in the list. This event is fired during a post-back when the value of a text box has changed. You could sink these events and update the database accordingly.

Checkout Processing and Security

When a customer is ready to commit to purchasing the goods that are currently in their shopping cart, they can click the Go to Checkout button in the shopping cart page, or click the shopping basket image located on the navigation bar. The security system used in Adventure Works takes advantage of cookie-based authentication (also called form-based security), as introduced in Chapter 6. When a customer hits any of the pages that require authentication, if they haven't already signed in, the page login.aspx is displayed:

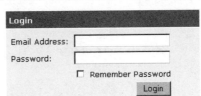

The ASP+ runtime knows to display this page if a user is not logged in because all pages that require authentication are located in a directory called **secure**. It contains a **config.web** file that specifies anonymous access is not allowed:

```
<configuration>
  <security>
    <authorization>
      <deny users="?" />
    </authorization>
    ...
  </security>
</configuration>
```

Remember that '?' means 'anonymous users'.

Using a specific directory to contain secure items is a simple yet flexible way of implementing security in ASP+ applications. When the ASP+ runtime determines that an anonymous user is trying to access a page in a secure directory of our application, it knows which page to display because the config.web file located in the root directory has a cookie element with a loginurl attribute that specifies it:

```
<configuration>
  <security>
    <authentication mode="Cookie">
      <cookie cookie=".wroxcookie" loginurl="/advworks/login.aspx"
              decryptionkey="0011223344556677" />
    </authentication>
  </security>
</configuration>
```

This configuration basically says if the `.wroxcookie` cookie is present and it has not been tampered with, the user has been authenticated and can therefore access secure directions if authorized. It not present, redirect to the URL specified by `loginurl`.

Cookie Based Authentication in Web Farms

For cookie authentication to work within a Web farm environment, the `decryptionkey` attribute of the `cookie` element must be set and not left blank or specified as the default value of `autogenerate`. The `decryptionkey` attribute should be set the same on all machines within the farm. The length of the string is 16 characters (as in the example above) for DES encryption (56/64 bit), or 48 characters for Triple-DES encryption (128 bit). If you do use the default value it will cause a different encryption string to be generated by each machine in the farm and cause the session authentication to fail between different machines as a user moves between servers. If this happens a `CryptographicException` will be thrown and the user will be presented with a screen saying data is bad or could not be decoded.

The Login.aspx Page Event Handlers

The Login button on the login form is created using an `asp:button` control which has the `OnClick` event wired up to the `LoginBtn_Click` event handler:

```
...
<td colspan="2" align="right">
  <asp:button Text=" Login "OnClick="LoginBtn_Click" runat="server" />
</td>
```

When the button is clicked the `LoginBtn_Click` event handler is invoked; it validates the users, and then redirects them to the original page. The validation and redirection code is shown here:

```
void LoginBtn_Click(Object sender, EventArgs e) {

  AdvWorks.UsersDB users = new AdvWorks.UsersDB(getDSN());
  AdvWorksCart.CartDB cart = new AdvWorksCart.CartDB(getDSN());

  if (users.ValidateLogin(UserName.Text, Password.Text)) {

    // Set Client Authentication Cookie
    CookieAuthentication.SetAuthCookie(UserName.Text, Persist.Checked);

    // Migrate any temporary shopping cart items to logged-in username
    cart.MigrateShoppingCartItems(Session.SessionID, UserName.Text);

    // Redirect user back to activating page
    Navigate(ReturnUrl.Value);
  }
  else {
    Message.Text = "Login failed, check your details and try again.";
  }
}
```

The code initially creates the two business objects that are required, using the 'code behind' function `getDSN` to collect details of the data source to connect to. Once the `UsersDB` object is created, its `ValidateLogin` method is invoked to determine if the user credentials are OK (the user details are stored in the `Account` table rather than the `config.web` file, as was the case in earlier chapters). If the details are invalid, the `Text` property of the `Message` control is updated to show the error. If the login is successful, the following steps occur:

1. The client is marked as authenticated by calling the `SetAuthCookie` method of the `CookeAuthentication` object, which we discussed in Chapter 6.

2. This causes the cookie named `.wroxcookie` to be sent back to the client, so we know from here on in that the client has been authenticated.

3. The user is redirected back to the page that initially caused the login form to be displayed.

If a customer has previously registered, they can log in via the Login page; after which, they will be redirected back to the original page that caused the Login page to be displayed. The redirection code is actually implemented by the Login page we have created, and does require some extra work on our part. We'll see this next.

Handling Page Return Navigation During Authentication

When the ASP+ runtime determines that a secure item has been accessed, it will redirect the user to our Login page, and include a query string parameter named `ReturnURL`. As the name suggests, this is the page that we will redirect the user to once we are happy that they should be allowed access to it. When displaying our page, we need to save this value, as it will be lost during the posts-back where we'll validate this user. The approach used in our page is to store the value in a hidden field during the `Page_Load` event:

```
void Page_Load(Object sender, EventArgs e) {

    // Store Return Url in Page State
    if (Request.QueryString["ReturnUrl"] != null) {
      ReturnUrl.Value = Request.QueryString["ReturnUrl"];
    }
}
```

The hidden field is defined as part of the Login form, and includes the `runat="server"` attribute so that we can programatically access it in our event handlers:

```
<input type="hidden" value="/advworks/default.aspx"
       id="ReturnUrl" runat="server" />
```

We have given the hidden field a default value, as it is possible for the user to go directly to the login page via the navigation bar. Without a default value, the redirection code that is executed after the login would not work. See Chapter 6 for more details of forms based authentication.

So when the customer clicks the Login button, we can validate their details and then redirect them to the page whose value is stored in the `ReturnUrl` hidden control.

First Time Customer – Registration

If a customer has not registered with our application before, they can click the Registration hyperlink - and they are then presented with a user registration form to fill in:

Please enter your details below:

Register	
Email Address:	v-rand@microsoft.com
Password:	******
Confirm Password:	******
	☐ Remember Password
	Register

We've kept the form simple for this case study, and only ask for an e-mail address and password. In a commercial application, this form would probably include additional information such as the name and address of the customer.

As the registration page (`Register.aspx`) is opened from a hyperlink in the login page (`login.aspx`), we have to ensure that we pass on the `ReturnUrl` parameter – so that the registration page knows where to redirect the user once they have completed the form. To do this we dynamically create the hyperlink in the registration form during the `Page_Load` event of the login page:

```
((HyperLink)RegisterUser).NavigateUrl =
    "Register.aspx?ReturnUrl=" + ReturnUrl.Value;
```

making sure that the hyperlink is marked as a server control in the `login.aspx` page:

```
...
<font size="2">
<asp:HyperLink NavigateUrl="Register.aspx" id="RegisterUser"
    runat="server" />
  Click Here to Register New Account
</asp:hyperlink>
</font>
...
```

Those of you with a keen eye will have spotted that customers can actually login at any time by clicking the 'Sign In or Register' hyperlink located in the page header. Once a user is successfully authenticated, the hyperlink changes to say 'Sign Out':

The sign in or out code is implemented in the header pagelet (`pagelets/header.aspc`) where the `Page_Load` event handler dynamically changes the text of the `signInOutMsg` control, depending on the authentication state of the current user:

```
<%@ Import Namespace="System.Web.Security" %>
<script language="C#" runat="server">

   private void Page_Load( Object Sender, EventArgs e ) {
     updateSignInOutMessage();
   }

   private void SignInOut( Object Sender, EventArgs e ) {

     if  ( User.Identity.Name != "" ) {
       CookieAuthentication.SignOut();
       Page.Navigate("/advworks/default.aspx");

     }
     else {
         Page.Navigate("/advworks/login.aspx?ReturnUrl=/AdvWorks/default.aspx");
     }
   }

   private void updateSignInOutMessage() {

     if  ( User.Identity.Name != "" ) {
       signInOutMsg.Text = "Sign Out (" + User.Identity.Name + ")";
     }
     else {
       signInOutMsg.Text = "Sign In / Register";
     }
   }
</script>
...
```

The updateSignInOutMessage function actually updates the text, and the SignInOut method is called when the user clicks the sign in/out text. If a user is signing out, the CookieAuthentication.SignOut function is called to invalidate the authentication cookie. If signing in, the user is redirected to the login page.

The SignInOut code is wired up as part of the control declaration:

```
...
<td>
  <asp:linkbutton style="font:8pt verdana" id="signInOutMsg"
       runat="server" OnClick="SignInOut" />
</td>
...
```

Checkout Processing

Once a customer is authenticated, they are taken to the checkout page (secure/checkout.aspx), presented with their shopping list, and asked to confirm that the list is correct:

Check Out

Please confirm you want to order the following items:

Product Code	Product Name	Description	Quantity	Unit Price	Unit Total
AW098-04	Everglades	medium-weight, waterproof leather boots, good traction, brown (br)	1	£98.00	£98.00
AW013-08	Petzl Spirit	Locking pear shaped	2	£13.00	£26.00
AW250-06	Campos	reinforced, waterproof, 2-layer nylon parka, interior/exterior pockets, blue (bl)	1	£250.00	£250.00

Total is £374.00

Cancel Order (Clears Basket)   Confirm Order

The checkout page uses very similar code to the ShoppingCart.aspx page, except we have omitted the controls that allow the customer to remove items or edit the order quantities. If the customer confirms an order by pressing the **Confirm Order** button, a new database record is created for the order containing the date and the total order value. Then the current shopping basket is cleared, and the customer is presented with a confirmation screen:

Order Confirmed

Thanks for placing an order. Your order has now been confirmed and your goods should be delivered within 5 working days.

You can view all of your orders to date by clicking   or clicking the 'Your Account' button shown in the navigation bar. Click here to go back to the   .

The code invoked for confirming an order is shown next:

```
void Confirm_Order(Object sender, EventArgs e) {

    AdvWorks.CartDB cart = new AdvWorks.CartDB(getDSN());
    double totalOrderValue;

    totalOrderValue = cart.GetOrderValueForCart(GetCustomerID());

    AdvWorks.OrdersDB orders = new AdvWorks.OrdersDB(getDSN());
    orders.AddNewOrder(GetCustomerID(), DateTime.Now.ToString(),
                   totalOrderValue );
    cart.ResetShoppingCart( GetCustomerID() );
    Page.Navigate("confirmed.aspx");
}
```

The total value of the order is calculated using the GetOrderValueForCart function of the CartDB object. The customer name that is passed into this function, as returned by a call to GetCustomerID, will always be the name that the user entered when registering, as it is not possible to access this page without being authenticated.

Once the total value of the order has been calculated, the AddNewOrder function of the OrdersDB object is called to create an entry in the orders table. Finally, the shopping cart contents are cleared from the database and the browser is redirected to the order confirmation screen.

> In a commercial application you would want to keep the contents of the shopping cart so you could actually process the order. As this is only a simple demonstration application, we have not implemented it here.

Canceling the Order

If an order is canceled, the current shopping basket is cleared and the customer is taken back to the Adventure Works home page (`default.aspx`). The code for canceling an order is shown here:

```
void Cancel_Order(Object sender, EventArgs e) {

    AdvWorks.CartDB cart = new AdvWorks.CartDB(getDSN());
    cart.ResetShoppingCart( GetCustomerID() );

    Page.Navigate("/AdvWorks/default.aspx");
}
```

Order History and Your Account

Customers can review their order history anytime by clicking the 'Your Account' image located at the top of each page. When clicked, the page displays all the orders they have previously placed to date, showing the date when the order was created and the total value of the order:

Your Account

You have placed the following orders to date:

Order Date	Order Value
06/11/2000 14:32:11	£914.00

`Clear Order History`

This page is generated using the `asp:Repeater` control, and just shows the entries in the `Orders` table for the current customer. The `PopulateOrderList` function data binds the controls just as in previous pages:

```
void PopulateOrderList() {

    // Populate list with updated shopping cart data

    AdvWorks.OrdersDB orders = new AdvWorks.OrdersDB(getDSN());
    DataSet ds = orders.GetOrdersForCustomer(GetCustomerID());

    MyList.DataSource = ds.Tables[0].DefaultView;
    MyList.DataBind();

    // Hide the clear button if there are no items to delete.
    if ( MyList.Items.Count == 0 ) {
        ClearButton.Visible = false;
        MyList.Visible = false;
        Status.Text = "No orders have been placed to date.";
    }
}
```

The last few lines of this code hide the 'Clear Order History' button if there are no orders for this customer. If there are orders, then clicking this button invokes the `ClearOrderHistory` function:

```
void ClearOrderHistory(Object sender, EventArgs e) {

    AdvWorks.OrdersDB orders = new AdvWorks.OrdersDB(getDSN());
    orders.DeleteOrdersForCustomer( GetCustomerID() );
    PopulateOrderList();
}
```

This code clears all orders for this customer by calling the `DeleteOrdersForCustomer` function provided by the `OrdersDB` object.

Summary

That's it, your first ASP+ e-commerce application.

In this chapter we have seen how clean and easy it is to write an e-commerce application using ASP+. The rich server–side control and event model makes ASP+ development much more like traditional VB event based programming which dramatically reduces the amount of code we have to write in our pages.

We have not had the space to cover every single feature that you could potentially use in an application in this chapter. However, hopefully the code presented here covers the most common aspects of an application, and when combined with all the information provided in the other chapters will give you the confidence to try build your own applications using ASP+.

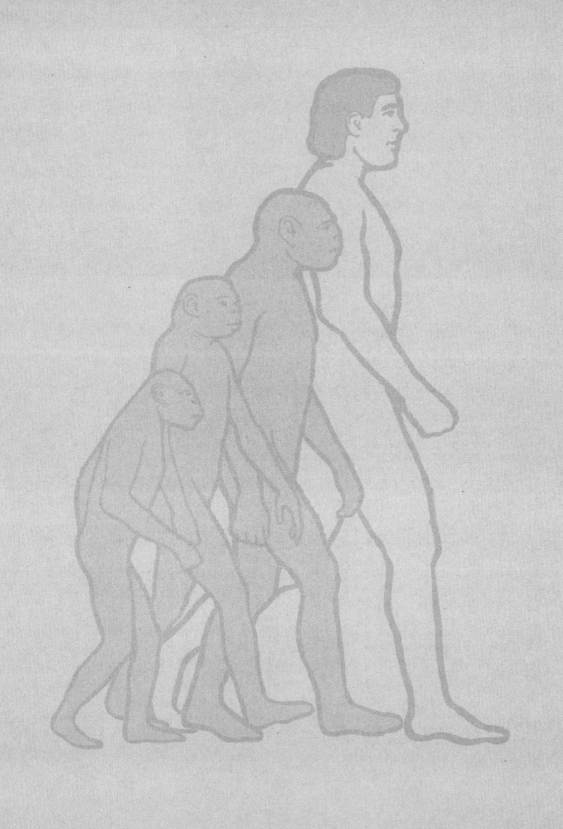

Moving from ASP to ASP+

While ASP+ is designed to provide maximum backward compatibility with existing ASP applications and Web sites, the fundamental changes to the core of the system mean that there are several areas where you will have to update your pages in order for them to work correctly under ASP+. And, probably more importantly, you'll want to update them over time to take advantage of all the new features in ASP+.

Instead of migrating immediately, however, you might consider running ASP+ alongside your existing ASP pages for the time being, and migrating as resources permit. And, of course, you may feel that it's time for a redesign of the site or application anyway, as Web sites can soon start to look 'tired', and there are often many new things that you want to add.

Your existing skills developed with ASP will still be of great benefit when you move to ASP+. However, you need to be constantly aware of the way that things have changed, and the 'gotchas' that can creep up and bite you when you least expect it.

The design goals of ASP+ have been discussed in earlier chapters, in particular in Chapter 1, so this appendix is devoted to simply documenting the important changes between ASP and ASP+. We'll also try to give technical reasons as to why things have changed where we can.

> Note that the special Web site supporting this book will be updated as new information or changes come along in the beta and release versions of ASP+. You can find this site at **http://www.wrox.com/beta**.

Changes to the Page Structure

There are a few issues that involve the way a page is structured in ASP+.

The Structure of Code Blocks

Previous versions of ASP allowed **either** the <script> element **or** the script delimiters <%...%> to be used to enclose any script code in a page. In ASP+, you must place **all** functions and subroutines within a <script> section. They cannot be placed within the <%...%> delimiters. See Chapter 2 for more details.

In the current release of ASP+, only one code language can be used per page, however, a pagelet or component can be written in a different language from the rest of the page.

Page Directives

Previous versions of ASP allow only a single page directive to be inserted into a page. It usually defines the language for any code sections in the page that don't specify this explicitly, for example:

```
<%@Language="VBScript"%>
```

This directive can also be used to set the 'transaction' state for the page, the character encoding to be used, and several other properties.

In ASP+, a page can accept multiple directive statements, and the 'default' directive is now identified with the name Page:

```
<%@Page Language="VBScript"%>
```

This directive supports the existing ASP attributes such as Transaction="Required", etc. There are also several new attributes available for use in the Page directive, such as Trace="True" and MaintainState="False". The following table lists these, with the default value underlined:

Attribute	Supported Values	Description
BUFFER	True | False	Specifies if response buffering is on.
CONTENTTYPE	Any content-type string	The HTTP content type for the output.
CODEPAGE	Any valid codepage value	The locale code page of the file.
CULTURE	Any valid COM+ culture string	The culture setting of the page.
RESPONSEENCODING	GetEncoding() values	The encoding of response content.
LCID	Any valid LCID identifier	The locale identifier for code.
DESCRIPTION	Any string description	A text description of page.

Attribute	Supported Values	Description
ENABLESESSIONSTATE	True | False (read-only)	The session state requirements.
ERRORPAGE	Any valid HTTP URL	The URL for unhandled errors.
INHERITS	Page-derived COM+ class	A 'code-behind' class for the page to inherit from.
LANGUAGE	VB | JScript | C# | {other}	The language used when compiling all <%...%> blocks in the page.
MAINTAINSTATE	True | False	Indicates whether viewstate should be maintained across page requests.
TRANSACTION	NotSupported | Supported | Required | RequiresNew	Indicates the transaction semantics.
TRACE	True | False	Indicates whether tracing is enabled.
SRC	Source file name	The 'code-behind' class to compile.
WARNINGS	True | False	Indicates whether compiler warnings should be treated as errors or ignored.

To provide backward compatibility, any directive statement encountered in a page that does not have a recognized directive name (such as Page, OutputCache, Register, etc.) will be treated as the Page directive statement. As Language and Transaction are not valid ASP+ directive names, this means that (in most cases) existing ASP pages that omit the Page directive name will still work, i.e.:

```
<%Language="VBScript"%>
```

is assumed to be:

```
<%@Page Language="VBScript"%>
```

and:

```
<%Transaction="Required"%>
```

is assumed to be:

```
<%Page Transaction="Required"%>
```

Unification of the Supported Languages

ASP+ provides **no** support for the **VBScript language**. Instead, you must code your pages in Visual Basic or one of the other supported languages (currently JScript, C# and C++, with others such as Cobol and Perl to follow). The good news is that the syntax of Visual Basic is very similar to that of VBScript, and so the compiler will often accept VBScript code as it stands. The default settings don't insist that you pre-declare all your variables (using `Dim`, for example), so pages that depend on implicit variable declarations will still work. You can add the statement `Option Strict` to the head of a page if you do want the compiler to check for variable declaration.

The reason for the language change, and many of the other changes documented here, is the unification of languages in the new runtime framework. All supported languages are compiled to a common intermediate language, and then the runtime framework executes this code directly. This means that there have to be common data types and structures for variables and objects such as collections, lists, etc.

So, each language has to adapt to use these new structures. VBScript really had nowhere to go, as all the Microsoft tools and applications now use Visual Basic or Visual Basic for Applications (VBA), and there is no client-side browser support for VBScript outside Internet Explorer. We've documented the main differences between VBScript and Visual Basic in Appendix B.

Default Properties, Methods, and Collections

There is no longer any concept of a default property or default method in VB7. So, like client-side script in an HTML page, you have to specify the property or method in your ASP code every time. For example:

```
strValue = objTextBox.value
strFieldValue = objRecordset("field_name").value
```

or

```
strValue = objTextBox.value
strFieldValue = objRecordset.Fields("field_name").value
```

instead of the 'lazy' way that worked in ASP:

```
strValue = objTextBox
strFieldValue = objRecordset("field_name")
```

Working with Request and Response Collections

The `Request` and `Response` object collections (i.e. `Form`, `QueryString`, etc.) are no longer based on the special `RequestDictionary` or `ResponseDictionary` objects, as they were in previous versions of ASP. Instead they use a new common dictionary object.

Each member of the `Form`, `QueryString`, and `ServerVariables` collections in previous versions of ASP is an array, so multiple values with the same name can be accessed using array syntax (i.e. values from a multi-select list box or a group of text boxes with the same `name` attribute).

In ASP+, the value of each member of these collections is of type `String`. The string is comma-delimited where there are multiple values with the same key (or name). The `Keys` method and the `HasKeys` property are no longer supported.

For backward compatibility, the `Contents` and `StaticObjects` collections are still supported for the `Application` object and the `Session` object (through special wrappers to the objects). So you can still use:

```
strValue = Application.Contents("key_name")
```

The new and recommended syntax, however, is just:

```
strValue = Application("key_name")
```

You can use the new `Params` property of the `Request` object to get a collection containing all the contents of the `QueryString`, `Form`, `ServerVariables`, and `Cookies` collections:

```
objEverything = Request.Params
```

However, the old syntax is still supported for backward compatibility:

```
objEverything = Request
```

Note that the technique of capturing all the request collection contents is not generally recommended on performance grounds.

The `Request.ClientCertificate` collection is replaced by the `Request.SecurityCertificate` collection. There is also less need to access the `Request.ServerVariables` collection, due to the range of new properties such as `Request.UrlReferrer`, `Request.UserAgent`, and `Request.PhysicalPath`.

Iterating Through the Collections in VB

In previous versions of ASP, the usual way to iterate through a `Request` collection, such as `Request.Form`, was like this:

```
<%
 Dim strItem as String
 For Each strItem in Request.Form
   Response.Write(strItem & " = " & Request.Form(strItem) & "<br>")
 Next
%>
```

This will work in ASP+, but notice that we have added the declaration of the variable used for accessing each member of the collection as a `String` type. However, there are also methods that return all the keys and values from the collections as separate arrays that we can iterate with a normal `For...Next` loop:

```
<%
 Dim arrNames As String()
 Dim arrValues As String()
 arrNames = Request.Form.AllKeys
 arrValues = Request.Form.All
```

```
  For intLoop = 0 To UBound(arrNames)
    Response.Write(arrNames(intLoop) & " = " & arrValues(intLoop) & "<br />")
  Next
%>
```

Runtime Changes

There are a few major issues involved at runtime when migrating to ASP+.

Server.CreateObject and Late Binding

Late binding can still be used to instantiate ASP+ components, so the code:

```
objThis = Server.CreateObject("some_progid")
```

will still work. However, where possible, you should declare the object as being of the specific type using the New keyword (early binding):

```
Dim objThis As New typename_or_progid
```

or

```
Dim objThis As typename_or_progid = New typename_or_progid
```

This provides better performance, and also allows development tools to display pop-up syntax help and object member lists.

Managed vs Unmanaged Components

The new runtime, and the underlying runtime architecture, specify two different types of executable code or component:

- ❑ **Unmanaged code**, where the x86 binary instructions are executed directly by the processor.

- ❑ **Managed code**, which is compiled to the Intermediate Language (IL) code and executed by the runtime in its own memory space. The runtime can therefore control and manage the code execution, provide error and failure handling, allow cross-language calls and inheritance, provide garbage collection, and implement proper code and object protection.

All the compilers provided with the new universal runtime create IL managed code. You can still use un-managed components as well, including 'classic' COM components. However, you can also convert these to managed code components and update the COM+ metabase with the component definition. This can be done either by rewriting and/or recompiling them using the new framework compilers, or by using the special **Type Library Import** utility (tlbimp.exe) that is provided with ASP+. This creates a managed wrapper around the existing DLL, and no changes to it are necessary. See the ASP+ SDK for more details.

If you use classic COM components that have been converted using `tlbimp.exe`, you should avoid calls between these components and native managed code wherever possible, as the overhead it incurs can reduce efficiency. Preferably, rewrite and recompile the components using the new runtime compilers to create fully managed code.

There is no need to register managed components – any components that are available in the application's `\bin` directory are automatically available to your ASP+ code.

Accessing the Object Context

The `ObjectContext` object that was introduced along with ASP 2.0 and MTS is no longer directly used in ASP+. Instead, a new `Context` object provides access to the ASP+ page and its execution environment. When you create your own components, you should use this object to obtain access to the intrinsic ASP+ objects such as `Request`, `Response`, `Server`, etc.

However, the legacy `OnStartPage` and `OnEndPage` events are still supported for passing the page context into a component. So even components written to work in ASP 1.0 can still be used. And the `GetObjectContext` method introduced in ASP 2.0 is still supported for use in transacted components, and will be supported for legacy use and backward compatibility in components written for ASP 2.0.

New Configuration Techniques

Many settings made in Internet Service Manager snap-in to the Microsoft Management Console for a virtual application directory, or Web site as a whole, do apply to ASP+ pages and components that reside in that application or Web site. This includes things like HTTP Headers, Security and Authentication, etc. Although the 'IIS' settings specified in Internet Services Manager continue to work with ASP+, the ASP specific settings do not (session state, default language, etc.). These settings are no longer stored in the IIS metabase, but are instead stored within `config.web` files.

The `config.web` file(s) for an application is always processed, but note that the `global.asax` file will only be processed if the directory it resides in is set up in Internet Service Manager as a virtual root directory.

Some ASP+ Tips and Tricks

Here are a few simple techniques that demonstrate some of the things that you can now do with ASP+.

Uploading Files to the Server

File upload is now natively supported by the ASP+ framework, using the `Request.Files` collection. There is also an ASP+ server control for the `<input type="file">` element:

```
<form enctype="multipart/form-data" runat="server">
  <input type="file" id="myfile" runat="server" />
</form>
```

On the server, the file can be accessed and saved to disk using the new `Files` collection of the `Request` object:

```
Request.Files("myfile").SaveAs("file_location")
```

or just:

```
myfile.PostedFile.SaveAs("file_location")
```

The 'MyWeb' Personal Tier

For the final release of ASP+, the universal runtime will be available on platforms other than just Windows 2000. This will allow code to be run completely on a client machine, with no server interaction required. To extend this ability, ASP+ introduces the concept of a **personal tier**, currently named **MyWeb** in the beta version and only usable on Windows 2000 machines.

This feature allows a Web site to be compiled and loaded onto a disk or CD-ROM for distribution. Everything runs sand-boxed inside the `IExplore` process, and so there is little security risk. When the user requests an application or resource that is not installed, it will automatically open http://*hostname*/*path*/myweb.osd for installation of the application. If a suitable **MyWeb** application is found, it is downloaded, installed, and run after a user confirmation prompt.

Accessing the Event Log

ASP+ includes many new object classes that you can instantiate from within your applications. The sample **Class Viewer** utility included with the other samples that are installed along with ASP+ can be used to view these object classes.

As an example, the following code uses the `EventLog` class, and shows how easy it is to add simple text messages to the **Application** section of the Windows Event Log:

```
Import System.Web.Util
...
Dim objLog As New EventLog
objLog.ReportError("Some error has occured")
```

B

Moving from VBScript or VB6 to VB7

As we saw earlier in the book, there is no intrinsic support for VBScript in ASP+. Instead, pages that define the language as VBScript (i.e. using `<%LANGUAGE="VBScript"%>` or `<script language="VBScript">`) will be compiled to the Intermediate Language (IL) binary code by the Visual Basic compiler. This means that you need to get used to the differences between VBScript and Visual Basic. However, Visual Basic 7 is also changing so as to meet the requirements of a cross-language runtime. Some of the major issues that you'll come across when using VB7 in your ASP+ pages are summarized below.

Set and Let No Longer Supported

The `Set` and `Let` assignment keywords are no longer supported (except when implementing properties in a class file). This is because the concept of default properties and default methods has gone, and so it's no longer necessary to use them. Because you have to provide the specific property or method name, the runtime can figure out what data type the object or variable is – and can therefore perform the correct assignment. So, assigning an object reference to another variable like this will produce a syntax error:

```
Set objThis = objThat
```

Instead, you now just use:

```
objThis = objThat
```

This is in line with the syntax of other languages such as JavaScript and C#.

Class Property Syntax in VB7

The format for defining properties in VB7 classes has also changed. In previous version of Visual Basic, you used the following form:

```
Private m_MyProperty As Variant    'this is the VB6 syntax

Public Property Let MyProperty(ByVal vData As Variant)
   m_MyProperty = vData
End Property

Public Property Set MyProperty(ByVal vData As Variant)
   Set m_MyProperty = vData
End Property

Public Property Get MyProperty() As Variant
   If IsObject(m_MyProperty) Then
      Set MyProperty = m_MyProperty
   Else
      MyProperty = m_MyProperty
   End If
End Property
```

In VB7 this has been rationalized, and follows the C# style more closely:

```
Private m_MyProperty As String              'this is the new VB7 syntax

Public Property MyProperty As String

   Get
      MyProperty = m_MyProperty
   End Get

   Set
      m_MyProperty = MyProperty
   End Set

End Property
```

The variable value is automatically supplied by Visual Basic 7.0, and it is the value supplied by the user when the property is Set. Notice that the private member variable is properly typed, and that the Get no longer needs to perform the IsObject check because of this.

Also changed from VB6 is the way you define read-only or write-only properties. Now you **must** put ReadOnly or WriteOnly at the beginning of the property declaration. For example:

```
ReadOnly Public Property MyReadOnlyProperty As String
   Get
      MyReadOnlyProperty = m_MyProperty
   End Get
End Property
```

```
WriteOnly Public Property MyWriteOnlyProperty As String
   Set
      m_MyProperty = MyWriteOnlyProperty
   End Set
End Property
```

Subroutines and Functions

There are several important changes to the way that you call and work with subroutines and functions.

Changes to the Method Calling Syntax

All method, function, and subroutine calls must now use parentheses to enclose the parameter list. VBScript and Visual Basic have previously allowed (and in some cases insisted) that parameters to a subroutine, or a function that takes no parameters, be used without parentheses:

```
'these work in previous version of ASP, but not in ASP+:
datTime = Now
DoSomething "MyValue1", intCount, "MyValue2"
```

Now parentheses must be used:

```
'in ASP+ you have to do this:
datTime = Now()
DoSomething("MyValue1", intCount, "MyValue2")
```

Watch out for this particularly with `Response.Write` and other common ASP statements:

```
Response.Write "Some text"      '<- results in a syntax error
Response.Write("Some text")     '<- correct
```

Parameters are ByVal by Default

Another area to watch out for is that VB now defaults to `ByVal` for all parameters that are intrinsic data types; previously the default was `ByRef`. This will affect any routines where you modify such a variable inside a subroutine or function, but do not specify `ByRef` for the argument:

```
Sub DoSomething(strValue1, strValue2, intDifference)   '<- won't work properly
   intDifference = Len(strValue1) - Len(strValue2)
End Sub
```

Instead, you have to use:

```
Sub DoSomething(strValue1, strValue2, ByRef intDifference)
...
```

In fact, it's a good idea to do the whole thing properly. This is the suggested syntax in VB7:

```
Sub DoSomething(ByVal strValue1, ByVal intCount, ByRef strValue2)
...
```

References to classes and interfaces, and array and string variables, still default to `ByRef` – in other words they are still passed by reference so that they can be modified within a subroutine or function.

A Full Range of Data Types

VBScript supports only the `Variant` data type. In Visual Basic 7.0, everything is an object – including the intrinsic data types. The `Variant` is just a special type of object, and allows the same kinds of syntax when declaring variables as VBScript. However, as Visual Basic supports a full set of rich data types, you should get into the habit of choosing an appropriate one, and declaring it as such:

```
Dim strValue1 As String
Dim intNumber As Integer
Dim arrStrings(20) As String
... etc ...
```

This makes code more compact and efficient. If you don't specify the data type, VB will default to using a `Variant`, which is much less efficient – unless you actually need the features that a `Variant` provides. For example, when working with things that may result in `Null`, the `Variant` data type can be useful. This is often the case with database recordsets:

```
Dim varFieldValue As Object    'or use: As Variant
varFieldValue = objRecordset.Fields("field_name").Value
If IsNull(varFieldValue) Then
   strValue = ""
Else
   strValue = CStr(varFieldValue)
End If
```

The intrinsic data types supported by Visual Basic 7.0 are:

Type	Data Type Name	Size	Default Value
Numbers:	Byte	1 byte (8 bits)	0
	Short	2 bytes (16 bits)	0
	Integer	4 bytes (32 bits)	0
	Long	8 bytes (64 bits)	0
	Single	4 bytes (32 bits)	0.0
	Double	8 bytes (64 bits)	0.0
	Decimal	12 bytes (96 bits)	0.0

Type	Data Type Name	Size	Default Value
Unicode Text:	String		" "
	Char	2 bytes (16 bits)	" "
Other Types:	Boolean		False
	Date		# 01/01/0001 12:00:00AM #

Note that the Currency *type is no longer supported. You should now use a* Decimal *type for currency and values that require extreme precision or very large numbers.*

Declaring Variables, Constants, and Arrays

Visual Basic 7.0 has added some new techniques for declaring variables and constants. Variables can be assigned values when they are declared – the declaration acts like an executable statement:

```
Dim x As Integer = 24
Dim y As Integer = x * 24

Const MY_NUMBER = 42
Const MY_NUMBER As Integer = 42
Const MY_STRING = "Hello World!"
Const MY_STRING As String = "Hello World!"
```

Note that, unlike VB6, variables that are declared within the same **statement** must have the same type. So, this is no longer allowed:

```
Dim x As Integer, y As String
```

However, the statement:

```
Dim x, y As String
```

now has the 'expected' result – both x and y are now String types.

The Dim statement can also be used to initialize an array:

```
Dim MyArray(20) As Integer
Dim MyArray(5) As Integer = (1, 2, 3, 4, 5)
Dim MyArray(3) As String = ("Bill", "Fred", "Mary")
```

Arrays must always be declared with Dim, though empty parameters are permitted to allow the array to be resized afterwards. ReDim can now only be used to resize an array. And ReDim cannot change the number of dimensions in an array:

```
Dim MyArray() As Integer
Redim MyArray(20)
```

```
Dim MyArray(,,) As Integer  '<- comma placeholder for dimensions
Redim MyArray(20, 10, 5)
```

You can assign one array to another using:

```
MyArray = YourArray
```

One major area of change is that, like most other languages, arrays can now only be zero-based. All arrays start with index zero. One 'gotcha' is that the statement:

```
Dim MyArray(10)
```

actually creates an array with 10 elements, and the index values run from 0 to 9. So, the assignment:

```
MyArray(10) = "Some value"
```

will cause an 'Index Out Of Bounds' error. This is not exactly intuitive to most VB programmers!

Using Appropriate Data Types

When defining subroutines and functions, take advantage of the data typing features of VB to declare the parameter data types – and the result data type for functions:

```
Sub DoSomething(ByVal strValue1 As String, _
                ByVal intCount As Integer, _
                ByRef strValue2 As String = "Initial value")
...
```

```
Function GetSomething(ByVal strValue1 As String, _
                ByVal intCount As Integer, _
                ByRef strValue2 As String = "Initial value") _
                As String
...
```

You might even like to take advantage of the Optional parameter support in VB – which must now always specify a default value (the IsMissing keyword is no longer supported):

```
Function GetSomething(ByVal strValue1 As String, _
                ByVal intCount As Integer, _
                ByRef strValue2 As String = "Initial value", _
                Optional ByVal strType = "Default Value" As String)
                As String
...
```

Integer and Long Data Type Changes

Note that the Integer data type is now 32 bits rather than 16, and the Long data type is now 64 bits instead of 32. This brings VB into line with other languages, and may break code that uses bit-wise arithmetic to manipulate individual bit values. It may also break code that accesses the Windows API functions or API functions in other custom DLLs.

When defining declarations of API functions you choose a data type based on the number of bits rather than the generic type name. You may have to change some to match the new bit counts.

Casting to Appropriate Data Types

In many cases, especially when using some of the built-in objects of the ASP+ runtime framework, you will have to convert values from one data type to another in places where this was not previously necessary. For example, when you write to the Request and Trace objects, you must ensure that the values are converted to a String first:

```
Dim intLoopCounter As Integer
...
Request.Write(CStr(intLoopCounter))
Trace.Write("My Category", CStr(intLoopCounter))
```

This requirement may be relaxed in future releases of ASP+, and the VB compiler and runtime. However, it is usual practice in other languages, and you should really be using it – especially when dealing with Variant data types.

The variable casting functions available in VB7 are listed below. If the conversion cannot be carried out, a runtime error occurs:

Function	Returns value converted to:
CBool (*value*)	Boolean data type
CByte (*value*)	Byte data type
CChar (*value*)	Char data type
CDate (*value*)	Date data type
CDec (*value*)	Decimal data type
CDbl (*value*)	Double data type
CInt (*value*)	Integer data type
CLng (*value*)	Long data type
CObj (*value*)	Object data type
CShort (*value*)	Short data type
CSng (*value*)	Single data type
CStr (*value*)	String data type

New Shorthand Assignment Syntax

At last, VB7 supports the shorthand syntax for assigning values that is a much-loved feature of many other languages:

```
MyValue = 10
MyValue += 10    '<- gives MyValue = 20
```

instead of the need to write:

```
MyValue = MyValue + 10
```

As well as 'plus-equals', there are the other three common operators:

```
MyValue -= 10    '<- minus/equals
MyValue /= 10    '<- divide/equals
MyValue *= 10    '<- multiply/equals
```

Using Early Binding

The rich data type support also allows you to use early binding to define objects as being of a specific type. This allows the compiler to detect errors, and also allows your development environment to provide support for pop-up member lists and syntax help:

```
Dim objThisRecordset As New ADODB.Recordset
```

Note that, although this is supported, what the compiler is actually doing is:

```
Dim objThisRecordset As ADODB.Recordset = New ADODB.Recordset
```

You can use either syntax, although the second is actually recommended.

Conditional Statements

The And and Or operators are now properly short-circuited, as is the case with most other languages. This means that when you have multiple conditions in a conditional expression, which uses And or Or, the first test to 'fail' will mean that any subsequent tests will not be carried out. For example, take the conditional expression:

```
If (x > 3) And (y < 10) Then
...
```

If x is **not** greater than 3, the first test will fail and the second comparison will not take place. The result of this comparison is not important because the entire expression must be False – irrespective of the result of the second comparison. This technique speeds up execution.

Likewise, in the conditional expression:

```
If (x < 21) Or (y < 10) Then
...
```

If x **is** less that 21 then the complete expression must be True – irrespective of the result of the second comparison. Therefore the expression short-circuits, and the second comparison is not carried out. The only time that this behavior is important is if you have a function in one of the subsequent parameters, for example:

```
If (intRange < 25) And (DoSomethingWithMyFile("myfile.txt") = True) Then
...
```

In this case, if `intRange` is not less than 25, the custom `DoSomethingWithMyFile` function will not be executed. If you are depending on it to do something that you later rely on, you've now got a bug to resolve.

Structured Error Handling

Visual Basic 7.0 supports structured error (or **exception**) handling that uses the `Try` and `Catch` and `Finally` statements common to other languages like JScript, C#, and C++:

```
...
Try
    ...
    ... do something here ...
    ...
Catch
    ...
    ... code that runs when an error occurs
    ...
Finally
    ...
    ... code that will always run, either after the Try block
    ... or after the Catch block if there was an error
    ...
End Try
...
```

It is also possible to use the `Throw` expression to throw an exception or error so that it can be handled by an error handler further up the execution tree – much like the `Err.Raise` statement.

> *The existing 'unstructured' error handling technique using On Error Resume Next and On Error GoTo 0 is still supported in VB7, along with the other VB6 error handling statements.*

Formatting Strings and Parsing Numbers

The common task of formatting numbers and dates into strings for display is carried out in VBScript using a range of specific functions, such as `FormatNumber`, `FormatCurrency`, `FormatDateTime`, etc. In Visual Basic 6, the generic `Format` function is used instead. To convert a string representation of a number into a number type, both VBScript and Visual Basic 6 offer a range of functions such as `CCur`, `CLng`, `CInt`, etc.

In Visual Basic 7.0, all variables are objects, and as such have methods that can handle formatting and parsing of their data. Each of the standard numeric data types has a `Format` method that returns a string representing that number, formatted in the specified way. They also provide a `Parse` method that returns a numeric variable containing the value represented by the string.

While it all sounds very different from current techniques, in fact (at least as far as formatting numbers into strings goes), the technique is very similar to the existing VB6 Format function. The new methods are also language-independent, so they can be used from VB, C#, C++, JScript, or any of the runtime-supported languages.

Formatting Numbers as Strings

Each of the standard numeric data types provides a Format method that returns a string containing a representation of the number in a specified format. The syntax of the Format method for all the numeric data types is:

```
Object.Format(ValueToFormat, FormatString, [LocaleInfo])
```

where:

❑   Object is one of the types SByte, Byte, Int16, Int32, Int64, Single, Double, Currency, or Decimal.

❑   ValueToFormat is the name of the variable to be formatted.

❑   FormatString is a string of characters that defines the format required.

❑   LocaleInfo is an optional parameter that defines the locale information to be used when deciding on things like the currency symbol, decimal and thousands separator, etc.

There are two types of format string that can be used with the FormatString parameter. **Standard format strings** use a single character and one or more numbers to specify the format as one of a standard set of number formats, while **custom format strings** are used to specify the actual characters that will appear in the result.

Standard Format Strings

Standard format strings consist of one of the special characters listed below, and one or more numbers that define the precision of the result, for example the number of characters after the decimal place.

The characters available for the FormatString parameter when specifying a standard format string are:

Character	Format	Character	Format	Character	Format
C or c	Currency	E or e	Scientific (exponential)	N or n	Number
D or d	Decimal	F or f	Fixed-point	X or x	Hexadecimal
G or g	General				

For **Currency, Scientific, Fixed-point**, and **Number** formats, the value of the precision character specifies the number of decimal places to be included in the resulting string representation of the value, with rounding automatically applied.

For **Decimal** and **Hexadecimal** formats, the value of the precision character specifies the total number of digits to be included in the string representation of the value.

Decimal and Hexadecimal values are left-padded with zeros to make up the number of characters specified by the precision format character.

The letter case of the type character is only important for Scientific and Hexadecimal formats, where the same case as the format character will be used for the characters in the resulting string.

The General format returns a string representing the numerical value in either Fixed-point format with trailing zeros, or Scientific format – whichever is more compact for the value and precision specified. The result is rounded where necessary.

The following examples show the effects of some of the different types of standard format string (assuming the default locale of 'United States'):

```
Double.Format(12345.6789, "C")     <- returns "$12,345.68"
Double.Format(-12345.6789, "C0"    <- returns "($12,3456)"
Int32.Format(12345, "D")           <- returns "12345"
Int32.Format(12345, "D8")          <- returns "00012345"
Double.Format(12345.6789, "E")     <- returns "1.234568E+004"
Double.Format(12345.6789, "E10")   <- returns "1.2345678900E+004"
Double.Format(12345.6789, "e4")    <- returns "1.2346e+004"
Double.Format(12345.6789, "F")     <- returns "12345.68"
Double.Format(12345.6789, "F0")    <- returns "12346"
Double.Format(12345.6789, "F6")    <- returns "12345.678900"
Double.Format(12345.6789, "G")     <- returns "12345.6789"
Double.Format(12345.6789, "G7")    <- returns "12345.68"
Double.Format(123456789, "G7")     <- returns "1.234568E+8"
Double.Format(12345.6789, "N2")    <- returns "12,345.68"
Double.Format(123456789, "N")      <- returns "123,456,789"
Int32.Format(&H2c45e, "x")         <- returns "2c45e"
Int32.Format(&H2c45e, "X")         <- returns "2C45E"
Int32.Format(&H2c45e, "X8")        <- returns "0002C45E"
```

Custom Format Strings

While the standard format strings are quick and easy to use, there are times when you want more control over the formatted result. Custom format strings allow you to specify exactly what appears in the result, including literal characters that are not part of the initial value.

The characters available for the FormatString parameter when specifying a custom format string are:

Character	Description
0	Insert a digit if one exists in this position in the resulting string, or a zero otherwise.
#	Insert a digit if one exists in this position in the resulting string, or nothing otherwise.
.	Insert a decimal point character (e.g. a period for the US and UK locales).
,	Insert a thousands separator character (e.g. a comma for the US and UK locales).
%	Insert a percent character and divide the result by 100 to display it as a percentage.

Table continued on following page

Character	Description
E+, E-, e+, e-	Format the number using scientific notation and insert 'E' or 'e' at this location. If '+' is included, always insert a plus or minus sign. If '-' is included, only insert a minus sign.
\	Treat the following character as a literal character instead of a format instruction.
'string' string	Insert the characters in *string* as literal characters exactly as they appear in the string. Any formatting instruction characters are treated as literal characters. Any characters that are not formatting instruction characters are automatically treated as literal characters by default.
;	Section separator, used when providing different formats for positive, negative and zero values, for example "$ #,##0.00;$ -#,##0.00; zero".

The following examples show the effects of some of the different types of custom format string (assuming the default locale of 'United States'):

```
Double.Format(12345.6789, "$#,###.00")          <- returns "$12,345.68"
Double.Format(-12345.6789, "$#,###.00;($#,###.00)") <- returns "($12,3456)"
Int32.Format(12345, "0")                         <- returns "12345"
Int32.Format(12345, "00000000")                  <- returns "00012345"
Double.Format(12345.6789, "0E+000")              <- returns "1.2345689E+004"
Double.Format(12345.6789, "0E-0")                <- returns "1.23456789E4"
Double.Format(12345.6789, "0e+00")               <- returns "1.2346789e04"
Double.Format(12345.6789, "0.00")                <- returns "12345.68"
Double.Format(12345.6789, "#0")                  <- returns "12346"
Double.Format(12345.6789, "#,##0")               <- returns "12,346"
Double.Format(12345.6789, "Total: $ #,##0.00")   <- returns "Total: $ 12,345.68"
Double.Format(12345.6789, "#0.00%")              <- returns "12.35%"
Double.Format(123, "'ID #:' 0000")               <- returns "ID #: 0123"
Double.Format(1, "\E\+\0:000")                   <- returns "E+0:001"
```

Date/Time Formatting

The `DateTime` object provides a special version of the `Format` method that can be used to convert any legal date or time into a string of any format. The syntax is:

```
DateTime.Format(ValueToFormat, FormatString, [LocaleInfo])
```

where:

❏ ValueToFormat is the name of the `DateTime` variable to be formatted.

❏ FormatString is a string of characters that defines the format required.

❏ LocaleInfo is an optional parameter that defines the locale information to be used when deciding on things like the date separators, time separators, AM/PM indicators, etc.

Like the numerical formatting method, there are two types of format string that can be used with the FormatString parameter. **Standard format strings** use a single character to specify the format as one of a standard set of date and time formats, while **custom format strings** are used to specify the actual characters that will appear in the result.

The standard single character values for the FormatString parameter are:

Character	Description
D	Long date only, e.g. "Sunday, October 31, 1999"
d	Short date only, e.g. "10/31/1999"
F	Long date and long time, e.g. "Sunday, October 31, 1999 2:00:00 AM"
f	Long date and short time, e.g. "Sunday, October 31, 1999 2:00 AM"
G	General date (short date and long time), e.g. "10/31/1999 2:00:00 AM"
g	General date (short date and short time), e.g. "10/31/1999 2:00 AM"
M or m	Month and day, e.g. "October 31"
R or r	RFC 1123 standard format, e.g. "Sun, 31 Oct 1999 10:00:00 GMT"
s	Format suitable for sorting by date, e.g. "1999-10-31 02:00:00"
T	Long time only, e.g. "2:00:00 AM"
t	Short time only, e.g. "2:00 AM"
U	UTC time with long date and long time, e.g. "Sunday, October 31, 1999 10:00:00 AM"
u	UTC time in format suitable for sorting, e.g. "1999-10-31 10:00:00"
Y or y	Month and year only, e.g. "October, 1999"

It's also possible to build up custom format strings using the individual characters described in the next table. If the format string contains more than one character, it is treated as being a custom format string:

Character	Description
h	The hour from 1 to 12 with no leading zero.
hh	The hour from 01 to 12 with leading zero.
H	The hour from 0 to 23 with no leading zero.
HH	The hour from 00 to 23 with leading zero.
m	The minutes from 0 to 59 with no leading zero.
mm	The minutes from 00 to 59 with leading zero.
s	The seconds from 0 to 59 with no leading zero.
ss	The seconds from 00 to 59 with leading zero.

Table continued on following page

Character	Description
t	The locale-specific AM/PM indicator as a single character, e.g. A or P for the US locale.
tt	The locale-specific AM/PM indicator as two characters, e.g. AM or PM for the US locale.
d	The day of the month from 1 to 31 with no leading zero.
dd	The day of the month from 01 to 31 with leading zero.
ddd	The day of the week as three characters, e.g. Mon, Tue, Wed. etc.
dddd	The day of the week in full, e.g. Monday, Tuesday, etc.
M	The month of the year from 1 to 12 with no leading zero.
MM	The month of the year from 01 to 12 with leading zero.
MMM	The month of the year as three characters, e.g. Jan, Feb, Mar. etc.
MMMM	The month of the year in full, e.g. January, February, etc.
y	The year as two digits with no leading zero, e.g. 99, 0, 1 etc.
yy	The year as two digits with leading zero, e.g. 99, 00, 01 etc.
yyy	The year as four digits, e.g. 1999, 2000, 2001 etc.
yyyy	– same as yyy above –
z	The time zone offset in hours from 0 to 12 with no leading zero, e.g. +4, -2, +10.
zz	The time zone offset in hours from 00 to 12 with leading zero, e.g. +04, -02, +10.
zzz	The full time zone offset from 00:00 to 12:00 with leading zero, e.g. +04:00, -02:00.
/	The locale-specific character for the date separator (e.g. '/' for US and UK locales).
:	The locale-specific character for the time separator (e.g. ':' for US and UK locales).
%	Treat the next character as a standard date/time format instruction character.
\	Treat the following character as a literal character instead of a format instruction.
'string' string	Insert the characters in *string* as literal characters exactly as they appear in the string. Any formatting instruction characters are treated as literal characters. Any characters that are not formatting instruction characters are automatically treated as literal characters by default.

The following examples show the effects of some of the different types of format string for dates and times (assuming the default locale of 'United States'). The time zone offset is 6 hours, and datDate is a variable that holds the value #6/20/2000 15:20:45#:

```
DateTime.Format(datDate, "D")    <- returns "Tuesday, June 20, 2000"
DateTime.Format(datDate, "%D")   <- returns "Tuesday, June 20, 2000"
DateTime.Format(datDate, "ddd dd MMM yyy")    <- returns "Tue 20 June 2000"
DateTime.Format(datDate, "dd/MM/yyy")         <- returns "20/06/2000"
DateTime.Format(datDate, "dd/M/yy")           <- returns "20/6/00"
DateTime.Format(datDate, "dd/MM/yy HH:nn:ss") <- returns "20/06/00 15:20:45"
DateTime.Format(datDate, "dd/M/yy h:nn tt")   <- returns "20/6/00 3:20 PM"
DateTime.Format(datDate, "yyyy-MM-dd")        <- returns "2000-06-20"
DateTime.Format(datDate, "HH:nn:sszz")        <- returns "15:20:45+06"
DateTime.Format(datDate, "Time now: h:nn tt") <- returns "Time now: 3:20 PM"
```

Parsing Strings into Numbers

To extract a numeric value from a variable, you can continue to use the conversion functions such as
CCur, CInt, CLng, etc. However, the new Parse method of each of the variable objects might be more
generically useful. The syntax is:

```
Object.Parse(StringToParse, [NumberStyle], [LocaleInfo])
```

where:

❑   Object is one of the types SByte, Byte, Int16, Int32, Int64, Single, Double, Currency
    or Decimal.

❑   StringToParse is the name of the string to be parsed for a number.

❑   NumberStyle is an optional parameter that provides extra information about the format of the
    string.

❑   LocaleInfo is an optional parameter that defines the locale information to be used when
    decoding things like the decimal and thousands separator, etc.

The optional NumberStyle parameter is a combination of any of the enumerated values listed below,
which can be used to specify the type of value that the string contains and extra information about how
to treat any non-numeric characters within the string. Together with the optional LocaleInfo parameter,
these values can provide hints to the method on how it should perform the parse operation:

AllowCurrencySymbol	AllowDecimalPoint	AllowExponent	AllowLeadingSign
AllowLeadingWhite	AllowParentheses	AllowThousands	AllowTrailingSign
AllowTrailingWhite	Any	Currency	Float
Integer	None	Number	Value

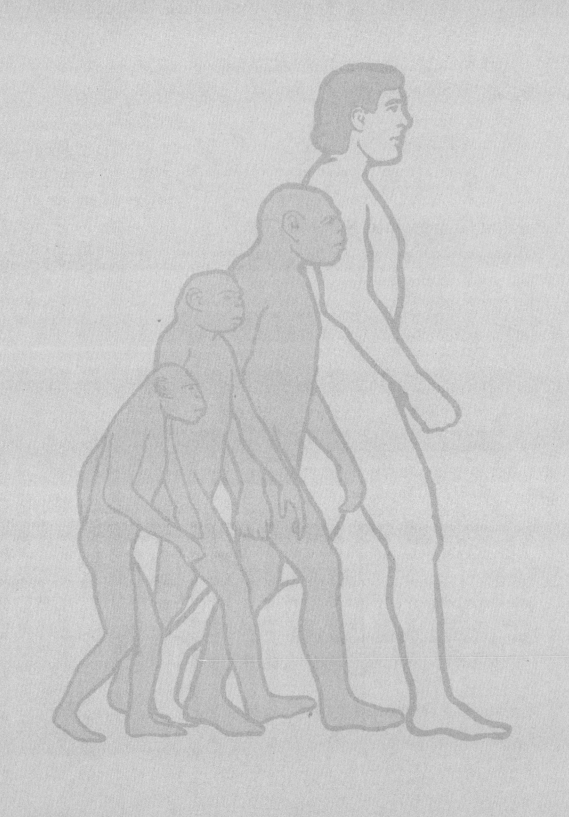

The ASP+ Object Model Reference

The fundamental changes in the overall structure and design of ASP+ when compared to previous versions of ASP means that the object model has changed quite considerably. However, the three core objects – Request, Response, and Server – are alive and well, and living in ASP+. They are broadly compatible with earlier versions, though there are a few issues. We documented these in Appendix A.

As earlier books and references predicted, the context in which an ASP page runs has become more important as ASP has evolved. In ASP 2.0 and 3.0, it was the 'proper' way to get access to the underlying ASP objects from within a component. It was referred to in previous versions of ASP as the ObjectContext object. In ASP+, the whole page is now a structured tree of objects that interact, and do so within the **context** of the page, as exposed by the HttpContext object.

We summarize the Request, Response, Server, and HttpContext object members in this Appendix, together with the members of the ASP+ Application and Session objects.

> Note that the special Web site supporting this book will be updated as new information or changes come along in the beta and release versions of ASP+. You can find this site at **http://www.wrox.com/beta**.

The ASP+ Request Object Members

The Request object gives access to all parts of the user's request for a resource from the server. It has gained 25 new properties and **3** new methods in ASP+. These are marked with an asterisk in the tables that follow:

Request Properties

Name	Type	Description
AcceptTypes	String Array	* Read Only. An array of client-supported MIME **AcceptTypes** sent by the client's browser.
Browser	HttpBrowserCapabilities	* Read Only. Provides browser capabilities information for the client.
ClientCertificate	HttpCertificate	Read Only. Enables a developer to query the client's security certificate. Same as the new **SecurityCertificate** collection.
ContentEncoding	Encoding	* Read Only. Character set data supplied by the client's browser.
ContentType	String	* Read Only. The MIME **ContentType** of the incoming request.
Cookies	HttpCookieCollection	Read Only. A collection of client's **Cookie** variables.
FilePath	String	* Read Only. The virtual path of the current request.
Files	HttpFileCollection	* Read Only. A collection of client-uploaded files (in multi-part MIME Format) Populated when the HTTP **ContentType** is "**multipart/form-data**".
Filter	Stream	* Read Only. Enables developers to attach a wrapping filter object to modify the HTTP body before it is read.
Form	NameValueCollection	Read Only. A collection of **Form** variables. Populated when the HTTP request **ContentType** is either "**application/x-www-form-urlencoded**" or "**multipart/form-data**".
Headers	NameValueCollection	* Read Only. A collection of all the HTTP Headers.
HttpMethod	String	* Read Only. The HTTP invocation type sent by client (**GET, POST**, etc.).
InputStream	Stream	* Read Only. A COM+ IO **Stream** that enables a developer to gain access to the raw contents of the incoming HTTP entity body.

Name	Type	Description
IsAuthenticated	*Boolean*	* Read Only. Indicates whether the HTTP connection is authenticated.
IsSecureConnection	*Boolean*	* Read Only. Indicates whether the HTTP connection is secure (i.e. https://).
Params	*NameValueCollection*	* Read Only. A combined collection of all **QueryString** + **Form** + **ServerVariables** + **Cookies** collection values.
Path	*String*	* Read Only. The full path of the current request.
PathInfo	*String*	* Read Only. Additional path information that follows the name of the host in the URL.
PhysicalApplicationPath	*String*	* Read Only. The file system mapped path of the current ASP+ application.
PhysicalPath	*String*	* Read Only. The file system mapped path of the current request.
QueryString	*NameValueCollection*	Read Only. A collection of **QueryString** variables. Populated when the method for a form is "**GET**", or the values are appended to the URL as a query string.
SecurityCertificate	*HttpCertificate*	* Read Only. Enables a developer to query the client's security certificate. Replaces the ASP **ClientCertificate** collection.
ServerVariables	*NameValueCollection*	Read Only. Exposes a collection of various server variables.
TotalBytes	*Number*	Read Only. The total number of bytes in the request.
Url	*HttpUrl*	* Read Only. Information about the URL of current request.
UrlReferrer	*HttpUrl*	* Read Only. Information about the URL of the page containing the link that loaded this page.
UserAgent	*String*	* Read Only. The client browser's raw **UserAgent** string.
UserHostAddress	*String*	* Read Only. The IP address of the remote client.

Table continued on following page

Name	Type	Description
UserHostName	*String*	* Read Only. The DNS name of the remote client.
UserLanguages	*String Array*	* Read Only. An array of client language preferences sorted alphabetically.
VirtualApplicationPath	*String*	* Read Only. The virtual root mapping of the current ASP+ application root.

Request Methods

Name	Parameters	Description
BinaryRead	count (*Number*)	Reads all or parts of the contents of the request when the data is sent using the POST method. The number of bytes to read is defined by **count**.
MapImageCoordinates	name (*String*) (*name of the form control*)	* Maps incoming parameters from an image button on a form into appropriate coordinate values. Returns x and y values as a two-element *Integer* array if found, or **Null** if not.
MapPath	virtualPath (*String*)	* Maps a virtual path to the equivalent physical path. Returns a *String*.
SaveAs	path (*String*) saveHeaders (*Boolean*)	* Saves the HTTP request to disk. No return value.

The ASP+ Response Object

The `Response` object gives access to all parts of the response that will be sent to the user. It has gained **9** new properties and **7** new methods in ASP+. These are marked with an asterisk in the tables that follow.

Response Properties

Name	Type	Description
Buffer	*Boolean*	Default **True**. *Deprecated*. This is a pointer to the **BufferOutput** property, provided for ASP compatibility.
BufferOutput	*Boolean*	* Default **True**. Indicates if page buffering is on or off.

Name	Type	Description
Cache	*HttpCachePolicy*	* Enables a developer to control the caching semantics of the page (i.e. expiration time, privacy, vary clauses, etc.).
CacheControl	`Public	Private`	Specifies if downstream proxy servers can cache the page (**Public**) or not (**Private**).
Charset	*String*	Appends the character set used for the response to the HTTP headers.
ContentEncoding	*Encoding*	* The HTTP character set of the content to be returned.
ContentType	*String*	Default "**text/html**". The HTTP MIME type of content.
Expires	*Integer*	Default **0**. *Deprecated.* The number of minutes that the client should cache the page.
ExpiresAbsolute	*DateTime*	Default **Now**(). *Deprecated.* A date and time on which content of the current page should cease being cached on the client.
Filter	*Stream*	* Enables developers to attach a wrapping filter object to modify the HTTP entity body before transmission.
IsClientConnected	*Boolean*	Indicates whether the client is still connected to the server.
PICS	*String*	Appends a PICS label in *String* to the HTTP response headers (not available in beta 1).
Output	*TextWriter*	* Read Only. COM+ IO **Writer** that enables custom text and HTML to be placed in the outgoing HTTP content body.
OutputStream	*Stream*	* COM+ IO **Stream** that enables binary output to be placed in the outgoing HTTP content body.
Status	*String*	Default "**HTTP 200 OK**". *Deprecated.* The complete status string. Retained for ASP compatibility.
StatusCode	*Integer*	* Default **200**. The HTTP status code for returned output.

Table continued on following page

Name	Type	Description
StatusDescription	*String*	* Default "**OK**". The HTTP status description string.
SupressContent	*Boolean*	* Default **False**. Allows a developer to prevent any HTTP content from being sent to the client.

Response Methods

Name	Parameters	Description
AddHeader	headerName (*String*) headerValue (*String*)	*Deprecated*. Retained for ASP compatibility. Equivalent to **AppendHeader**.
AppendCookie	cookie (*HttpCookie*)	* Adds an HTTP cookie to the output.
AppendHeader	headerName (*String*) headerValue (*String*)	* Adds an HTTP header to the output.
AppendToLog	logEntry (*String*) – text to add	Adds a custom entry to the IIS log file.
Clear	*none*	Clears all headers and content from the page buffer.
ClearContent	*none*	* Clears all content from the page buffer.
ClearHeaders	*none*	* Clears all headers from the page buffer.
Close	*none*	* Closes the connection to the client.
End	*none*	Sends all currently buffered output to the client, terminates the page, then closes the connection.
Flush	*none*	Sends all currently buffered output to the client.
Redirect	newUrl (*String*)	Redirects the client to a new URL.
Write	value (various types)	Writes values to the output stream.
WriteFile	filename (*String*)	* Writes the contents of a file directly to the output stream.
WriteFile	filename (*String*) offset (*Long*) byte to start from length (*Long*) no. bytes to output	* Writes the specified section of the contents of a file directly to HTTP content output stream.

The ASP+ Server Object

The `Server` object provides a series of methods that are used to carry out routine tasks while processing the page, such as converting strings into the appropriate format for use in HTML. It has gained **1** new property and no new methods in ASP+ (although two have been extended). These are marked with an asterisk in the tables that follow.

Server Property

Name	Type	Description
MachineName	*String*	* Returns the name of the server machine that is executing the page.
ScriptTimeout	*Number*	Read/write. The number of seconds after which the page will timeout if execution of the code it contains is not complete.

Server Methods

Name	Parameters	Description
CreateObject	progid (*String*)	Creates an instance of the object with the specified **progid** using late binding. Where possible you should use the appropriate new operator instead.
Execute	urlPath (*String*)	Executes a new request for the page or resource specified in the **urlPath** parameter. Execution of the original page continues after the 'executed' page completes. No return value.
GetLastError	*none*	Returns an instance of the ASPError object, which exposes details of the last error that occurred in the page (not implemented in beta 1).
HTMLEncode	stringToEncode (*String*)	Converts all non HTML-legal characters in the supplied string to their legal HTML entity equivalents. Returns a *String*.
HTMLEncode	stringToEncode (*String*) output (*TextWriter*)	* Converts all non HTML-legal characters in the supplied string to their legal HTML entity equivalents and writes the string to the specified **TextWriter** object. No return value.
URLEncode	stringToEncode (*String*)	Converts all non URL-legal characters in the supplied string to their legal URL entity equivalents. Returns a *String*.

Table continued on following page

Name	Parameters	Description
URLEncode	stringToEncode (*String*) output (*TextWriter*)	* Converts all non URL-legal characters in the supplied string to their legal URL entity equivalents and writes the string to the specified **TextWriter** object. No return value.
MapPath	virtualPath (*String*)	Maps a virtual path to the equivalent physical path. Returns a *String*.
Transfer	urlPath (*String*)	Terminates execution of the current page and begins execution of the page or resource specified in the **urlPath** parameter. No return value.

The ASP+ Application Object

The `Application` object provides access to the contents of variables stored within the ASP+ application. It allows developers to share state across multiple requests, sessions and pipelines. It has gained **2** new properties and **4** new methods in ASP+. These are marked with an asterisk in the tables that follow.

Application Properties

Name	Type	Description
Contents	*Dictionary*	Returns '**this**'. Provided for legacy ASP compatibility only.
Count	*Integer*	* Read Only. Returns the number of items stored in the **Application** object.
StaticObjects	*Dictionary*	Exposes all objects declared via an **<object runat=server />** element within the **global.asax** file for the application.
[this](*String*)	*String*	* Allows access to an **Application** value by name, enabling developers to add, remove, and update values.

Application Methods

Name	Parameters	Description
Add	key (*String*) value (*String/Object*)	* Adds the specified item to the **Application** object with the specified value. No return value.
Clear	*none*	* Removes all items from the **Application** object. No return value. Replaces the ASP **RemoveAll** method.

Name	Parameters	Description
GetDictionary Enumerator	*none*	* Returns a **DictionaryEnumerator** object containing all items (and their appropriate keys) within the **Application** object.
GetEnumerator	allowRemove *(Boolean)*	* Returns an **Enumerator** object containing all items stored within the **Application** object. At present **allowRemove** must always be **False**.
Keys	*none*	Returns an array of the keys of the items stored within the **Application** object (not in beta1).
Lock	*none*	Used by developers to synchronize access to application state variables. No return value.
Remove	key *(String)*	Removes the specified item from the **Application** object. No return value.
RemoveAll	*none*	Removes all items from the **Application** object. No return value.
UnLock	*none*	Used by developers to synchronize access to application state variables. No return value.

The ASP+ Session Object

The `Session` object provides access to the contents of variables stored in an ASP+ user session. It allows developers to share state across multiple requests from a specified user. It has gained **7** new properties and **4** new methods in ASP+. These are marked with an asterisk in the tables that follow. The existing ASP `Session.CodePage` property and the `Session.LCID` property are not currently supported, though they may be added back in to the final release version of ASP+.

Session Properties

Name	Type	Description
All	*Object Array*	* Returns an snapshot array of all the values in the session.
Contents	*Dictionary*	Returns '**this**'. Provided for legacy ASP compatibility only.
Count	*Integer*	* Read Only. The number of values stored in the session.
IsNewSession	*Boolean*	* Read Only. Returns **True** if the session has been created by the current request.
IsSeparateProcess	*Boolean*	* Read Only. Returns **True** if the session is stored in an external state store process.

Table continued on following page

Name	Type	Description
Key(*Integer*)	*String*	* Returns the key of the item at the specified index as a *String*.
SessionID	*String*	Read Only. The unique identifier of the session.
StaticObjects	*Dictionary*	Exposes all objects declared via an **<object runat=server />** element within the **global.asax** file for the application.
[this](*Integer*)	*Object*	* Default Property. Allows access to a session value by its index.
[this](*String*)	*Object*	* Default Property. Allows access to a session value by name.
Timeout	*Integer*	The number of minutes allowed between requests before the session will terminate.

Session Methods

Name	Parameters	Description
Abandon	*none*	Terminates the current session.
Add	key (*String*) value (*String/Object*)	* Adds the specified item to the **Session** object with the specified value. No return value.
Clear	*none*	* Removes all items from the **Session** object. No return value.
GetDictionary Enumerator	*none*	* Returns a **DictionaryEnumerator** object containing all items (and their appropriate keys) within the **Session** object.
GetEnumerator	*none*	* Returns an **Enumerator** object containing all items stored within the **Session** object.
Keys	*none*	Returns an array of the keys of the items stored within the **Session** object (not in beta 1).
Remove	key (*String*)	Removes the specified item from the **Session** object. No return value.
Remove	index (*Integer*)	Removes the item at the specified index from the **Session** object. No return value.
RemoveAll	*none*	Removes all items from the **Session** object. No return value.

The ASP+ HttpContext Object

The HttpContext object gives access to all parts of the page that we are creating, and the environment in which ASP+ is executing. It is available through the Context property within an ASP+ page. The HttpContext object is broadly equivalent to the ObjectContext object in ASP2 and ASP3, but has gained **8** new properties and **9** new methods in ASP+. These are marked with an asterisk in the tables that follow.

HttpContext Properties

Name	Type	Description
AllErrors	*Exception Array*	* An array of all errors accumulated during the request processing.
Application	*HttpApplicationState*	A reference to the **Application** object for the current request
Error	*Exception*	* The first error (if any) accumulated during the request processing.
Handler	*IHttpHandler*	* A reference to the **HttpHandler** class for the current request.
Items	*HashTable*	* A key-value collection that can be used to build-up and share data between **HttpModules** and **HttpHandlers** during the request.
Request	*HttpRequest*	A reference to the **Request** object instance for the current request.
Response	*HttpResponse*	A reference to the **Response** object instance for the current request.
Session	*SessionState*	A reference to the **Session** object instance for the current request.
TimeStamp	*DateTime*	* The initial date and time of the request.
Trace	*TraceContext*	* A reference to the **Trace** object for the current request.
User	*IPrincipal*	* A reference to the security information object for this request.

HttpContext Methods

Name	Parameters	Description
AddError	error (*Exception*)	* Registers an error for the current request. No return value.
ClearErrors	*none*	* Clears all errors accumulated for the current request. No return value.

Table continued on following page

Name	Parameters	Description
CreateObject	progid (*String*)	* Instantiates a classic COM object identified via a *progid*. Returns a reference of type *Object*.
GetConfig	configSection (*String*)	* Returns the requested configuration information for the current request from **config.web**. Returns a reference of type *Object*.
GetConfig	configSection (*String*) path (*String*)	* Returns the requested configuration information for a particular URL. Returns a reference of type *Object*.
URLDecode	stringToDecode (*String*)	* Decodes a URL-encoded string. Returns it as a *String*.
URLDecode	stringToDecode (*String*) output (*TextWriter*)	* Decodes a URL-encoded string and sends it to the specified COM+ **TextWriter** object. No return value.
URLEncode	stringToEncode (*String*)	* Converts all non URL-legal characters in the supplied string to their legal URL entity equivalents. Returns a *String*.
URLEncode	stringToEncode (*String*) output (*TextWriter*)	* Converts all non URL-legal characters in the supplied string to their legal URL entity equivalents and writes the string to the specified **TextWriter** object. No return value.

The ASPError Object

This object is not available in beta 1 of ASP+, but is planned for re-introduction in later versions and the final release. It is identical to the `ASPError` object provided by ASP 3.0. It has the following read-only properties:

Name	Type	Description
ASPCode	*Integer*	The error number generated by IIS or ASP.
ASPDescription	*String*	A detailed description of the error if it is ASP-related.
Category	*String*	Indicates the source of the error, e.g. ASP itself, the code compiler, or an object or component.
Column	*Integer*	The character position within the line of the file where the error was detected.
Description	*String*	A short description of the error.

Name	Type	Description
File	*String*	The name of the file that was being processed when the error occurred.
Line	*Integer*	The line number within the file where the error was detected.
Number	*Integer*	One of the standard language/COM/COM+ error code numbers.
Source	*String*	The actual code, where available, of the line where the error was detected.

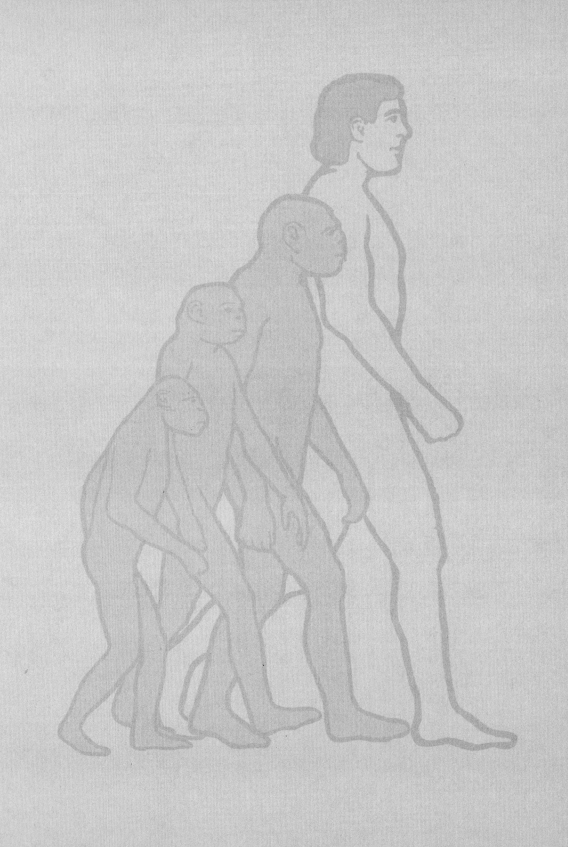

Using Classic COM components in ASP+

Components are a fundamental part of most Windows DNA applications. Many companies have followed the Window DNA blueprint laid out by Microsoft, and have subsequently benefited from the scalability it gives enterprise applications. However, this adoption means that a lot of time and money has been invested into component development that must be usable in the NGWS runtime **without** change.

Realizing this component investment exists, and understanding that not everybody will instantly adopt the new runtime for various reasons, Microsoft has provided a sophisticated interoperability layer between the new NGWS runtime and classic COM. This allows existing COM components to be in the new managed runtime (and therefore ASP+), and for managed components to be used by classic COM applications.

In this appendix we are going to take a brief look at how a classic COM component can be used in an ASP+ application, after which we'll discuss some of the implications of doing this.

Type Library Importer

The new runtime SDK ships with a utility called the Type Library Importer (**TlbImp** – `tlbimp.exe`). This takes a standard COM type library and creates an assembly that contains equivalent NGWS metadata. This metadata can be used in managed code to create and use an instance of any unmanaged component that was defined in the original type library, seemingly as if they were managed components created by a managed language. Other definitions within the type library (such as enumerations) can also be accessed.

TlbImp is designed to enable managed code to **early bind** to unmanaged components and their interfaces. This results in excellent interop performance, but, if you just want to late bind to unmanaged components using `Server.CreateObject` and `CreateObect`, you do not need to use the `TlbImp` tool. The late binding syntax/code that worked in ASP will work without change in ASP+.

> **All managed code requires metadata descriptions of the various types (classes etc.) it uses. This is similar to metadata held in a traditional type library, but it is much richer and it is also extensible.**

Using a VB6 component in ASP+ (early binding)

To see `TlbImp` in action I've created a simple VB6 ActiveX DLL project called `ClassicCOM` that contains one component called `myComponent`. This exposes its standard default VB interface (`_myComponent`) and a custom interface called `_myInterface`. The default interface has one method called `Add` that takes a number and adds a specified amount it. The `_myInterface` interface has one method called `Subtract` that number and subtracts a specified amount it.

Both interfaces are implemented in the way you'd expect, and the component code *really* couldn't be much simpler:

```
Implements myInterface

Public Function Add(number As Long, valueToAdd As Long) As Long
    Add = number + valueToAdd
End Function

Private Function myInterface_Subtract(number As Long, _
                                      valueToSubtract As Long) As Long

    myInterface_Subtract = number - valueToSubtract

End Function
```

> **Although this component is very simple, the basic techniques we are showing should work for any COM server/type library including those published by Microsoft.**

Once the project has been compiled and **registered**, we can use the TlbImp utility to create an assembly for our VB6 DLL:

```
TlbImp ClassicCOM.dll /out:Wrapper.DLL
```

To view the contents of the assembly we can use the ILDASM tool:

Looking at the IDLASM output we can see that the namespace `ClassicCOM` has been created, which matches the name of the DLL containing the type library. The first two definitions within this namespace match our VB6 definitions (remember VB adds the underscore behind the scenes), and the following definition for the component also matches. The final definition is slightly confusing, as our original VB6 COM server did not contain a component called `myInterface`. However, as VB6 hides the underscore and actually lets you type `myInterface` rather than `_myInterface`, the type library converter is working on the principle that it should also support both naming conventions.

Once the assembly is created we can copy it into the `bin` directory of an ASP+ application and use it.

Using a TlbImp-created Assembly

Create a new Web application, and in it create a page called `default.aspx` that looks like this:

```
<%@Import namespace="ClassicCOM" %>

<script language="VB" runat="server">

    protected Sub Page_Load( sender as object, e as EventArgs )

        ' First time through set current value to 100

        If (Page.IsPostBack = false ) Then
            currentValue.Text = "100"
        End If
    End Sub
```

```
    ' increment the value

    protected Sub DoAdd( sender as object, e as EventArgs )

        dim test as myComponent
        test = new myComponent()

        dim total as Int32
        dim value as Int32

        value = int32.Parse( change.Text )
        total = int32.Parse( currentValue.Text )

        total = test.Add( total, value )

        currentValue.Text = total.ToString()

    End Sub


    ' decrement the value

    protected Sub DoSubtract( sender as object, e as EventArgs )

        dim test as myComponent
        test = new myComponent()

        dim total as Int32
        dim value as Int32

        value = int32.Parse( change.Text )
        total = int32.Parse( currentValue.Text )

        total = test.Subtract( total, value )

        currentValue.Text = total.ToString()

    End Sub

</script>

<h2>ASP+ using a 'Classic COM' component</h2>

<form runat="server">

  <asp:TextBox id="change" runat="server" Text="10"/>
  <asp:Button Text="Add" OnClick="DoAdd" runat="server" />
  <asp:Button Text="Subtract" OnClick="DoSubtract" runat="server" />

<br>Current value is: <asp:label id="currentValue" runat="server" />

</form>
```

When viewed in the browser the pages will look like this:

The ASP+ code is relatively straightforward, so we'll just focus upon the important sections. The first point to note is that the namespace ClassicCOM has been imported into the page, which saves us having to prefix all of our declarations with ClassicCOM. :

```
<%@Import namespace="ClassicCOM" %>
```

The component within this namespace is then used within the DoAdd and DoSubtract functions. If we look at the DoAdd function we can see that there really is no special code needed to access and use the unmanaged component:

```
protected Sub DoAdd( sender as object, e as EventArgs )

    dim test as myComponent
    test = new myComponent()

    dim total as Int32
    dim value as Int32

    value = int32.Parse( change.Text )
    total = int32.Parse( currentValue.Text )

    total = test.Add( total, value )

    currentValue.Text = total.ToString()

End Sub
```

We are just calling the Add function and the runtime is taking call of all the interop issues.

Late Binding

The NGWS interop layer supports late binding in the same way as classic ASP, so we can still create and access unmanaged components using Server.CreateObject and CreateObject functions:

```
protected Sub DoAdd( sender as object, e as EventArgs )

    dim test as object

    test = Server.CreateObject("ClassicCOM.myComponent")
```

```
        dim total as Int32
        dim value as Int32

        value = int32.Parse( change.Text )
        total = int32.Parse( currentValue.Text )

        total = test.Add( total, value )

        currentValue.Text = total.ToString()

    End Sub
```

Late bound code like this should be avoided in ASP+ because it will not execute as quickly as early bound code, and it is more error prone – just like traditional ASP code. For example, if you mistyped a method name, the error will occur at runtime, and not compile time.

Error Handling

In the world of COM all methods return HRESULTs (although this is hidden in higher-level languages such as VB). Because the new runtime does not support HRESULTs directly, the interop layer automatically converts any errors (failed HRESULTs) returned from your components into ComException exceptions. These should be caught and processed in your code:

```
Try
   someClassCOMObject.SomeMethod()
Catch e As ComException
   ...
End Try
```

For well-known error code, other exceptions will be thrown, such as ArgumentNullException for E_POINTER and NotImplementedException for E_NOTIMPL.

Performance

Although we have showed you how to use classic COM components inside of an ASP+, **we must make it clear** that doing this incurs a number of performance penalties that you should consider from day one. Ideally, we recommend that you recompile your components using the new compilers where possible, and only use the interoperability where you really have no other choice (such as a dependency of a third party component).

Calling into unmanaged code from managed code

Calling from managed code into unmanaged code requires some special processing, so creating an instance of an unmanaged component and calling its methods from within a managed application such as ASP+ is not as quick as creating and calling other managed components. The performance overhead will vary depending upon the complexity of the individual parameters used in components interfaces, as certain types require more conversion and processing (marshaling) than others.

Runtime Callable Wrapper (RCW)

As the new managed runtime is so radically different to classic COM, a **Runtime Callable Wrapper** (RCW) is used to bridge the communications between managed code and an unmanaged class COM component:

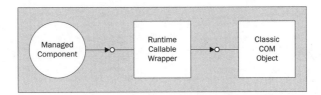

The RCW is a managed component with which managed code like ASP+ interacts. The RCW consumes the interfaces exposed by a classic COM component and re-exposes them as if they were part of a native managed component. Each time an unmanaged component is created, or any of an unmanaged component's interfaces returns an object reference, an RCW will be created to managed it. In many ways the RCW is like a standard COM proxy, except that it lives by the rules of the NGWS runtime and is therefore garbage collected.

Not all interfaces of unmanaged components are re-exposed by an RCW; no classic **standard** COM specific interfaces such as `IUnknown` and `IDispatch` are accessible, only custom interfaces.

> If you are a VB programmer the new managed runtime really isn't a radical concept as VB has primarily worked this way since its incarnation (p-code). However, if you are a C/C++ programmer you'll appreciate that the RCW has to do a lot of tricks to enable the interop, such as lifetime management, identity management, etc.

Calling into managed code from unmanaged code

Although not the primary topic of this appendix, calling from unmanaged code into managed code also requires some special processing, and can effect ASP+ developers. Like the RCW discussed earlier, classic COM objects use a COM Callable Wrapper (CCW) when accessing managed components to bridge the differences between them:

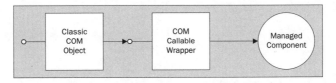

Like the RCW, the CCW is created each time a classic COM component interacts with a managed component. If you create an unmanaged component within an ASP+ page and pass it a reference to a managed component via an interface method, a CCW will be created. However in theory, CCW are less of an overhead in real terms, as the new runtime promises to generate code that is more efficient and scalable than the existing range of unmanaged compilers (especially VB6), so the overhead is compensated for by the performance of the new runtime. Microsoft realizes that performance of the new runtime is the crucial key requirement for the new runtime to be accepted, so you can be sure that this interop layer and managed code in general will be **lightning** fast. Initial tests have already shown ASP+ to be to 2-4 times faster than ASP today.

ASP+ is built on an MTA thread pool

ASP+ under the hood is built on top of a thread pool, where each thread is registered as a Multiple Threaded Apartment (MTA). Any calls to classic COM components that are apartment threaded (e.g. all VB6- components) will always require proxy/stubs to be used when they are invoked. This overhead is quite significant and will dramatically reduce the performance of your unmanaged components in a managed application.

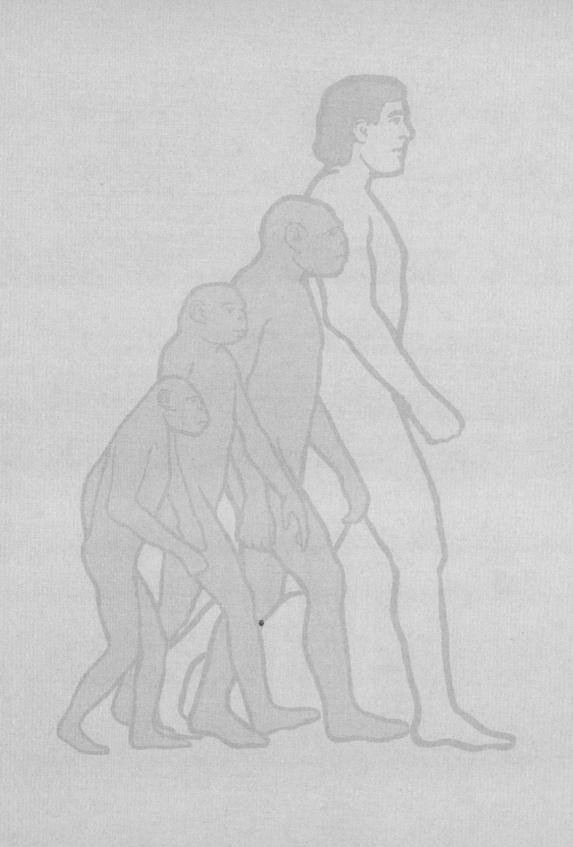

Index

A Guide to the Index.

The index is arranged hierarchically, in alphabetical order, with symbols preceding the letter A. Most second level entries and many third level entries also occur as first level entries. This is to ensure that users will find the information they require however they choose to search for it.

D

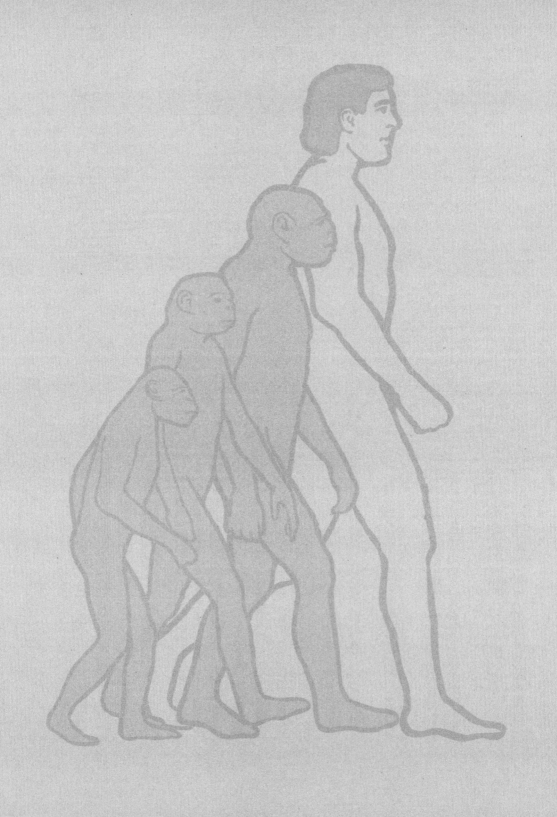